Praise for *The Last Stone*

"With its blistering descriptions of an American special-forces operation gone wrong, Mark Bowden's 1999 nonfiction book *Black Hawk Down* made for excellent action-movie fare. The story told in his latest work, the deeply unsettling *The Last Stone,* unfolds more slowly but is no less potent. Bowden displays his tenacity as a reporter in his meticulous documentation of the case." —*Time*

"Like all great true crime, *The Last Stone* finds its power not by leaning into cliché but by resisting it—pushing for something more realistic, more evocative of a deeper truth." —*New York Times*

"Riveting true crime from the ever-capable author . . . A keen synthesis of an intricate, decades long investigation, a stomach-churning unsolved crime, and a solid grasp of time, place, and character results in what is sure to be another bestseller for Bowden." —*Kirkus Reviews*

"Bowden delivers a narrative nonfiction masterpiece in this account of fiercely dedicated police detectives working to close a cold case. This is an intelligent page-turner likely to appeal even to readers who normally avoid true crime." —*Publishers Weekly* (starred review)

"The book is well-researched and well-written, and those interested in crime and police interrogation methods will find it most interesting." —*Washington Times*

"Bowden returns to the story that catapulted his career with a horrific portrait of a sociopath and honors the dedicated officers who were determined to get justice for two innocent girls and their grieving family." —*Booklist*

"Mesmerizing . . . *The Last Stone* will leave readers on the edge of their seats as a group of indefatigable detectives tries to unearth the carefully concealed, unspeakable truths behind a decades-old tragedy." —*BookPage*

Also by Mark Bowden

Doctor Dealer

Bringing the Heat

Black Hawk Down

Killing Pablo

Finders Keepers

Road Work

Guests of the Ayatollah

The Best Game Ever

Worm

The Finish

The Three Battles of Wanat

Hue 1968

THE LAST STONE

A MASTERPIECE OF CRIMINAL INTERROGATION

MARK BOWDEN

Grove Press
New York

Photo credits are as follows: p. 1: Montgomery County Police; p. 8: the *Washington Post*; p. 29: Montgomery County Police; p. 65: Photo by James K. Atherton / the *Washington Post* via Getty Images; p. 91: Photo by Ricky Carioti / the *Washington Post* via Getty Images; p. 115 Montgomery County Police; p. 134: (Left) Montgomery County Police (Right) WDBJ News; p. 155: © Jay Westcott / The News & Advance; p. 192: Montgomery County Police; p. 217 © Neal Augenstein / WTOP; p. 243 Montgomery County Police; p. 280 Montgomery County Police; p. 305: Photo by Sarah L. Voisin / the *Washington Post* via Getty Images; p. 341: Family photos via the *Washington Post*.

Published simultaneously in Canada
Printed in the United States of America

First Grove Atlantic hardcover edition: April 2019
First Grove Atlantic paperback edition: March 2020

This title was set in 12-point Arno Pro by Alpha Design & Composition of Pittsfield, NH.

Library of Congress Cataloging-in-Publication data is available for this title.

ISBN 978-0-8021-4891-9
eISBN 978-0-8021-4731-8

Grove Press
an imprint of Grove Atlantic
154 West 14th Street
New York, NY 10011

Distributed by Publishers Group West

groveatlantic.com

20 21 22 23 10 9 8 7 6 5 4 3 2 1

To Gail

It's a good deal like chess or boxing. Some people you have to crowd and keep off balance. Some you just box and they will end up beating themselves.

—Raymond Chandler

PENNSYLVANIA
Pittsburgh
Harrisburg
Wilmington
MARYLAND
Baltimore
Smyrna
Dover
Gaithersburg
Wheaton
Hyattsville
DEL.
W. VA.
66
Washington, D.C.
VIRGINIA
Charlottesville
81
95
64
29
Richmond
Thaxton
Bedford
Lynchburg
460
Roanoke
85
NORTH CAROLINA
Greensboro
Durham
Raleigh
60 MILES

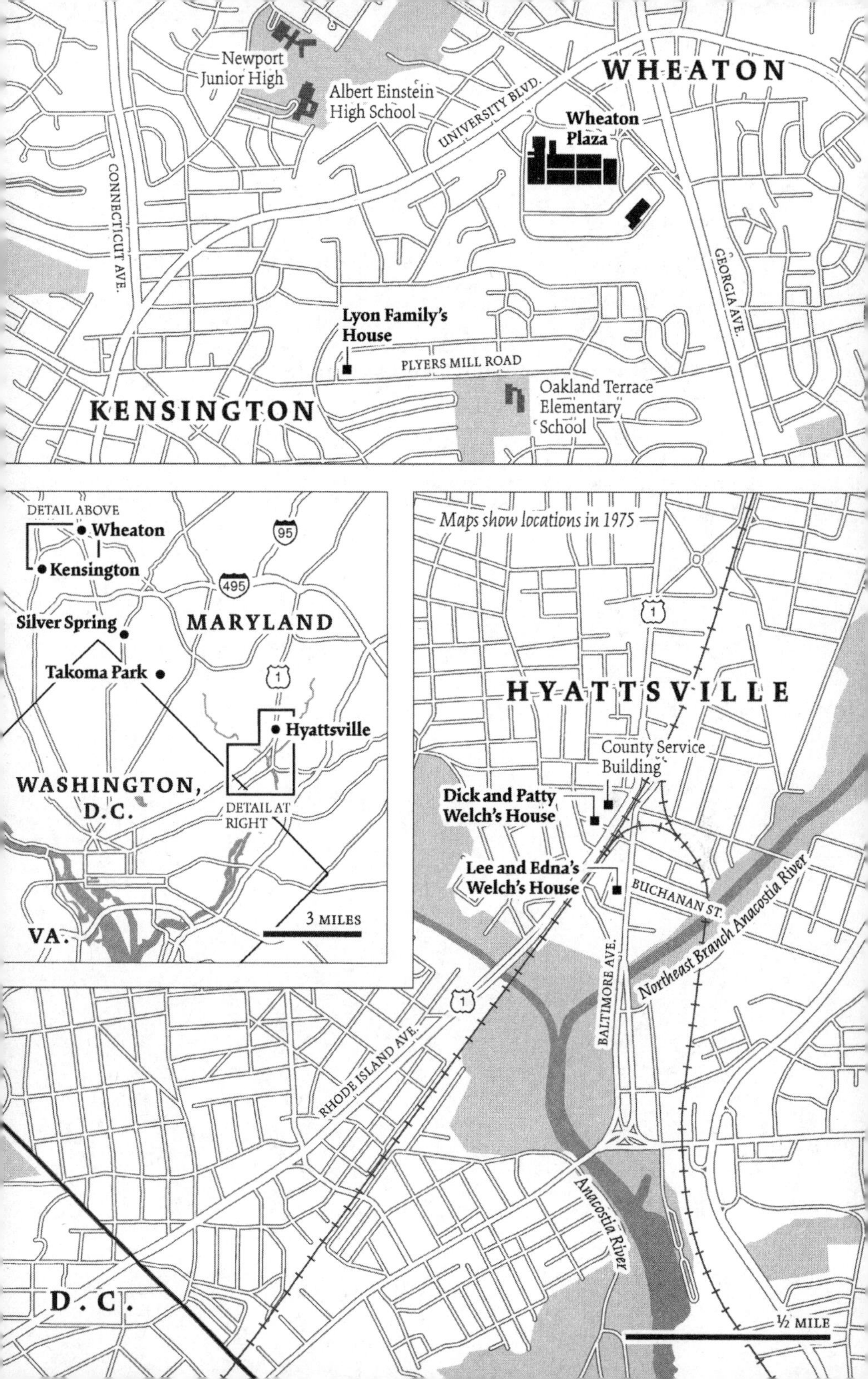
WHEATON
Newport
Junior High
Albert Einstein
High School
UNIVERSITY BLVD.
Wheaton
Plaza
CONNECTICUT AVE.
GEORGIA AVE.
Lyon Family's
House
PLYERS MILL ROAD
Oakland Terrace
Elementary
School
KENSINGTON
DETAIL ABOVE
Wheaton
Kensington
95
495
Silver Spring
MARYLAND
Takoma Park
1
Hyattsville
WASHINGTON,
D.C.
DETAIL AT
RIGHT
VA.
3 MILES
Maps show locations in 1975
HYATTSVILLE
County Service
Building
Dick and Patty
Welch's House
Lee and Edna's
Welch's House
BUCHANAN ST.
Northeast Branch Anacostia River
BALTIMORE AVE.
RHODE ISLAND AVE.
Anacostia River
D.C.
½ MILE

Most of the dialogue in this book was recorded.
I have edited it for concision and clarity.

1

The First Lie

Lloyd Lee Welch, 1977

April 1, 1975

Lloyd Welch got himself good and high before he went back to Wheaton Plaza on April Fools' Day. He was stoned enough not to listen when his stepmom, Edna, warned him, "Don't get mixed up in this."

But Lloyd was already mixed up in it, enough to scare him. He needed to do something, even if it meant running a big risk. The marijuana buzz, he figured, would soothe him and help him think straight. Such was his teenage logic.

Screwing up came naturally. He was a seventh-grade dropout with, at age eighteen, a pathetic whisper of a mustache. His long, thick dark brown hair was parted in the middle, strapped down with a headband. He was scrawny and acned and mean; life had treated him harshly, and it showed. And, man, could he talk. Lloyd was a con artist. Words tumbled from him pell-mell, as if their sheer number and urgency could persuade. Whatever was true in what he said came wrapped in slippery layers of guile.

The story Lloyd planned to tell that day concerned two little girls who had gone missing from Wheaton Plaza a week earlier—Sheila and Kate Lyon. Their disappearance had created a media storm. Every newspaper and TV and radio station between Richmond and Baltimore was reporting on the hunt. Children were on lockdown. The Lyon girls' father, John, was a local radio personality, and this gave the crisis even more notoriety. After a week, past the point where odds favored ever finding the girls alive, the police in Montgomery County, Maryland, were desperate. The public had flooded them with tips, none of which had helped. The girls had vanished. In the days since their disappearance, both had had birthdays; Sheila had turned thirteen, and Kate, on Easter Sunday, eleven. The heart of every parent ached.

The plaza was a Main Street of sorts for the suburban sprawl northwest of Washington, DC. An enormous cross-shaped structure that had opened eight years earlier, it had stores on both sides of two partly sheltered promenades. The longer of the two was anchored at its ends by the department stores Montgomery Ward and Woodward & Lothrop; it had a roof open to the sky along the center and was ornamented at intervals with bush-filled brick planters, the sides of which doubled as seating areas. Where the two promenades intersected was a square with a fountain and a modernist sculpture, then decorated for Easter. The mall's style was futuristic, with the long horizontal lines, sharp angles, and neon hues that artists and filmmakers associated with the space age. It was more than a place to shop; it was a social center, a place to see and be seen. Unlike traditional small towns, few of the residential communities that sprouted outside big cities in the 1950s had anything like a nucleus. So the mall filled a need beyond commerce, and like those being built in suburbs all over America, Wheaton Plaza was an immediate and enduring sensation. A towering sign above its vast parking lot spelled out its name, each huge black letter set in a giant orange ball that glowed at night. There were specialty shops, a three-screen cinema, a Peoples drugstore, and plenty of food outlets, including a Roy Rogers, an ice cream shop, and a popular pizza joint called the Orange Bowl.

With schools out for spring break, unseasonably warm weather, and sunshine, the plaza was a magnet, especially for children.

Lloyd walked in by himself, looking for a security guard. His plan was to tell his story to a mall cop and leave, but he had a poor sense of situation. Any scrap of new intelligence about the Lyon sisters at that point was a very big deal. The mall cop immediately called the police. “Now I’m screwed,” Lloyd thought. “My stepmom was right.” Two detectives, Steve Hargrove and Mike Thilia, came promptly. Lloyd was taken to police headquarters, and as soon as a tape recorder was turned on, he did what he did best.

He told them he was twenty-two. He said he had finished high school. He had been at the mall with his wife, Helen. None of this was true. He had seen two little girls who fit the Lyon sisters’ description—the same ages, blond hair, the elder one (Sheila) with glasses—talking in the mall to an older man with a tape recorder. All of this was unremarkable; pictures of the girls had been everywhere, on TV, in newspapers, and on telephone poles—the police had posted thousands of leaflets. The unknown “tape recorder man” had been widely reported as the prime suspect. Lloyd offered a detailed description: hair gray around the ears, black and thick on top; a dark, stubbly face—“like a heavy shaver”—about six one, six two; wearing a brown suit, white shirt, and black tie; and carrying a brown briefcase that held the portable recorder. He said he’d overheard the man explaining to the girls that he recorded people’s voices and then put them on the radio. This same story had been in all the news reports and was known by just about everyone breathing within a radius of two hundred miles. Lloyd said he later saw both girls leaving the mall with the man and had seen them again outside as they drove off.

“All right, let me ask you a couple of questions before we get to the second time you saw him,” said Hargrove. “What brought your attention to the man and the little girls in the first place?”

“Well, because an older man talking to two small girls, just walk up and talk to them, the girls wouldn’t know exactly what to say if he was asking some kind of questions," Lloyd said, words spilling out awkwardly. "And the girls looked pretty young, [one] about twelve, the other ten, a little younger than that maybe. I'm not sure how old they were, because I didn't see their face[s], and they just caught my attention when he said he was putting them on the air, and he looked pretty old to be talking to someone that young"—as if it were uncommon for adults to speak with children.

"Did he appear to be alone?"

"Yes, he was alone."

"Working by himself?"

"Right, until he started talking to those two girls."

Lloyd said he saw the man pull the tape recorder out and show it to the girls, and that he himself watched them for five or ten minutes, which is a long time to sit and watch three strangers.

"I was sitting down at the time because I was walking around so much I was tired, and I sat down and that's when I saw him talking to them." He said he had been walking around the mall applying for jobs.

"Did you hear him ask the girls any specific questions?" Hargrove asked.

"Not at the time I was there, no. I didn't hear that."

"Did you hear the girls say anything?"

"One of the girls laughed, you know. Giggled, like."

"Which one? The taller one?"

"The taller one."

Lloyd was a fount of particulars about the girls' departure.

"I came through the Peoples drugstore, and he was standing there, and they were getting ready to cross the street. Me and my wife, we both, she came and got me, and we cut through the store and we got in the car, and he left before us and he went west on University [Avenue], and we went west toward Langley Park. And the car that he got into was a red Camaro, and it had white seats, lining, and the girls had gotten in the back, and he got in the front, and there was a dent in the right rear end, and the taillight was busted out."

"How did you know the taillight was busted out?"

"Because when he started to pull off, then he stepped on the brakes easy, and his taillight didn't go on, just one of them."

"Which one went on? Which side?"

Lloyd said the left-side light came on, the right side was broken, and then went on to offer a startling spate of additional details about the car—oversize shocks, high suspension, wide tires, chrome wheel covers—"and he had pinstripes on each side, and they were about one inch apart and they were black, and he had something written like an advertisement thing in the right-hand corner."

"The front?"

"The back of the windshield. And it looked like it was on the outside or inside, I couldn't really tell, and then his mufflers sounded really loud, and I noticed they sounded like glasspack mufflers, and he had square coming out, you know the muffler which at the end was a square, and I told my wife, Helen, I said, 'Ain't that a nice car, a souped-up car?' and she said, 'uh,' she wasn't paying that much attention to it. She was really tired from walking around so much and looking for a job, so she didn't pay much attention. I don't know if she saw the car or not. And we were pulling out, and he was right in front of us, and we were at the light and we stopped, and the light turned green, and I wasn't really looking at the car when the light turned green, when he took off, that's what got me to look again, because I was listening to the muffler and talking to her, and then he went west. And we went toward Langley Park, and that was the last time I had seen him since."

"Why didn't you come forward with this information when you first heard about it?"

"Because I wasn't really positive and sure if it was the same guy and the same two girls at the time, and that's why I was up in Wheaton Plaza today, looking at the picture and listening around to see if it was the same two girls and the same guy, and then I saw a captain, he was a security guard, and he remembered me there last Tuesday in a brown fur jacket."

"You were wearing a brown fur jacket?"

"Yeah, I was wearing a brown fur jacket, and he talked to me again today. I mean, he didn't talk to me last week, but he talked to me, and I told him about what I saw. That's when he contacted you all. That's when you got ahold of me."

Lloyd said he might be able to identify the girls and the man if he saw them again. He could describe what the weather was like that earlier afternoon: "A little windy, but it was nice." He said the Camaro had white Maryland tags.

"Okay, Lloyd, are you telling me, the police department, all this of your own free will?"

"Yes, I am."

"No one has asked you?"

"No. I came forward of my own free will because I have been worried about the girls, even though I don't know them, but I just can't stand to see anybody hurt, two little girls, or anybody hurt."

Hargrove and Thilia warned him that giving a false statement to the police was a criminal offense.

"Now, with that in mind, are you willing to say everything you told us is correct?" asked one of the officers.

"Yes, I am. I am telling you the truth. I can't afford to lie because I have a baby on the way and a wife to take care of, and I can't afford to lie about anything."

"Are you nervous right now?"

"I am a little nervous talking to the tape recorder, yes."

In a final flourish, Lloyd added that the man he saw leaving with the girls "walked with a little limp."

Lloyd was then given a lie detector test, which he flunked. Flustered, he admitted that he'd made up everything about the car and about seeing the tape recorder man with the girls outside the mall. He had told them nothing that anyone listening to news reports wouldn't know, gussied up with a peculiar flurry of made-up particulars. Lloyd thought for sure he'd be arrested then, but instead the detectives dismissed him, no doubt annoyed.

The officers missed something about Lloyd Welch that day, something big. Days earlier, Danette Shea, a girl slightly older than Sheila Lyon, who had seen Sheila at the mall that day, had described a man who had been following and staring at Danette and her friends. He had been so obnoxious that one of the girls had taunted him: "Why don't you take a picture? It'll last longer." Shea had described the man as eighteen or nineteen years old, five eleven to six foot, dark brown hair in a shag, medium mustache. A police artist had even produced a sketch, which was in the growing file. It looked a lot like Lloyd.

Before leaving, Lloyd was given a lecture about lying to the police. He was enormously relieved. The Montgomery County police were swimming in useless tips just then. Given the urgency of the situation, the kid wasn't just a nuisance, he was a serious waste of time. They had no doubt sized him up as a local knucklehead, obviously high, trying to insinuate himself into the story, play the hero, and collect a reward—WMAL, the radio station that employed John Lyon, had just upped its offering to $14,000, and the Wheaton Plaza Merchants' Association had put up $5,000 more. Lloyd seemed stupid, not suspicious. How much sense would it make, after all, for someone involved with a kidnapping to draw attention to himself by claiming to be a witness and telling an elaborate lie? The six-page typed transcript of the interview went into a ring binder with all the other stray bits. A one-page report was written up. At the top, Hargrove wrote, "LIED."

After that, the department didn't give Lloyd Welch a second thought.

Not for thirty-eight years.

2
Finding Lloyd

John and Mary Lyon, 1975

One Shot

One shot was all they were likely to get with Lloyd Welch. So the Montgomery County Police Department's Lyon squad had gamed the meeting for months, all through the summer and fall of 2013. They had even driven down to Quantico, Virginia, to consult with FBI behavioral analysts, who drew up impressive charts and summoned comparative data to pronounce Lloyd a classic hard case. The analysts predicted he would clam up as soon as he learned what the squad wanted to ask him about.

At that point all they knew about Lloyd Lee Welch came from files. His criminal record sketched a rough time line before and after he had walked into Wheaton Plaza in 1975 with his bogus story—or so it had been considered then; now the authorities were less certain.

Lloyd's record traced a heroic trail of malfeasance. In Maryland: larceny (1977), burglary (1981), assault and battery (1982). In Florida: burglary in Orlando (1977), burglary in Miami (1980). In Iowa: robbery in Sioux City (1987). Then he'd moved to South Carolina: public drunkenness and then grand larceny in Myrtle Beach (1988), burglary in Horry County (1989), sexual assault on a ten-year-old girl in Lockhart (1992), drunk driving in Clover (1992). Then on to Virginia: sexual assault on a minor in Manassas (1996), simple assault in Manassas (1997). He'd finally landed hard in Delaware: sexual assault of a ten-year-old girl in New Castle (1997). After that the list ended. This was typical. Waning hormones or better judgment often overtook even the slowest learners by their mid-thirties, after which they avoided trouble. Either that or they got killed or locked up. In Welch's case it was the latter. He was deep into a thirty-three-year sentence for the Delaware charge, housed at the James T. Vaughn Correctional Center in Smyrna.

All that interested the squad, however, was the story he'd told in 1975. Here was a potential eyewitness, albeit a sticky one, to the kidnapping of Sheila and Kate Lyon. He had failed every part of that old polygraph except his claim to have been in Wheaton Plaza at the same time the girls had disappeared, which was the part that most interested the detectives. If he had seen the girls with their abductor, he might be able to corroborate, all these years later, evidence against the squad's prime suspect, a notorious pedophile and murderer named Ray Mileski.

But Welch's own history with little girls made them wonder. Could he have been involved? Did he know Mileski? Welch was under no obligation to talk and had every reason not to. For a convicted pedophile, the slightest link to the Lyon case might mean serious trouble. Any attorney worth retaining would advise him to stay silent. On the other hand, showing some willingness to help with an old case might earn him grace down the line with the Delaware parole board. It was a delicate situation. To prepare, the detectives had talked with several members of Welch's family, few of whom seemed to know him well. Those who did remembered him with grudging kinship and scorn. The detectives didn't know what to expect and weren't sure how to proceed. At weekly staff meetings, their captain kept asking, "When are you guys going to do this?" But with only one shot, they weren't going to just wing it. Thirty-eight years after the girls vanished, Welch was the last stone unturned. The two biggest questions they wanted answered were, in order: Could he identify Mileski? Had they worked together?

From Montgomery County police headquarters in Gaithersburg to Delaware was a two-hour drive. The investigators bypassed Annapolis; crossed the long, high Chesapeake Bay Bridge; and then eased into the flat farmland of the Eastern Shore. Fields of brittle, head-high brown corn lined both sides of Highway 301. As he drove, Sergeant Chris Homrock talked last-minute strategy in the front with Montgomery County deputy state's attorney Pete Feeney. In the back was Detective Dave Davis, the one who would actually be in the room with Welch. At the Dover, Delaware, police headquarters, to which Welch had been brought from the prison that morning, they would be joined by an FBI agent.

Moving Welch to the police station was part of their strategy. Prisoners did not like to be seen talking to cops, and there were eyes and ears everywhere in a maximum-security prison. It had taken high-level persuasion to get Delaware's corrections department to agree. This would be Welch's first trip to the outside world in years. But he might become eligible for work release in just two years, and with freedom on his horizon the drive south from Smyrna might give him a taste of it and encourage helpfulness. They knew his instincts would make him wary. In an inmate's world, an unscheduled summons from the Law rarely meant good news.

Welch had not been told who wanted to see him or why. The squad wanted to catch him cold. First reactions were often revealing. Could the detectives get him talking? Lloyd would see the danger, so they had to entice him. But with what? He was under Delaware's supervision, and they had no sway with that state's prison system or parole board. With no carrot, they needed a stick, a way to convince Welch that it was more dangerous to stay silent than to talk. With nothing to hold over him, leverage would have to be invented.

The longer they'd planned for this day the less likely it seemed they would succeed. Spooking Welch was just their first worry. If he agreed to talk, how should they proceed? Should they read him his Miranda rights, or would that alarm him? If they didn't and he incriminated himself, they couldn't use his evidence. Should they tell him about Mileski? Their theory of the case? How much? How little? If he balked, how could they keep him in the room?

As the sergeant and prosecutor rehashed these questions in the car, Dave Davis clapped on earphones and tuned them out. He watched the flat farmland fly past. They weren't going to come up with anything new. Dave was a wiry, boyish-looking man with an engaging, toothy smile. His close-cropped dark hair was beginning to show flecks of gray, but he still wore it spiked in front like a teenager, and he was always meticulously groomed—his colleagues teased him about it. Even when he was dressed informally, as was his norm, his slacks and sport shirts were spotless and unwrinkled. His weekend passion for extreme mountain biking kept him tan and very fit. After graduating from Florida Southern College with a criminology degree, he had worked for his father's heating and air-conditioning company before becoming a cop, and he still supplemented his paycheck with carpentry and general contracting. He liked his job, but for him, unlike many of his colleagues, it was just a job, not his mission in life. When asked what he did for a living, Dave would answer, "I work for local government," because if he said he was a cop, the mood instantly stiffened. As Dave saw it, the work was what he did, not who he was. He came from a military family and as a teenager had seriously considered West Point or the US Naval Academy—he was a good athlete, which would have helped—but he had decided against military service because it was too *defining*. Being a civilian—"a regular guy," as he put it—was a conscious choice. Many of the cops he knew found ways to moonlight in work related to policing—security work or consulting—but Dave did not. He preferred time away from it. Off duty, he liked himself better. That didn't mean he took the job less seriously; in fact, it made him better at it. People didn't see Dave as a cop; they saw him as just a friendly, outgoing guy, but this sunny demeanor hid a quick, calculating mind.

Chris considered him the best interrogator in the department. It was work that particularly suited Dave. Criminals saw the man, not the badge, and they liked him, sometimes enough to tell him surprising and damaging things. As one of his colleagues put it, "Dave is very genuine, even when he isn't genuine." The department had nabbed a gang of armored-car robbers after a string of violent, sophisticated heists—in which the gang had stolen hundreds of thousands of dollars at a time. The ringleader, a man with an extensive record that included murder, had, at the end of a long conversation with Dave, not only confessed but also told him where the loot was buried. They dug it up at two in the morning on a golf course in Howard County, right where he'd said it would be. Years later Chris was still amazed by that. He didn't understand how it had happened. He just knew that when they met Lloyd Welch, he wanted Dave to be the man in the room.

The earphones bought Dave some time to relax. He was anxious. He knew there was no road map for this session. That was not how interrogation worked. Conversations were improvisational. You never knew when an offhand remark might give you the answer you needed, when a poorly worded question might instantly shut down a suspect, or how an important insight might leap from a slip of the tongue. Chris and Pete would be in an adjacent room watching and listening. Dave would be able to consult with them at intervals, but what happened in the moment would be up to him.

It wouldn't just be an interview—it would be a performance.

A Pebble in the Shoe

The taking of Sheila and Kate Lyon had cried out for justice over decades. It wasn't just a mystery; it was a regional trauma. The crimes that most terrorize us are those that occur where we feel happy and safe. This one struck to the hearth, a shock to anyone who has ever loved a child or remembered being one.

For the Montgomery County Police Department, it was also an embarrassment, a blot both professional and personal. Professional because it was unsolved, the most notorious such case on its books in a half century. Personal because one of the girls' two brothers, Jay, had grown up and joined the force. With its fierce fraternal tradition, that had made it a *family* tragedy.

It was a pebble in the department's shoe. Generations of county detectives had come and gone, and many had taken a crack at it. Periodically, a new cold case team would start over, combing through the many boxes of yellowing evidence, hoping to find something missed. Ed Golian, now retired, had worked the case off and on for his entire career, from before he had even earned his badge. He had been in the academy when the sisters disappeared. His entire cadet class was pressed into the search, striding an arm's length apart in long rows through wet spring fields, beneath the staccato thrum of a helicopter that swept a moving spotlight. Golian and the others had manned long tables late into the night sorting the flood of tips and sightings. They were also asked to assemble a list of every known sex offender in the area, compiling, they were told, something called a "database." At the time, Golian wasn't sure what that meant.

Fruitless suspicion had fallen at first on the girls' father, John Lyon, for no reason other than statistics—most crimes against children were committed by family members—and sheer desperation. But the Lyon family was a happy one. Their photos—four sunny children posing on the beach or dressed in their Sunday best in the front yard or peering out happily from the back window of the family station wagon—depicted a contemporary suburban ideal. Sheila stood out in all the pictures, with her glasses and bright blond pigtails, from early childhood to the picture taken of her dressed all in white, her legs grown long and lean, posing before a shrub on the day of her First Communion. Kate looked like more of a tomboy, with even brighter blond hair, cut shorter than her sister's, and a spray of freckles across the bridge of her nose. The drawings and cards and notes the girls left behind in their bedrooms were heartbreakingly innocent and joyful. John and Mary were loving parents, guilty of nothing more than letting their girls walk unsupervised down the street to the mall to buy slices of pizza. They were bereft.

That much was plain to anyone who saw them those first days, as I did, working the story as a new reporter for the *Baltimore*

News-American. Knowing that any attention might help, the couple opened up their small white stucco house on the corner to everyone, family, friends, and even reporters. They passed out cans of beer and cups of coffee. Mary was unusually composed—she was on a diet of tranquilizers—but her face was red and drawn. John was a study in well-contained panic, a man with a wry sense of humor about himself, someone *cool*, trapped in a circumstance for which there was no cool way to behave. I remember sitting with him in the enclosed side porch of his house as he vacantly strummed a guitar and tried patiently to answer my useless questions.

They were a handsome pair, John rugged and hip, Mary pretty, small, and slender, with short dark hair. Both were in their thirties. They had met at Xavier University in Cincinnati, when John had been a full-time student and Mary a part-time one. He was from Chicago, and she was from nearby Erlanger, Kentucky. They married in Erlanger and had their first child, Jay, shortly before moving to Chicago, where they lived with John's parents while he completed his degree by taking night classes at Columbia College. He worked days at Sears in the Loop. After graduation he'd gotten a job at a radio station in Ohio, where Sheila was born, and then one in Streator, Illinois, where Kate was born, and then a bigger job, in Peoria—"The big city!" Mary joked—where John worked in both radio and TV. He appeared on a daytime kids' show, introducing movies with his guitar and banjo. He and Mary sometimes performed with a folk band in those years, during which she gave birth to their youngest, Joe. The job at WMAL was a big step up. It was the most popular radio station in Washington, DC, and by now John was a seasoned on-air personality. He had long, dark hair beginning to show strands of gray and a droopy mustache and spoke with the deep, melodious tones of a radio pro. He worked as a fill-in disc jockey and sometimes read the news and still performed with a band, called Gross National Product, that played gigs in the area. John and Mary were charming and witty and fun, accustomed to the spotlight, which helped explain their remarkable poise at the center of this awful one. Tragedy felt like a complete stranger in their home, a reminder of the most banal of truths: you can do absolutely everything right and still be rewarded with unconscionable cruelty.

In those first days there was disbelief and hope. Maybe it was all a snafu and the girls would turn up. John went on the air at WMAL the day after they vanished, speaking calmly and modestly.

"I'm sure we're going to feel stupid about this," he said. "They probably told us they were going to a sleepover and we forgot. If anybody knows where they are, please send them home."

Kensington, where the Lyons lived, was north of Washington, well outside the Capital Beltway, adjacent to the booming edge city of Silver Spring. It had been farmland until the end of the nineteenth century, when an Anglophile DC developer bought lots and replicated a Victorian village, which would lend a quaint character to the suburban homes that sprang up around it. First popular as an escape from the swampy district summers, it was overtaken by the suburban explosion that followed World War II. By the 1970s Kensington was a bedroom community for Washington commuters, most of them government workers, nearly all of them white, and still something of an escape, not so much from DC's climate as from its crowded, increasingly black, restive, and troubled core. Together, Kensington and the larger, adjacent suburb of Wheaton were home to fifty thousand people and distinctly middle to upper class. They were like thousands of other suburbs ringing American cities, havens for whites fleeing the black urban migration, seeking comfort in racial and demographic homogeneity. Largely new, green, clean, and prosperous, Kensington was considered an idyllic place to raise a family.

Before the age of continuous cable TV news and the Internet, children's disappearances were primarily local tragedies and did not automatically attract strong news coverage. In big cities like Washington and Baltimore, newspapers were the primary medium, and they had come a long way from their sensationalist roots. Journalism was now a white-collar profession. Reporters for the big papers saw their work as public service—the *Washington Post* was fresh off the triumph of Watergate. In Baltimore, the most respected paper was the *Baltimore Sun*, a dignified modern daily that headlined those stories its editors deemed important—an amendment to a piece of tax legislation in Annapolis would get better play than a lurid local crime. With its news bureaus all over the country and the world, the *Sun* was in the business of educating and informing readers. My paper, the *Baltimore News-American,* on the other hand, was a throwback. It was part of the Hearst chain. It had nothing like its competitor's resources (or talent), took itself less seriously, and, for better or worse, still showed its yellow roots. Its priority was still *whatever sells.* In keeping with that approach, my job was to show up in the newsroom at four in the morning and phone every police barracks in the state, asking whether anything interesting had happened overnight. This was a mind-numbing task and usually produced nothing, but when, on the morning of March 26, 1975, the desk officer in Wheaton told me about the missing children, I drove directly to the scene. Ours was an afternoon paper, so if the story was interesting enough—which this clearly was—and I moved fast enough, it was possible to slap a story on the front page later that day. It was sure to attract attention. Millions of families in the region lived in neighborhoods just like Kensington, shooing their kids out the door in the morning and catching up with them at mealtimes, unconcerned about where they went, because every house on every block was inhabited by families just like their own. A story like this struck at suburbia's idea of itself.

My first story ran on a Thursday, two days after the girls vanished, under the headline, "100 Searching Woods for 2 Missing Girls." It had photos of Sheila, in pigtails and glasses, and Kate, with her hair cut in a cute bob. By the next morning, Good Friday, the FBI and the Washington, DC, police department had joined the effort, and the story led the local news in the *Washington Post*: "Police Press Search for Missing Girls." As days passed with no good news, the tale turned grimmer. No one wanted to imagine the girls' fate. In my newspaper the story was still on the front page at the end of the week: "Hope Fades in Search for Girls." Every TV and radio news broadcast led with it, sparking a huge public response. More than three hundred people phoned the police in the first three days alone to say they had seen the girls, and all these tips had to be checked out. The family heard from everyone they'd ever known.

"We've had hundreds of phone calls from well-wishers," John told me, two days after the girls had disappeared. "Most are from perfect strangers. They want to know what they can do to help. I wish I knew what to tell them."

Every stand of woods or weeds was searched. Storm sewers were explored, as was every vacant house for miles. The residents of a nearby nursing home were interviewed, one by one. Scuba divers groped through mud at the bottoms of ponds. John stood by one chilly afternoon, shivering, his hands thrust deep into the pockets of his white Levi's, as divers disappeared into a small lake on the grounds of the nearby Kensington Nursing Home. He waited awkwardly . . . for what? How did one both want and desperately not want to find something? Nothing was found. Nothing came of anything the police did, despite occasional moments of excitement. Thirteen days after the girls vanished, on April 7—long after hopes of finding them alive had faded—there was a call from an IBM employee who, on his way to work in Manassas, Virginia, had stopped at a red light behind a Ford station wagon. He had been startled to see in its rear the head of a blond child, bound and gagged. He jotted down the license-plate number, all but the last digit, which he couldn't see because the plate was bent. The driver of the station wagon, apparently noticing the other driver eyeing him from behind, had suddenly accelerated through the red light and sped off through the intersection. In that pre-cell-phone era, the IBM man phoned in the tip when he got to his office and later that day was questioned and polygraphed. He wasn't sure whether the plate had been from Maryland or North Carolina—the new bicentennial plates of these states were similar—but his story was sound. Lists were compiled of all cars with plates that matched the description, from both states, and efforts were made to find them. Nothing came of it.

This nightmare unfolded in the context of larger national unease. Ground was shifting under enduring institutions of American life, and the promise that had propelled the country so dynamically through the

1950s and '60s had soured. Jobs were scarce, and paychecks didn't go as far—a phenomenon dubbed "stagflation." Americans had stopped buying stocks—they were no longer betting on the future. The Vietnam War was spiraling to humiliating defeat after dominating headlines for more than a decade. President Nixon had resigned in a scandal, and each week another top member of his administration went to jail. There were revelations of domestic spying and of troubling American involvement in foreign coups and assassination plots, both ludicrous and disturbing. Government suddenly appeared not just untrustworthy but inept. Violent crime in nearby Washington had nearly doubled in the previous five years. The Summer of Love had degenerated into drug abuse and violent radicalism. Strange groups were setting off bombs and abducting people—tracking dogs used in the hunt for the Lyon sisters had been used a year earlier to look for kidnapped heiress Patty Hearst. On TV, the most popular character was Archie Bunker, a blue-collar American male railing hilariously against the collapse of his preferred social order.

The day Sheila and Kate went missing was an early taste of spring. There had been two snowfalls that March, but the weather before Easter week had turned warm and muggy. That Tuesday morning John worked the midnight-to-six shift, after which he drove home and went to bed. He woke up at one in the afternoon to an empty house. Off school for spring break, Sheila and Kate had gone to the mall. They had left with about two dollars between them, complaining that the cost of a pizza slice at the Orange Bowl had recently gone up five cents. There had been a time when Sheila did not want her younger sister with her, but in recent months Mary felt they had begun to play happily together again. Mary had gone bowling, and the Lyon boys were off with friends in the neighborhood. Mary and Joe were home soon after John got up, and when he went back to bed for a mid-afternoon nap, she took a rake to the matted leaves in the backyard that had been buried in snow just weeks before. At dusk she began missing the girls. She assumed they were with friends and having fun. They were usually prompt at dinnertime, and ordinarily Sheila would call if they were delayed. But she had not called. John and Mary ate dinner with their boys, two empty chairs at the table, Mary now annoyed. With still no word after they'd finished, they started calling all the girls' friends. Nothing. They drove around the neighborhood with a mounting sense of alarm. Then they called the police.

Many teenagers and even children go absent from their homes—there had been eighteen hundred reported cases in Montgomery County alone in the previous year, but most involved slightly older children, and in nearly every case they were quickly found. That this report was different was rapidly becoming apparent, and when the girls remained missing through that night it became a crisis. According to John and Mary, this was utterly out of character. Both girls were obedient. They were honor roll students. Kate was the outgoing, athletic, silly one. She was a fifth grader at Oakland Terrace Elementary School and had a poster of pop singers Loggins and Messina in her bedroom. Her mother had just given her permission to get her ears pierced. Sheila was the dreamy one, quieter and more of a homebody. The poster in her room was of the romantic folk balladeer John Denver. She had started to help her mother cook, had begun wearing eye shadow, and had recently taken her first babysitting jobs. A seventh grader at Newport Junior High, she was hoping to make the school's cheerleading squad. Neither girl had taken money from her piggy bank or extra clothing, telltale signs of a runaway.

"No," John told me, with crisp certainty. "They did not run away. I really wish there was a reason for believing they did."

As a green, twenty-three-year-old reporter, I tried to see the Lyon case as a *story*, my first chance to write front-page news. The people I wrote about were subjects, and tragedy was a thing that happened to others. But the Lyons were people I liked, even admired. I could not witness their pain dispassionately.

Of the thousands of missing children cases reported each year, those involving children taken by a stranger number only one one-hundredth of one percent—on average about one hundred cases a year in the United States, a number that has changed little for as long as such statistics have been kept. Nearly all missing children are found quickly. For two to be taken at once and to disappear completely is a thing so rare that it's almost true to say it never happens—the numbers are so low they cannot be meaningfully framed as a percentage of overall kidnappings. Needless to say, very few people are ever touched personally by such crimes, but today's omnipresent tabloid-style journalism and social media so magnify every occurrence that people are unduly afraid. American children in the twenty-first century lead far more sheltered, supervised lives than children of earlier times. Only thirteen percent still walk to school. Parents who leave a child untended for even a short time may find themselves reported to the police. While today we can all too readily imagine the disappearance of a child, in 1975 it was shocking—and all the more so in this case because it was two children. Imagining how or why was difficult. The problem of controlling two alarmed children at those ages suggested more than one kidnapper, which raised the question, why? What would motivate two people or a group? A sex-trafficking ring? A circle of pedophiles? Just speculating about it conjured scenarios that made you ashamed to be human.

A few weeks after the girls vanished, as if to underscore the potential for cruelty, opportunists began to surface. There were psychics who claimed to have "seen" where the girls were. There were extortionists. One man called the Lyon home and said he would return Sheila and Kate for a payment of $10,000. John drove to the appointed location, a bus station in Annapolis, with a briefcase—in it was just $101, enough to make the crime a felony. He was told to wait there for a pay phone to ring. It did. The caller, a man, instructed him to walk across the street to the county courthouse and put the briefcase in a trash can inside the first-floor men's room. The man said he would then drop the girls off in front of the building. With police watching from a distance, John did as instructed. He then stood expectantly for hours before the courthouse, hopefully eyeing every car that passed. He and his police escort only gave up when the courthouse shut down for the day. They retrieved the briefcase and drove home. John was desperately disappointed and furious. The same man phoned the next morning and said that he hadn't followed through because there were too many cops around. John pointed out the stupidity of selecting a courthouse if he was trying to avoid cops.

He told the man not to call back unless he could put one of the girls on the phone. They did not hear from him again.

There were other, even less sophisticated extortion attempts. One caller told John and Mary to drop $6,000 in an air vent outside the Kensington Volunteer Fire Department, and another instructed them to stand with exactly $1,050 outside the Orange Bowl at Wheaton Plaza. Two months after the girls disappeared, a tip from a Dutch psychic who claimed to have helped solve the Boston Strangler case sent 150 police and National Guardsmen on a daylong search of nearby Rock Creek Park. They found nothing. John and Mary gradually closed themselves off from such contacts, stopped giving interviews, and worked to avoid being consumed with bitterness. The loss of a child is a shattering experience for any family. For the Lyons—John, Mary, Jay, and Joe—it would be a hard task to salvage what was left.

To me, the story was sad and beyond understanding. Like everyone else, I waited for the police to find something and explain the mystery. In time, the story moved off the front page and then out of the news completely, overtaken by fresh outrages. As the decades passed I wrote thousands more stories, big ones and small ones. I raised five children of my own. I experienced tragedy and loss in my own life. I became a grandfather—of two little blond-haired girls, as a matter of fact. Few stories haunted me as this one did.

When he was nearing retirement, Ed Golian, who had joined the search effort as a cadet thirty years earlier, was assigned to the department's cold case team in 2011, typically a last stop before hanging up the badge. As had other detectives before him, he reopened the Lyon files, ending his career with the same case that started it.

Today police have new tools for old crimes. DNA testing offers seemingly magic solutions to decades-old mysteries as long as physical evidence has been preserved. With no bodies and no crime scene, there would be no such magic for this one. Computers held promise. No longer a novelty, they cast a far wider net than even the massive application of manpower applied in those first weeks to finding Sheila and Kate. The machines made it inestimably easier for Ed to complete the old sex-offender lists, to compile time lines, and to cross-check names and incidents for intersections with Wheaton Plaza in 1975. The old list of car registrations that met the IBM man's description was broadened and rechecked. More than three decades later Ed found, of course, that most of these cars had vanished to junkyards. Many owners were no longer alive. Still, all the leads were tracked down, yielding nothing.

This is what cold case teams do. They embrace the tedium. They are the turners of last stones, laboring in a landscape beyond hope. The task is Sisyphean. By its nature, investigation continually churns up new leads, prolonging both the work and the frustration. The Lyon file filled thirty boxes. Golian worked with four other detectives: Chris Homrock, who at forty-one had twenty years of experience in the department; and three who, like Ed, were nearing retirement, Joe Mudano, Bobby Nichols, and Kenny Penrod.

Instead of adding more to the files, the squad decided to weed them. The detectives set out to identify every plausible suspect and reinvestigate enough to either eliminate him or keep him. That work took two years. All the detectives were working on other cases at the same time—Chris was running the department's robbery section, and Kenny led the homicide section—but the puzzle was such a noteworthy challenge that it was always on their minds. The suspects included a fellow named Fred Coffey in South Carolina, whom Kenny favored; another suspicious predator, Arthur Goode; and the infamous sexual sadist and serial killer James Mitchell "Mike" DeBardeleben, all of whom had stories with potential links to the Lyon girls. None could be completely eliminated.

But one jumped out—Ray Mileski, who had died in prison in 2005.

Mileski

By 2013, Chris Homrock was the only one left in the Lyon squad. One by one, Ed Golian, Joe Mudano, Bobby Nichols, and Kenny Penrod had retired. Chris had become obsessed with the case. He talked about it constantly with his wife, Amy, also a police officer, and she encouraged him. If anyone could crack the mystery, she thought, Chris could. He was a natural. He always seemed to know what question to ask next; he could think on his feet better than anyone else she had ever met. No matter how long and hard he worked, no matter how elusive the answers, Amy would have been the last to tell him to stop. Just a few years younger than Sheila and Kate, and having grown up in nearby Potomac, Maryland, she remembered their disappearance well. Her parents referred to the case as a "permanent loss of innocence." Now she and Chris had two daughters who were roughly the same ages Sheila and Kate had been. They could only imagine John and Mary's suffering. So Amy was all in, even if for Chris it meant working long hours, losing sleep, and not eating right. Not that she didn't try to tamp down his intensity now and then, reminding him that the girls were not tied to a tree somewhere awaiting his rescue. His job was to figure out what had happened, to find who had taken them, perhaps to bring the story of their terrible last days—and maybe their remains—home at last to the Lyon family.

But by the early summer of that year, Chris was ready to give up. He felt weighed down with both responsibility and futility. Despite his years of effort, the trail, if anything, had grown colder. Mileski was the one thing that had kept him going.

A petty criminal, killer, and audacious pedophile, Mileski had inserted himself into the investigation. In 1975, he had called the Montgomery County police twice: first with a suggestion—they should offer immunity to the person who kidnapped the girls if he returned them—and then, two weeks after the girls vanished, with a tip. He said he had seen the widely publicized suspect, the gray-haired man with a tape recorder, weeks before the Lyon sisters disappeared, trying to lure children into his car at another mall. He gave the police a detailed account. Then, two years later, the same Ray Mileski shot and killed his wife and one of his sons. In prison for those crimes, he had talked a lot about the Lyon sisters, telling other inmates that he knew where the girls were buried. Police investigated these claims in 1982, partially excavating Mileski's old backyard and basement. They found nothing.

That had stalled active work on Mileski, but when the squad took another hard look at him in 2011, interest in him deepened. Reviewing old witness interviews from after he was arrested for murder, the detectives learned that one possible motive for the killings had been to prevent his wife and son from revealing his connection to the Lyon case. On his bedside table, the night of the murders, police had found a slip of paper with John Lyon's phone number on it.

And the more Chris looked, the more he found. Witness after witness said Mileski was known to pick up young boys and girls for sex. One said he had done this once at Wheaton Plaza. Another said he had seen two little blond girls in Mileski's basement. One woman said that Mileski had raped her on two different occasions when she was a teenager and that he had held sex parties at his suburban home. Men admitted, under hard questioning, that as boys they had been intimidated by Mileski into engaging in sex acts. Chris learned that Mileski had been part of a group of men who engaged in such activities, sometimes gathering at parties to share young victims.

It all fit. Mileski had been a pedophile associated with other pedophiles who swapped child pornography and groomed and shared victims. In time, Chris came to believe in his bones that this was his man, but the case was all circumstantial. He had talked the young couple who owned Mileski's old house into letting him rip out the carpeting in their basement to inspect the concrete floor. He found nothing (and paid to recarpet the floor). At one point Chris learned that Mileski had purchased undeveloped land in Lancaster County, Virginia. Chris then spent weeks there, living in a motel, supervising a dig on the property in a futile search for remains. He would come home and tell Amy how close he felt, almost as if he could hear the Lyon girls calling to him from their graves. He found nothing. Now he wanted to go back to the old Mileski basement and tear through the concrete, but no judge was going to okay that without a strong justification. The gut feelings of a veteran detective didn't count.

Chris had run out of moves. Continually paging through the files, he felt as if he were wearing deeper ruts in a well-worn road. No lead had gone unpursued, no witness unquestioned. It made him angry and stung his pride. He considered himself a pro, and he had struck out. He was at his desk one evening, early that summer, reviewing documents so familiar he could almost recite their contents, when it struck him. He was finished. He had done everything he could do. He was not a man to give up, but he had reached a dead end. The feeling surprised him. He walked to the lavatory and splashed water on his face. It was not so much a decision as a *recognition*. There was nothing left for him to do. It was deeply disappointing but also a relief. He would put the burden down. If Sheila and Kate were still alive, they would both be middle-aged, a good bit older than John and Mary had been in 1975. Like all those before him, Chris had failed. At least he could tell the Lyons, in good conscience, that he had done everything possible.

But when he returned to his desk, staring at him from a stack of old familiar files was one he could not remember having seen—the six-page transcript of Lloyd Welch's April 1, 1975, statement. He was first astonished that he had somehow missed it. How could that be? And how had it come to sit on top of the papers on his desk? Could someone else have put it there? No one was working nearby. It had clearly come from his own collection. He read it for the first time, somewhat amazed, and felt a jolt when he reached the end. This witness had told the detectives that the man who led the girls from the mall "walked with a little limp."

That *had* to be Mileski! During a lifetime of run-ins with the law, Mileski had once been caught in a home burglary and had been shot in the leg by police. Afterward, he limped.

Chris could not believe he had never seen this. Here was someone, this Lloyd Welch, who may have actually seen Mileski in the mall with the girls! If this was true—an eyewitness!—it might be the break he needed.

He showed the old statement to two robbery detectives who worked for him, Dave Davis and Kari Widup.

As they read it, Chris could hardly contain his excitement.

"See the part about him walking with a limp?" he said. "He's describing Ray Mileski!"

Both detectives agreed that it was intriguing, but neither knew enough about the case to fully share Chris's excitement. Dave, the seasoned interrogator, noted that the witness's recall in this old statement seemed suspiciously detailed. In his experience, it went well beyond what any normal teenager would have to offer. Most would never look twice at two little girls. Still, he could see the importance of a potential living witness.

"He would be in his fifties now," said Dave, which meant there was a good chance he was still around.

Welch's old flunked polygraph didn't mean much to Dave; he put little stock in the device. He told Chris he thought it was a good find. Running to a meeting, Chris asked him to do some Internet sleuthing to see whether he could find the man.

A quick scan of state criminal records disclosed Welch's repeated run-ins with Montgomery County. There was a photo attached to a 1977 arrest, showing Welch staring sullenly into the camera. He looked older than his years, kicked around, hardened, a man with scars on his broad face and wide, crooked nose. His thick brown hair was parted in the middle, held down by a dirty, rainbow-colored headband.

Dave confirmed that Welch was still living by calling family members, some of whom were named in the police records. He called an old number in Tennessee, and Welch's elderly stepmother, Edna, answered. Dave identified himself. "We're doing an investigation," he said. "It's from a very long time ago." Edna sounded confused and said she could not hear him well—he suspected that she was trying to get rid of him. She told him to call her son Roy, Lloyd's younger half brother.

"I know he's incarcerated," said Roy, with what sounded like a chuckle—wouldn't a cop know this already? "He's in Delaware for something to do with little kids."

Those words rang loud. Roy didn't offer any more, but Dave now cast a wider digital net. Using a national police database, he found all of Welch's arrests and his disturbing history of sex crimes against children. He had worked for a traveling carnival, which explained the wide-ranging geography of his criminal past. The most recent photo, a prison shot, showed the same face grown older and thicker, sneering down at the lens. Lloyd had lost his hair, his youth, and his freedom. He had a gray mustache and goatee.

When Chris didn't pick up his phone, Dave texted him: "We've located him. Issues with sexual stuff with kids. Currently incarcerated."

That brought Chris out of the meeting. When Dave showed him the old arrest photo, Chris's face paled. He took Dave upstairs and found the old police sketch based on the description given by Danette Shea, the thirteen-year-old girl who had seen a man staring at girls in Wheaton Plaza that day. They were a virtual match. *How could this have been missed?*

They had seen Welch as a possible witness. Now they were even more intrigued. Chris knew Mileski had groomed young victims to help attract other children. Could he and Welch have worked together? Two little girls would be far more likely to follow a teenage boy than a middle-aged man. Both Welch and Mileski had come forward years earlier to volunteer information about the Lyon sisters—how could that be a coincidence?

The find rejuvenated the case. Over the following months, Dave began working it with Chris. They waded back into the piles of paper looking for links between Mileski and Welch. Welch did not fit the profile of a child kidnapper in every way or as neatly as Mileski. There were three instances of child sexual abuse in Welch's record, all with young girls, but all involved children he knew—daughters of girlfriends—in their homes. While bad enough, these incidents were a far cry from kidnapping two unknown girls from a public place and likely killing them. Still, here was a man sexually attracted to little girls. If he had been working with Mileski, it might explain why he'd gotten involved in something more extreme.

There was more. The FBI helped the squad build a Lloyd Welch time line, cross-checking his travels against unsolved missing children cases around the country. There were a number of curious hits. One was spookily reminiscent of the Lyon sisters' case. Welch's carnival made an annual trip through Texas in the winter months, and in December of

1974, in Fort Worth, Texas, three teenage girls had disappeared from a mall, never to be seen again.

Could they have stumbled on a serial killer? The FBI thought it was possible. Chris and Dave then spent months fleshing out their understanding of Welch. They interviewed other members of his family, a collection of odd characters in Maryland and Virginia who had preserved their rural accent and outlaw attitude over generations.

All this provided insight for their sit-down. Despite the other intriguing clues, Welch remained important to them, first, as a witness, someone who might be able to identify Mileski as the man "with a little limp." Whether or not the 1975 statement was true, and whatever his motivation had been in giving it, Welch had clearly been present. Shea's testimony and the drawing confirmed that. Beyond this potential, however, was a richer possibility. Had the two men known each other? After all, if teenage Welch knew Mileski, how likely was it that both men had just happened to have been in the mall at the same time the girls were taken?

The only way to find out was to ask Lloyd Welch. Because the detectives felt he would be more likely to confirm his connection to Mileski if he did not know they were investigating the Lyon case, Dave would start by trying to establish a connection between the two men. Only then would he ask about his old witness statement and try to nail down the vital Mileski ID.

That, at least, was the plan.

3

In All "Honestly"

Lloyd Lee Welch, 2013

OCTOBER *16, 2013*

The plan did not survive the first thirty seconds. Dave met Lloyd Welch in an upstairs hallway of the Dover police headquarters. Before him stood a pale, bald old man with a potbelly in baggy white prison denim, shackled hand and foot. He had big features and a ponderous brow over clever, liquid blue eyes and a wide nose that had been broken and healed bent. He had an unsettling forwardness. This was unmistakably the man in the old arrest photo, bulked out over three decades, especially in the middle. The word that came to Dave was *hard,* a shell baked by years of lockup. He immediately threw the detective off balance.

"I know why you're here," he said with a sly grin. "You're here about those two missing kids."

So much for surprise and for gauging Lloyd's first reaction. If he intended to rattle Dave, it had worked. The detective's mind raced. How could he know? It had to have come from his family, yet the detectives had taken care to avoid saying exactly why they were looking for Lloyd. They'd said, at most, that he might have witnessed a very old crime. Of course, the police do not actively investigate old *minor* crimes, and the Lyon case was notorious, but it was still a highly specific assumption. What did it mean that Lloyd had been given a heads-up?

Then Dave realized that part of the responsibility was his. That morning, without thinking, he had pulled on a dark blue polo shirt with a gold crest that read, "Montgomery County Police / Major Crimes Division."

They were shown to a bare interview room, a small windowless space with gray walls and black trim, olive carpeting, a table, and two chairs. Lloyd was visibly disappointed. When he had been awakened early that morning, he had hoped the interview would be about a pardon petition he had filed recently. The emblem on Dave's shirt had dashed that hope.

The detective asked about prison life.

"It sucks," said Lloyd. "It sucks."

"How much longer do you have?"

"I'm waiting to go for a pardon recommendation, and if I get that, right now I've got nine, about nine and a half years." He was requesting that the final five years of his sentence be dropped as a reward for good behavior, which, according to the intricate algebra of detention, meant he might be eligible for work release in just two. Dave ran with it.

"Do you think prison has been that rehab that they talk about, or do you think you're gonna fall right back into whatever it was that you were doing back then?"

Once freed, Lloyd said, he hoped to go to Tennessee, "out in the country," near where his stepmother, Edna, lived.

Lloyd was nothing at all like the man the FBI analysts had led them to expect. He appeared to enjoy talking for its own sake, and even though he knew Dave was working on the old Lyon case, he seemed indifferent to the risk. He talked like a man addicted to talk, free-associating, and Dave, who had worried for so long about how to get him going, just sat back and listened. Riffing at length about prison life, Lloyd got around to contrasting Delaware to Maryland, where he'd served an earlier stretch. Dave's state, he said, was "ten times better."

"I mean, the staff is a lot better, the food is a lot better, the pay's a lot better [he was being paid eighteen cents an hour for his work detail in the Delaware prison kitchen]. They're more concerned about rehabilitating people. This place isn't."

He then launched into the sort of lament cops hear often from inmates, so routine it was rote, about how awful his life had been, how events had forced him into crime, about how he had learned his lesson, turned his life around, found the Lord, and become a productive citizen who didn't belong behind bars. Dave nodded agreeably.

"I'm fifty-six years old," Lloyd said. "I've lost a lot in life because I had a screwed-up life. You know, I had a screwed-up father. I never knew my real mother. So at fifty-six, if I can get out, I could probably give a lot to the community. I'd prefer to help law enforcement in finding these sons of bitches and drug dealers."

Lloyd was like a burst dam. Words cascaded. Unprompted, he came to the offense that had gotten him locked up for so long. Such injustice! He was, he wanted Dave to know, a good guy. He had been grossly over-punished. His "crime" had been a simple misunderstanding. He was not a child molester. His victim was the daughter of his girlfriend, a child he cared about and would never harm. His crime had been, at worst, a momentary lapse.

"I got drunk. I got high. You know, the girl had me in her trust and everything like that. I was stupid for doing what I did. I admit it. I had all the remorse in the world for what I did to that child, you know? She was gonna be my stepdaughter, you know? I thank God that I didn't go all the way with what happened and shit like that. Even though they say I penetrated, in the state of Delaware, if you put your little pinkie in there [a vagina] or your tongue, you're considered to have penetrated."

Dave swallowed his bile. He had children of his own. His daughter was just nine. Here was a man arguing that the sex acts he had performed on a ten-year-old were trivial. Dave pretended to be surprised.

"It's considered penetration?"

"Right. My penis never went in her. She was still a virgin because I stopped myself, you know? And I feel bad about what I did to her."

"How old were you then?"

"I was forty."

Dave shook his head.

"Yeah," said Lloyd. "Stupid. Very stupid."

"Uh-huh."

"You know what I'm sayin'?" Lloyd said.

Dave nodded and then got to work: "Along those same lines, minus the sex part of it, when you were talking about your upbringing and your family, believe it or not, that's why we're here to talk to you."

"Okay."

Dave told Lloyd that he could take a break whenever he wished, and that if he wanted to order food—a special treat for an inmate—"We can make that happen. I mean, this is very informal." But before they got down to business, even though they were just friends talking here, Dave was a cop and Lloyd was an inmate, so there were formalities. Lloyd had to give written consent. Despite the fears this might arouse, Deputy State's Attorney Pete Feeney had insisted on it. Dave had the statement before him on the table.

"I'm going to read it to you, we'll sign it, we'll put it away, and then we'll start to talk a little bit," he said. "Like I said, we have all day."

He read: "You have the right now to remain silent. Anything you say may be used against you. You have the right to a lawyer before or during any questioning. You can't afford a lawyer, one will be appointed for you."

Dave reassured Lloyd that this was just red tape; he was only a witness. There would be no charges. Lloyd listened, nodding, and squinted skeptically. Dave—and his colleagues in the next room, watching on-screen—waited nervously.

"As long as I'm not being charged with nothin'," Lloyd said finally, and then, to the relief of all, signed.

He then resumed holding forth about . . . his life . . . his travels . . . his jobs . . . his girlfriends . . . the children he had left in his wake. His childhood was troubled and lonely. His most significant relationship had been with a woman named Helen Craver, whom he had met when he was just sixteen and she was twenty, a chubby woman who shared his appetite for drugs and drifting. They had stuck together through the 1970s, traveling and using drugs and making babies. Helen lost one child and gave birth to three during those years. After he was sentenced to a second stretch in prison in 1981, they both relinquished parental rights, and Helen went her own way. Lloyd had seen neither her nor his children since.

"They're all adults now," Lloyd said. "I should have grandchildren by now. You would think. I mean my oldest daughter's thirty-four years old. But do you have any idea where they're at?"

Dave shook his head.

"No? And if they married, their names?"

Again, Dave shook his head.

"I would love to establish a relationship with them, let them know that I did love them and everything, but I thought it was in their best interest to put them in foster homes and get adopted out. Margaret at the time was six, and Amy was just turning five, and Tanya was a little baby."

"You know, you impress me," said Dave. "I mean, to be able to—I know they're your kids but just the amount of time that's passed—how you're not only able to name them, but you're able to say how old they were. I mean, you obviously cared back then."

"I did. I did. It was just one of them things. It was hard but, you know, in the end it was probably the right thing to do. The only reason I did it was because at the time I was an ugly person. I was an alcoholic. I was a drugger. I was in prison. And I was thinking about how I was treated when I was a kid, all that I was put through, and I figured the best thing for me to do is to have these children go to a home that would love them and care about them and raise them right."

"Right."

"I was my father's son."

"We talked to some of Helen's sisters to try to get some insight." Lloyd nodded and listened here with particular interest. "[They said] you were like the nicest guy one day, and then the next day, you know, they were fearful of you. They were scared to death of you."

"Yeah."

"They didn't know what was going on. They said you guys moved around a lot. All this stuff is as intriguing as hell." Dave encouraged him to reconnect with his children. "You know, you still have time. You're gonna get out of here."

"Well, I'm hoping. I mean, good Lord willing, I'm hoping to be out of here. I don't wanna die in prison. I really don't, you know? I really wanna get my life. Like I said, I've really seriously thought about going into law enforcement. This is not the life for me. I don't want it. I really don't. I'm tryin' everything I can to get out of prison. This is my second time putting in a pardon package, and I'm just asking for five years. I'm not asking to be set out on the street right away."

Dave asked what sort of work Lloyd hoped to do when released. Lloyd said landscaping, so they talked about that. The detective then gently steered the conversation back to Helen and the 1970s, which he hoped might lead them to Ray Mileski, the priority.

"How did you get to Helen's house? Did anyone ever bring you over there or anything? Do you remember back then any names that you might have been hanging out with?"

"One time. I can't remember his name, though. He drove an old Plymouth. It was a station wagon. He brought me over a couple of times."

"Do you recall his name?"

"No, but I can—I mean, he had a bald head."

Mileski had not been bald. Dave asked for more. Lloyd said the man was old, "but everybody looks old when you're that age." He had picked Lloyd up outside a church. He thought the man might have been a minister—Mileski had not been. He drove a "dark-colored" car. When Dave pressed him for more details, Lloyd quickly grew irritated. He didn't understand why such an insignificant thing, a man who many years earlier had given him a ride, was so important. It was a lifetime ago. He had been a druggie. He had taken many acid trips and taken a lot of speed.

"My mind's almost shot on a lot of things," he said.

Dave changed the subject. He asked about Lloyd's father.

Lloyd said he'd been abused.

"How many times do you think he abused you?"

"Oh, I'll never forget it. Ten times."

Dave sighed.

Lloyd said it had happened every time Edna had left him alone in the house with his father. He would be berated, then beaten. "It just got to the point where I just didn't say nothing, you know?" When he did complain about his father to others, he said, no one believed him. He said he still had "a hatred of him."

Dave was sympathetic. He said. "Yeah, because, I mean, minus that in your life, who knows the potential you may have had."

In All "Honestly," Part I

They took a break. Dave went next door to confer with Chris, Pete, and Ray Young, the FBI agent. They had expected to be paddling upriver with Lloyd; instead, Dave was navigating rapids. They decided to show him a picture of Mileski. When the interview resumed, Dave placed it on the table.

Lloyd reacted with surprise. "That's the freaking guy that had the damn car I was telling you about! The one who was the minister!"

He said he was certain. In the next room Chris rose from his chair in excitement. Here was the connection he had been looking for, the primary reason for this interview. He was so pumped that he began pacing. Enormous time and effort had been invested in this session on the hunch that the two men had known each other—and bingo! A big piece of his long-stalled case against Mileski had just clicked into place. Now, what was the true nature of the connection?

"Did he ever offer you anything?" Dave asked.

"He never offered me anything."

"Never to work for him?"

Lloyd insisted that the man had given him a ride once or twice to Helen's house. That was it.

"Okay," said Dave. "He is the focal point of why we're here. In talking to people that surrounded him—you would have no idea who these folks are—we came up with you, and then we said, 'Well, look, you know, he [Lloyd] comes from that background of abuse, and what he [Mileski] did to his kids and other folks, he manipulated. He picked up young boys on the street, offered them sex for drugs and alcohol, that sort of thing.' "

Lloyd nodded.

"And that's why we came here to you, saying, hey, this may be a good day for you. It may be a great day for us."

"Right."

"And it may explain things that happened way back when, right? That may never ever get explained without your help."

"But he never offered me anything like that," Lloyd said. "I mean, he gave me the ride. It was just something hairy about him I didn't like. That's why I didn't get in the car with him anymore. I got in twice and that was it."

"You never recall seeing him in, like, a uniform or anything of that nature where he looked like he might have been maintenance for the church? Because it's weird that this guy, knowing who he is and knowing his background and what he was involved in—and he was involved in some pretty horrific things. Anything else that you can think of?"

Lloyd had no more to offer. He said the man who drove him listened to country music on the radio. He said he found the man "eerie" and didn't talk to him much. Eventually he decided to stop taking rides with him. He kept looking at the picture and shaking his head with amazement.

"Definitely looks like him."

"With all that being said, and him being the focus of this investigation, we said we have to go talk to you. I think at the time you wanted to help out," said Dave, referring to the statement Lloyd had given the police thirty-eight years ago. Lloyd warmed to this memory.

"I did!" he said. He said he had called the police to tell them he'd seen a man putting two girls into a car, "and the cops looked at me like I was some young little punk-ass drunk or whatever."

"Tell me what happened with that conversation and why they treated you the way they did and didn't pay attention to you," Dave said. "Tell me what you remember, what actually happened."

"I told him what I saw. I told him about where I saw it, and I guess because I looked like a young, dumb person or whatever, I didn't have, I guess, the smarts or whatever, dressed nice or whatever, they basically looked at me, like, *Yeah, okay, right.* I don't remember the officer's name. He wrote a little information down and said he'd get back and [I] never heard anything, never heard from him since."

Dave asked Lloyd to repeat what he had seen that day. Lloyd now launched into a story completely at odds with his old statement. He said he had been standing on a sidewalk near Helen's house in Takoma Park—this was miles from Wheaton Plaza—when he saw, "a guy putting two girls in the back of a car, and I told them [the police] that it didn't look right. It was dark. The way the girls were acting and stuff like that. I was walking up the street when I seen it, and that's all I saw, and that's exactly what I told them."

He fleshed out this story in more detail under Dave's questioning, adding specific memories: that the man was dressed all in black and wearing a black hat; that the man put the girls in the back seat of a car, slammed the door, and drove off fast; and how he had told Helen about it when he went back to her house. When Dave asked him about Wheaton Plaza, Lloyd said he had never been there and, in answer to another question, that he had not visited a police station to give his statement. He said he had called the police from a sidewalk phone booth at Helen's urging, and that an officer had come to him.

Dave showed him pictures of the Lyon girls. Lloyd said he couldn't tell if they were the ones he'd seen. It was dark, he said. The girls had their backs to him. One of them, the smaller one, had been crying. He described the car in detail, but he could recall no more.

"Now, these two little girls here, they have been missing," said Dave. "They have never been found. And their parents are damn near eighty years old and have no idea what happened to their daughters. That's why we're here to talk to you, and that's why I said I think it's gonna be a good day."

"Right."

"For both of us. You had some information that should have been explored back then. And I can't make excuses. What happened back then is what happened. The only thing I can do is just offer you this and say, look, this is where we are with this thing, and you, you are what we have left. He [Mileski] is the focal point of this thing and these two little girls, whether they're—stranger things have happened—whether they're alive or dead."

"Yeah, look at that guy who had those three women locked in his house," Lloyd said, referring to an abduction and rape case that had recently been in the news.

"Right. And before these people pass away—"

"They want to know where their children are," said Lloyd.

"Right."

"And I don't blame them. I wish I could honestly say that that was them. I wish. But, like I said, I did not get to see their faces. I couldn't tell you if one girl had glasses on or not." After giving his statement to the police, he said, "that was honestly the last time I ever thought about it."

Dave shifted gears. He asked how Lloyd had known today that they wanted to talk to him about the Lyons. Lloyd said his sister Darlene and his niece had told him about having been contacted by Maryland cops, and that his stepmom in Tennessee also had been contacted.

Dave explained the squad's hope that he could help them link Mileski to the crime.

"We were hoping, one, that you were still alive; and, two, that we would be able to sit down in a restaurant and have dinner. We didn't know that you were here."

"Take me to Maryland," Lloyd said, abruptly.

Dave laughed, startled.

"I'll help y'all out, man. Get me transferred to Maryland. I'll help you out on anything you want. Or I'm gonna clam up."

This was a startling shift. In the next room, Chris thought, "Why 'clam up' if he knew nothing more?" It was odd enough for Lloyd to lie about his 1975 statement. Anyone could misremember—it had been a long time—but he had just offered a spate of new details, clearly invented, to flesh out this false account. Why do that? What else might he be lying about or holding back?

Dave appealed to Lloyd's pity for the girls' parents. "They have no idea what happened to their daughters," he said. "It would be something if we can knock on their door and say, 'Look, we haven't found them, but we know that they passed,' you know? And we have some answers. This guy here," pointing to the photo of Mileski, "without a doubt, there's some involvement."

"Have y'all talked to him?"

"We have not."

"Okay."

"We started here."

"Okay."

"You know, we start with the best and go to the worst."

Lloyd again insisted, "in all *honestly*"—he continually mispronounced the word *honesty*—that he could not say who the man or the girls were that he had seen that night. "I don't want to say something just because [you] want to hear it."

"That doesn't do me any good," agreed Dave.

"And it ain't gonna do me no good. I mean, okay, I'm a criminal, but I'm not going to sit here and say, Let's make a deal," although that was what, in so many words, he had just done.

"Right. No."

"I'm not into all that. I can't honestly say that's the two girls or not."

In All "Honestly," Part II

It was Dave's turn to surprise Lloyd. He pulled his old statement from a folder and placed it before him.

"I want to bring this to your attention," he said, "and this is not in any way to jam you up, it's just what we have to go with, and maybe it will help bring back some memories. What we have here is your actual statement that you gave to the police about this particular case. And it's back from the mall—"

"From a mall?"

"From a mall, and it's actually a polygraph that you took in the police station where you were brought back, and they asked you some pretty specific questions."

Lloyd leaned back, startled. He had just been caught in a detailed lie.

"I don't remember this," he said, shaking his head and bending over to scrutinize the document.

"And you admit, after you take the polygraph, that, 'Hey, maybe some of the things I told you weren't exactly accurate.' "

"Right."

"Maybe you tried to embellish because you're trying to make it look good, or you were trying to tell them something without getting involved. When I look at where you came from and your upbringing and where you're at now, and trying to understand how all that took place, we got to a point where we said we just need to go talk to him. We need to see if he'll help us in this thing, help answer some questions for these people. We're not here to jam you up. You're already in trouble, you know, unfortunately, and there's nothing we can do about that. But this is the situation you're in. I'll let you read this thing."

Taken aback, Lloyd seemed momentarily at a loss. He leveled a serious look at Dave.

"I just don't remember going to a police station and giving a statement and taking a polygraph test. I mean, I honestly don't believe that. I mean, well, not believe, I just don't remember it. It was at a mall? What mall?"

"Wheaton Plaza."

"We never went to Wheaton Plaza that much."

The last two words were a concession. Moments earlier he'd said he had never been there. Dave reviewed the contents of the old document, in which Lloyd described going to the mall with Helen to look for jobs, and then added some more of what they knew. He told him about the girls who had said he had been staring at them. He showed Lloyd the old drawing based on Danette Shea's description.

Lloyd seemed unfazed. He joked: "Well, that's funny. You know why it's funny? 'Cause I didn't have a mustache. I didn't start growing a mustache until I was forty years old."

In fact, he had a mustache in the 1977 arrest photo, taken when he was just twenty. Dave didn't contradict him or show him the old photo. He just waited.

"And that's supposed to be me?" Lloyd asked, and then laughed dismissively, as if he had convincingly debunked it. Listening in the next room, Chris found everything about Lloyd's behavior strange—the lying, the laughter, the way he would protest how damaged his memory was and then come up with highly specific details from almost four decades past. If he was playing games, he didn't seem to be very good at it. There was much that seemed off about this guy.

Concerned that the sketch would make Lloyd believe he was a suspect, Dave reassured him. The drawing was just "informational." It wasn't, "an attempt to charge anybody. It was just an attempt to say, Hey, we need this guy. He has information."

Lloyd continued to insist he had no memory of giving the old statement. He stuck with the Takoma Park story. He protested again that he had done "a lot of drugs" and had been "an acidhead back then" and that there were holes in his memory.

"Well, it's all in here," said Dave, tapping the statement. There was no mistaking it. The address he had given was where his father and stepmother were living in 1975, and he had talked about Helen.

He read from Lloyd's old description of the man with a tape recorder who had been talking to the girls.

"Man, I honestly can't remember."

"This was one hundred percent you," said Dave. "You're talking about Helen, looking for jobs. You're pretty detailed in this statement, about hearing what he said to the girls. You were sitting on a bench watching this take place."

Lloyd looked away. Thinking. He appeared unsure how to proceed.

"Phew," he said. "I'm trying to jog my memory. I honestly am. Because I really do wanna help. I really do."

"This could be the most important thing," said Dave. "Some of the answers to these questions only you hold."

"Got a hypnotist? On a stack of Bibles, I don't remember that," Lloyd said, and stayed with his Takoma Park story.

Dave tried to loosen him up. "Would it help if I told you—some of this stuff I hold back because I don't want to just give it to you to hear you give it back to me—that this guy that I showed you a picture of that picked you up in the car is actually dead? If you were to tell me that, 'Hey, I was there with him, I saw what he did, I know what he did,' we're not going to be calling you as a witness. This guy is dead. He died in prison in 2005. So we've come up with these theories."

He said he believed Lloyd knew more. Lloyd insisted he didn't.

"I can't remember," he said. "And I'm serious."

Dave upped the ante. While Lloyd was not yet considered a suspect, if he continued to deny what was demonstrably true, he might become one. He didn't want to go down that road. For now, they were, "Just two dudes sittin' down and talkin'," he said. "Don't you find it weird that this guy's picking you up from a church and dropping you off at Helen's in a black car, and all of a sudden these two girls go missing, and he's the focal point of the investigation, and you guys are—if he truly is the person we believe he is, which we're damn sure, ninety-five percent—that you're in the mall together that same day that these girls go missing? What are the chances of that?"

Lloyd laughed nervously.

Dave said, "I mean, think about it that way."

Lloyd saw that the stakes had gone up. His memory began to improve.

"Am I involved in it? No. The first thing that would go through somebody's mind, Is he involved in it? No. I'm not involved in it. I have never killed anybody. I have never hurt anybody in my life as far as that's concerned. I have never kidnapped anybody, and I never would. You know? I'm an asshole for what I did to be incarcerated right now, and I feel bad about that every day, but as far as killing and kidnapping—"

"Let me stop you there," said Dave. "We're not putting you as killing these girls." He explained Mileski's methods, picking up hitchhikers, using them to help lure young girls, "because he liked to have sex with the younger crowd. And he would use these guys and give them drugs and give them alcohol to lure these girls, and then he would do what he did with them after the fact." He was trying to make it clear to Lloyd that if he admitted he'd been involved with Mileski at age eighteen, he may have been just another of the man's victims, not a killer or kidnapper. He was offering Lloyd a way out.

But Lloyd didn't bite. Mileski was just someone who had given him a ride now and then. Nothing more.

He said: "And very first thing I'd do if somebody said, 'Hey, go get those two girls for me?'—I would find that very strange to begin with—I wouldn't be involved in something like that. I'm not into that, and I would never be involved in something like that." Curiously, as he explained further, he would have refused not because taking two little girls from the mall would be wrong but because it would have been ill-advised. "The first thing I would do is, 'Well, why can't you go get 'em?' You know? 'Why you want me to go get 'em?' 'Cause I'm a very questionable person. I'll ask questions. I just won't go out and do something."

In All "Honestly," Part III

They took another break, and Dave left Lloyd alone in the room with the copy of his original statement. He leaned down and read it very carefully, lingering a long time over each page. A guard came in and set a large cup of coffee on the table and removed the chain that ran from Lloyd's hands to his waist. He stayed absorbed in his reading. He could now reach up with both hands for the cup and more easily turn the pages.

"Phew," he said at one point, very quietly, and then remarked, "Oh my God."

When he finished he sighed heavily, took a gulp of coffee, and sat for a long time with his head down, sighing at intervals. His old statement placed him in the mall at the scene of the kidnapping. They had caught him lying. What could he say?

When Dave returned, he stuck to his bad-memory defense.

"I mean, that's me," he said, gesturing to the document. "No ifs, ands, and buts about it. But, honestly, I can't remember anything. I can't even remember making that statement to be honest with you." He asked Dave, "Did you talk to Helen about this at all?"

Dave was silent for a moment. He was torn. Helen, it had turned out, was dead, and Lloyd might not know that. Should Dave build trust with him by telling him the truth, or would it be more useful for them if Lloyd didn't know? Later, it would become clear why Lloyd was concerned about what Helen might say, but for now, they had not anticipated the question. Dave had to decide. He opted for honesty.

"Helen has passed away," he said.

Lloyd was shocked.

"Are you serious?"

"Yes, I'm dead serious," he said. Dave explained that she had remarried. When they'd gone looking for her they'd found her husband, who told them she had died.

"I didn't know that," said Lloyd. "That's why nobody in the family could find her. She's dead. Wow." Apart from whatever else he felt about the death of his old partner, the mother of three of his children, Lloyd had to have been feeling *relieved*.

They talked more about the disparity between his stories. Lloyd continued to insist that his memory of seeing two girls being put into a car in Takoma Park was correct. Dave ignored this. Without question, the 1975 statement was the one that mattered, so he proceeded on that basis.

"You look back from a neutral standpoint, how is this possible? How are two people [Lloyd and Mileski] from different backgrounds, and y'all are in the same place at the same time and calling in information after the fact" (both men had contacted the police with a story about the kidnapping).

"Oh Lord, this is goin'—I can see myself gettin' charged now."

"Nah, no. No. Listen, look, we're not here to build a case against you."

"Right."

Dave talked about what an "animal" Mileski had been, how he had killed his own wife and child. He soothed Lloyd by telling him how impressed he was, that before they'd met he had imagined Lloyd as very "harsh" and "disturbed."

"But I come into this room. I sit down with you. You're drinking coffee, we're getting ready to have lunch, and I've got to be honest with you. I like you. But I have to stay neutral and take my personal feeling away from you. And when you can remember all this stuff but you can't remember *this*," pointing to the statement, "like I said, you sit on this side of the table and you start to say—"

"I know."

"It doesn't look good. I mean, you know, it makes it look like maybe you did have something to do with it."

"Right."

"And I don't want to go down that route."

Again, Lloyd pleaded that his brain had been addled by drugs. His memory had holes. But when he recognized the futility of denying his old police statement, it abruptly recovered.

"Me and him were not together," he said. "Let's get that straight, right? Me and him were not together. Me and Helen went to the mall and was looking for work. I don't remember the day or anything like that. I honestly . . . but me and him were not together. Oh Lord, please don't put us together." He laughed nervously. "Please! I did a lot of bad shit in my life, but I've never hurt anybody." He admitted what he had done to the little girl, the crime that had landed him in jail, "but as far as literally kidnapping somebody or allegedly getting involved with something like that and literally seeing somebody get hurt, I couldn't do it."

Dave offered, "There's no doubt in my mind that not only were you there that day and saw them in the mall, but I think your interpretation of what you remember with the black car and the two girls is one and the same." He was giving Lloyd permission here to simply merge the two stories. "You can put this asshole in the middle of what we already know because you were there. That's the best way I can explain it. You are fighting it right now because I think you are trying to determine what is the right thing and what's the wrong thing because you have to protect yourself."

Lloyd squirmed in his chair. They had been talking for three hours. He was floundering. He kept talking affably but with mounting incoherence.

"I mean, I'm not saying he wasn't at the mall that day, and I'm not saying I didn't see him that day, it's just that I can't honestly remember seeing that asshole or something like that, that happened." Lloyd had picked up Dave's use of the word *asshole* to refer to Mileski and immediately offered it back, something that would become a pattern. He continued, "Now as time goes on, and I start—because now this is bringing fresh to my memory of remembering stuff—I might be able to, but you gotta figure I got almost forty years of time behind me."

They took a break for food. The session was wearing on Lloyd. Left alone again, he leaned forward, elbows on his knees, and put his head into his hands. He sighed heavily, "Oh man!" Then again, head bent to his cuffed hands, "Oh man!" His head was down for long minutes until Chris brought him a meal from McDonald's.

When Dave resumed, after conferring with his colleagues, he said they all believed Lloyd was withholding information. They believed not only that he knew Mileski, but that he had worked with Mileski to kidnap Sheila and Kate Lyon.

"It's weird that there's an association," Dave said. "And that's the best way I can put it. I know you told me a couple of times that you guys weren't together, but there was an association. I mean, maybe, who the hell knows? Maybe you decided to look for a job, and this clown was there and doing his thing. We're here—guy's dead—and that's gonna be the focus of this investigation from here on out."

Lloyd continued to insist that he had nothing to do with Mileski and had no memory of seeing him at the mall. They went around and around.

"Even if you could just give me that little bit, well, yeah, I was in the mall," Dave said, almost pleading. "We know you were in the mall because you gave a statement. And you're thinking, man, even if I associate myself with that, I can be looking at additional time, and that's not—we're not here to jam Lloyd Welch up."

Dave showed him pictures of others who were in Mileski's circle, and he did not recognize any of them. Mileski was just the guy who had taken him to Helen's house once or twice. Dave leaned on him harder and harder. Lloyd could either be a witness or a suspect, his choice. He showed again the old police sketch, and Danette Shea's old statement about being followed and stared at. Then Dave laid out more explicitly their theory: Mileski groomed teenage boys, like Lloyd, to help him pick up little girls. If Lloyd would help them make that case, he might avoid being charged himself.

"That's the thing," insisted Lloyd. "The only time I ever saw that person was at that church and he never, ever offered me anything. He never said I want you to do this for me."

Lloyd talked on, making little sense. One minute he would repeat the Takoma Park story, and in the next breath acknowledge that the older statement was his. Then he began to recall more details about the day: how he and Helen had arrived, by bus; where they had applied for jobs; where they'd stopped to eat. But he continued to stress that he had no connection to Mileski.

"I can't honestly say that I saw him at the mall," he said. "I ain't gonna lie about it." He firmly denied following girls. "I'm baffled," he said.

The detective and the inmate kept at it for an hour more. There was a curious contradiction to Lloyd. He kept denying that he knew anything but also kept hinting that he could tell Dave more if he chose.

Dave kept trying to make the Mileski connection.

"I think in the back of your mind, if you did ID him as the person in the mall, you're saying, 'I'm fucked.' Because you put yourself in the mall already. You put yourself with this guy, and if you ID him as the one with the girls, you're thinking, 'Man, that dude across that table is gonna fuckin' walk out of here, and in about six months I'm gonna be looking at how much more additional time.' Tell me I'm not right?"

"Yeah, you are right," said Lloyd, laughing. "I done told you, that piece of paper I signed in there with you, that could be torn up, and my name could be signed on a new piece of paper."

"I wouldn't do anything crazy like that."

"No, no, I'm just saying. I mean, you gotta look at my perspective. Right? Yeah, I'm incarcerated. Okay, this guy's dead. Well, okay, we can pin this on somebody else and boom!"

They were at an impasse.

"We're stuck," said Dave.

"Right."

"I'm just putting it all out there for you. We need you, and we're not here to say okay, you ID this guy and we're gonna run out of here and say thank you and then turn around and charge you. That's not the goal here. What the hell will that do for me? You're already in jail."

"Right."

"I don't get a bonus. It doesn't do anything for me."

Lloyd laughed.

"You know what I'm saying? I think we both have established that you're only gonna give up so much because you have an absolute right to protect yourself, and I get that."

"But, see, the thing is, I'm trying to do the right thing," said Lloyd. "I'm trying to change my life around and get out and live a good life and have a normal life, and if I can take this mind of mine and push everything that happened thirtyeight years ago and push it all up front and give you the information right now, I would. I didn't think about it until I sat down in this office. Actually, I didn't think about it until we got back in that van there from the prison, and I said, 'Where the hell am I going?' And they said, 'Dover Police Department. Goin' for an interview.' I'm like, 'What the hell? An interview?' And that's when it all started coming together. And then I'm like, 'Oh shit, they're gonna pin some shit on me.' And it ran through my mind."

"Yeah, it has to."

"You know?"

"I mean it. It absolutely has to."

Lloyd complained bitterly about his experience with the law, how unjust his current sentence was.

"I was kind of surprised," said Dave. "It's a lot of time."

"I mean, the medical records show that the girl was a virgin. All's I did was put my little finger in, put my tongue in, I ate her, and that was it! I got thirty-three years! You know? I've talked to guys who have literally raped women, literally raped kids and stuff like that, and they did ten to fifteen years. So, yeah. It worries me. I ain't gonna lie. It worries me. Yeah, I feel like I'm going to get railroaded for sure. I feel like I'm gonna do this time because he's dead. For something that I didn't do."

Lloyd complained that he was tired. He'd been awakened early. Perhaps if he had time to rest he might be able to remember more.

"Somehow, we need to take that next step," said Dave. He explained that the department already had some ideas about where the girls might be buried—he was referring to the basement of Mileski's old house. "If you can say he was in the mall, that would give us the ability to go out and look for those girls."

"Even if I think about it and relax my mind and get a good night's sleep, and it all starts coming back to me, I couldn't tell where he put them or what he did to them."

"I'm going to put this out to you," Dave said. "We don't have any hard-core evidence on anyone. None. So what your role or no role or full involvement is, only you will know. So if you came to me and said, 'All right, enough's enough, I'm gonna tell you just this little much: I know that guy; I know him by name; I was in the mall with him; he took those girls.' That would give us enough to go find where we think they are, to spend the money, to fill the paperwork out and justify doing what we need to do to find these girls. It would have no bearing on you because you didn't give us any knowledge."

Lloyd said he didn't have the answers they wanted.

"Think about it," he said. "If I was in cahoots with somebody to take two little girls, why'd I stop at them two little girls? I'm just a stupid person who got myself caught up in this." He agreed that he'd probably stared at girls that day in the mall. "I mean, I was young. I probably did!"

"I appreciate that," said Dave. "If I were to say, are you holding out on me because you're worried about being charged with it? Answer that honestly so I can get a judgment call on maybe what we need to try to do next."

Lloyd offered to take a polygraph to show his innocence.

"I ain't gonna lie. I'm scared to death. I mean if you brought a piece of paper in here that [said] I wasn't going to be charged with anything, would I believe that piece of paper? No. No. For the simple reason, 'cause you'd go right down the hall and tear it right up. And it disappears. And it disappears, and now you've got Lloyd Welch going to court in Maryland and getting all kinds of time. I mean, I don't want to sound cruel. No. I really seriously want to help you, but I am scared to death."

Dave made a suggestion: "If I were to try and come up with a solution—and I can't make any promises, just as I can't threaten you in any way. I just need to know what I have to work with." He didn't want to go through the process of obtaining blanket immunity for Lloyd unless he had something material to offer. If he did, "Would you have additional information? There's no sense in me trying to sell something to somebody if you don't have anything to offer."

Lloyd suggested that he was prepared to give Dave exactly what he'd correctly divined the squad was after.

"I'll put it to you this way," he said. "He [Mileski] was in the mall. Okay? And I'll leave it at that."

"Okay, that's fair enough. That's what I need to know."

"I'll put it to you that way. In all honestly, I'll put it to you this way. He was in the mall. I was not with him."

Most people caught in a lie are ashamed, but not Lloyd. He was utterly unfazed. Most people made excuses. Lloyd, apart from his repeated plea of faulty memory, did not seem to feel any were necessary. He just slid into a completely different story, and then pretended—and sometimes insisted—that it was what he had said all along. It was just another item on a growing list of his peculiarities. Dave didn't call him on it. He just wanted Lloyd to keep talking.

Dave presented the old arrest photo, the one showing the mustache Lloyd claimed he hadn't grown until decades later. "Oh, so *I am* starting to get a mustache!" he said. "But I shaved it off." Again, his previous false statement, about which he had made a show of certainty, was ignored. He stared at the photo. "Wow, that's me!"

After five hours they took another break. Dave conferred with the others. This was tricky. If Lloyd were just a witness, someone who had seen Mileski leave the mall with the girls, then his statement would be invaluable, and he would need no immunity. The fact that he was insisting on immunity as the price for going ahead deepened their suspicions about him. If they offered him immunity now, it would prevent them from using anything he said against him—and they had no one else! They wanted his statement badly, but the price was too high—precisely because he was *asking* for it. When Dave came back he told Lloyd that he and his colleagues might be willing to give him blanket immunity in return for useful information, but first they would need permission from the Lyon family.

"It's not a done deal yet," the detective said. "It's gonna be a hard selling point."

"Yeah, because they want to charge me."

"Well, no."

"Let's be honest."

"No, they [his colleagues] don't want to charge you. What they're afraid of is, once they give you that letter they can't take it away."

Lloyd nodded.

"The state's attorney is not saying that you're involved in it right now," Dave said, and then explained Pete's reluctance to make the promise.

What if further investigation revealed that Lloyd *was* responsible? The prosecutor would have tied his own hands. He would have been duped. "So it's a hard selling point," Dave said.

"I'm *not* involved in it," said Lloyd, "and I stop talking as of now. You can send me on back to the corrections department. I was sitting here willing to talk freely, but I'm not involved with it. I never hurt nobody and don't even want it thought of that I hurt somebody. That's what I'm worried about."

Dave scrambled. He was *so close* to getting the ID of Mileski that they had come for.

"That's why we're trying to solve it," he said. "I went to him [Pete] and I said, 'Let's stop here, let's do the paperwork to make him feel covered, because we're not going to ever find him being in any way involved with it.' You see what I'm saying? It's a win-win for both of us. A win-win for you. A win-win for the whole damn thing. So let's make this happen. Let's make this work for everybody. I don't think you're involved."

"You got me scared now."

"No, no. I didn't mean to do that. Maybe I explained it wrong. I didn't mean it to come across that way. I was trying to say this is a good thing. We have to be able to protect you and us. That way we can sit down and we can put our feet up. I can get you a goddamn steak. We can talk about whatever the hell it is you have, and you're protected, I'm protected. We're at that point where I gotta respect you and what you have. You see what I'm saying? And I understand if I was in your situation, I'd do the same damn thing."

"Yeah, because I've been screwed over so many times, man."

"I hear you, I understand that."

"And I told you, I don't trust a lot of people."

"Right, and why would you?"

There ensued another long break. Despite his threat to demand a return to Smyrna, Lloyd stayed in his chair, waiting patiently for Dave to work out an agreement. The detective returned with a sheet of paper, a revision. Lloyd scanned it and pointed to a paragraph that allowed for the possibility that he had been involved in the crime.

"Why would they put that in there if I had no involvement?" he asked. He refused to sign it.

"I didn't kill anybody. I didn't rape anybody. I didn't do nothin' to those girls. I mean, I really don't have much to tell."

For another hour, Dave was in and out of the room trying out different wording on him. He kept insisting that he was working on Lloyd's behalf, trying to persuade a skeptical prosecutor that Lloyd was *just a witness*. Finally, he delivered a new document. It set forth six enumerated points: (1) Lloyd had agreed to talk to them about the Lyon case. (2) He had stated he was not involved. (3) "The immunity offered you is conditioned on your being truthful, candid, and complete." (4) His statements would not be used against him "in any criminal proceeding." (5) "This agreement does not grant you immunity for any crimes you may have committed against Sheila and Kate Lyon." (6) No other promises or conditions had been set. There were some obvious contradictions here. The subject of their conversation would be a crime. The offer of immunity implied that Lloyd was somehow directly involved; that was the only reason to offer it. The document then went on to say that if he admitted that involvement, the agreement was void. The document effectively canceled itself out. Pete was trying to give Lloyd reassurance enough to keep him talking without giving him what he wanted.

Lloyd saw right through it. He heaved a heavy sigh.

"No, it's a good one," said Dave. "It's basically saying you're a witness. And I think everybody's on the same page. We truly believe you were a witness to this, and anything that you tell us about this, you're covered. Because you're gonna tell us from a witness side, you see what I'm saying? And when we talk about it, I'm gonna make sure you tell us from a witness side instead of saying, 'Hey I did this; hey, I did that.' You didn't do that. And I'll remind you that you're a witness in this case."

"I still ain't signing it because *that's* in there," said Lloyd, pointing to the fifth point. "You can come back and get me for murder or rape? Isn't that still the same one?"

Dave examined the paragraph and said, no, the paper promised "not to use your statement" in the event he was ever charged. "What he's saying is, this covers you," said Dave. In the adjoining room, Pete was aghast. The agreement was designed to do the exact opposite. Dave was offering a far broader guarantee, and it mattered. What he told Lloyd in the room was as important as what was on the page. For his part, the detective knew he was pushing the limits, but he was ready to believe Lloyd was directly involved, so the guarantees mattered less than being able to get confirmation of Mileski's role. He wanted Lloyd to feel safe enough to take that step.

"This is absolute," Dave said—again, Pete winced. "I think it's the right thing to do. We've come a long way today, not only with you, but with the state's attorney, because before we came down here they were adamant that they weren't going to do this."

Lloyd sighed heavily once more, and then signed. Sucking up his reservations, Pete entered the room and signed it as well.

"He is the man," Dave said, after Pete left. Dave promised to leave Lloyd with a copy when he left.

"Now, let's cut to the chase," he said. "Tell me what's been bugging you."

Lloyd then said that Mileski, whom he did not know by name but recognized in the police photo, was the man he saw at the mall that day, "in a suit, with a briefcase, and he was talking to some girls. And there were no ifs, ands, or buts about it. Definitely was him. And I told Helen, I said, 'Remember that guy that brought me over the very first time that I started seeing you?' And she said, 'Yeah.' I said, 'Ain't that him over there?' And she looked. She said, 'It looks like him, but he's got hair.'" Here Lloyd deftly accounted for his earlier description of the man as "bald." He continued, "And I kept on staring and kept on staring, and then Helen said, 'Let's go put some more applications around.' We put some more applications around. We came back. He was still talking to [them]. Now I can't say that he really did have a tape recorder or not, because he had something in his hand that was small. I don't know what it was."

"Okay."

Lloyd said that he later saw the same man leading the girls from the mall. His memory had completely recovered.

"I said to Helen, 'Man, that just, he just doesn't look right, you know?' And we saw him in the parking lot area, and he had them two girls with him and he was putting them in the car and he started up the car, and I heard this loud muffling sound, and I didn't think much about it, and I told Helen, I said, 'Man, something just ain't right. I just don't feel comfortable about that.' But there was nothing I could do, because I didn't know what was going on. We left. I felt for five days that something was uncomfortable. I did go back to the mall, and I did make out a statement. The girls that said they saw me staring at them, they might have thought I was staring at them because they were around him at the time, but I wasn't staring at them. That's what I actually know about the whole thing. I never saw that guy after that because me and Helen left. We moved away. And that's the whole thing."

"What was his name?" Dave asked.

"I don't remember it."

"You don't remember?"

"I don't remember it."

"The first name or nothing?"

"I don't really remember his name. I really don't. I'm not good on a lot of names."

At this point, Dave went back to the story Lloyd had told him at the outset of this long conversation, the one about standing on a sidewalk in Takoma Park and seeing two little girls being put into a car.

"No disrespect, because I understand, was that horseshit?"

"Yeah," Lloyd confessed. "Well, no."

Then he said the scene of the girls being put into a car was what he had seen in the mall parking lot, adopting the out Dave had handed him.

"That was for real. I couldn't really say what color the car was. I knew it was a loud car. It was a little distance away. I did see them get into a car. I can't remember the name of the car. It was more of a maroon. I remember telling her [Helen], 'Damn, that car is loud,' you know? I saw it was a loud car and it was him."

Dave said he was concerned that Lloyd had now just adapted his story to correspond to the statement he gave in 1975—a concern which seemed obviously true.

"Why did you go back to the mall?" he asked.

"Why?"

"Yeah."

"Because I didn't feel right, that he was family with them or anything. I just didn't feel right."

"Did you see it on the news?"

"No."

This was hard to believe. The disappearance of the Lyon sisters had been on every radio and TV broadcast and in every newspaper for days.

Dave asked why he had not told the police in 1975 that he recognized the man with the girls.

"I was scared," Lloyd said. "They didn't ask everything. They didn't ask if I knew him. I felt more like I was being rushed than anything. And back in them days, still to this day, I don't trust a lot of men. Because of what my dad did and stuff like that. You know, it's plain simple English. If I didn't drink with you or smoke a joint with you, I didn't trust you."

"I can believe it."

"You know? And I was scared to death to talk to the Law. I really was. Because I had been in so much trouble and stuff like that before. And all I was really concerned about was, 'Man, they're gonna put me in jail. They're gonna think I did something.' And that's why we're been sitting here for the last five hours, because, man, I've been scared. I still am a little scared. Even though that paper's right there. I'm still a little scared that they're gonna say, 'Well, you know, that's not enough information.'"

Dave took him back through the story. Was Mileski alone at the mall? He was. Were the girls he was talking to the Lyon girls? Lloyd could not be certain.

"If I could honestly say this is where they are, this is what happened to them, and even though he's dead and I would take the blame for it, I would, but I can't. I didn't do nothing to them."

Dave reassured him. He had been a big help.

"You may not realize it, but what you did today is absolutely huge," he said. "This was a big to-do. It took a lot of preparation for us to get to this point to talk to you."

"If you had brought that [the immunity agreement] to me three hours ago, we wouldn't be sitting here now."

Dave offered to order out for dinner, and they took another break. Lloyd, his shoulders curled forward because of his cuffed hands, left for the bathroom and then returned to the interview room by himself. He paced for a few minutes, swinging his manacled wrists from side to side, and then he sat, sighing repeatedly. Eventually he put his glasses back on and pulled over the statement he had signed, to read it more carefully. He shook his head.

"Wait a minute," he said to himself softly, still reading. Then he said, "Oh, they got me. Oh, they got me." He read from the form, "This agreement does not grant you immunity . . . ," then exclaimed with disgust, "Oh!"

I'm Done

Chris Homrock was not as sunny and obliging as Dave. He's a shorter, darker, thicker man, older by about a decade, with a heavy brow and balding dome. Here at long last was a witness who seemed capable of proving his case against Mileski, a case he had been carefully constructing for years, an ending at last to the long mystery, not to mention a career-defining triumph, and Lloyd was tiptoeing around what really happened. Chris was convinced that Lloyd had been working with Mileski. His evasions and obvious dishonesty were exasperating. The sergeant entered the interview room with purpose, carrying a chair, which he placed close to Lloyd. He sat and fixed the inmate with a solemn stare. With Chris there would be no "Lloyd"; he addressed all his questions curtly to "Mr. Welch."

He started by explaining what he knew about Ray Mileski, that Mileski had a habit of picking up hitchhikers for sex, mostly boys "down on their luck." These victims were sometimes pulled into a criminal sexual underworld. Before the Internet made porn, even child porn, universal, pedophiles formed furtive social clubs. Members were cautiously recruited by word of mouth. At meetings they swapped or sold rare pictures and films and sometimes even victims, renting hotel rooms for their forbidden parties. Chris noted that Lloyd, a drifter, abused by his father, ever looking to get drunk or high, was low-hanging fruit for a ring like this.

"It kind of made sense to us that you may have been a victim," he said. "You weren't born like this. You were sexually abused too. It's a cycle. You were just an innocent kid who was abused by his own father, and you ended up doing the same to another girl, a younger girl, so it's a cycle. We didn't come charging out here expecting to meet a monster. We look at you as no different than those other dozen teenagers that we interviewed that he abused also. The only difference is, you gave a statement that you were in the mall that day and that you saw him. Okay? We're not trying to further a case against you. We're just trying to find out exactly what he did to those girls. Because there's no doubt in my mind that he did it."

Chris said he believed Mileski was not just some man who had dropped Lloyd off at Helen's house a few times. If he could get Lloyd to admit that he'd been one of the teenage boys Mileski abused and *used*, he would likely make his case. Chris believed it was true. He was not going to leave without it. "We still think there may be more that you need to tell us about how you met him and what he did to you," he said. "Is there anything more there?"

"He didn't offer me any money," said Lloyd. "He didn't try anything with me. As soon as he pulled up to the house, I got out."

Chris said the other men he had interviewed, who had known Mileski as teenagers, all initially denied that they had been molested but then ended up admitting it.

"You see," Lloyd protested. "That's the thing. He did not have sex with me. He never came on to me."

Chris pressed, and Lloyd grew adamant. This insinuation touched a nerve. He was insulted.

"I'm telling you he *did not* abuse me," he said sternly. He hammered on the table for emphasis. "What do you want me to say? He screwed me? I'd be sitting here lying—"

"No, I want—"

"Now you're pushing me."

"No, no, no. I don't want you to lie," said Chris. "We've never met before, and it's hard to take your word for it on face value."

"Believe me, if he sexually abused me, I would sit here and tell you he sexually abused me," said Lloyd, his voice becoming high-pitched with annoyance. "I was right up front about the way my father abused me. So I would definitely say you're crawling up the wrong tree on that."

Chris bore in, leaning forward in his chair, undeterred by Lloyd's denials, urging the scenario. Lloyd just grew more irate.

"He never did! He never, ever abused me! He never touched me in any way, and that's all I can say about that."

Chris wasn't buying it. "I'm kind of at a loss right now, because I think we're almost to a point now where I believe that you have more information about what happened."

Lloyd bowed his head and made a dismissive gesture with his cuffed hands.

"No, no. I know you're going to disagree with me, but hear me out," said Chris. He explained how surprised he was that Lloyd could recall so many particulars of a man who simply picked him up and gave him a ride once or twice thirty-eight years earlier.

"I'm confident that you have more information about this guy," he said. Then he walked Lloyd through the details of the story one more time. Lloyd stuck to his story. He was now "one hundred percent certain" that the man who had given him rides was the same one whom he saw with the girls at the mall and who had walked out with them. The car was maroon and loud. He insisted that he had not known anything about the girls' disappearance when he went back to the mall to tell what he had seen.

"Well, why did you go back to the mall if you didn't even know the girls were missing from the mall?" asked Chris. "That doesn't make a whole lot of sense."

Wounded now, Lloyd glared at Chris.

"I'll say it a little slower." He explained that he went back to the mall seven days later because "something didn't look right" about the man leaving with the girls. "So I felt bad about it, because I had just had a child [in fact, Helen wouldn't give birth to their first until months later], and if somebody [saw] who walked off with my child, I would want them to say something." He said he first learned that two girls were missing when the cop told him after he came in. This continued to defy belief. What about a man with two little girls, even if one of them was crying, would prompt him to call the police? It sounded like a weak link in a larger lie. Detectives are connoisseurs of untruth.

Chris leaned in once more and explained to Lloyd, intently and calmly, that he had certain doubts and reservations about his story. He asked about the differences in his three statements, the old one in 1975, the first one he had told here, and the most recent one.

"Why did you lie about the car?" Chris asked. "You said it was a Camaro they left in."

"I said it was a Camaro?"

"Yes." In fact, Lloyd had practically painted a picture of it.

"I guess I was scared," he said. "I didn't want them to think that I was involved or anything like that, because I wasn't."

"But the car?" Chris asked. "Why make up something about a different car?"

"I was scared, I guess. I don't know. I was young. I was dumb. I was high. I was a druggie."

"Mr. Welch, enough's enough," said Chris. "Here we go. If you read the fine print of this"—gesturing toward the document Lloyd had signed—"this only applies if you tell us the complete and honest truth right now." He explained that when they left him, their investigation would continue and might well lead to serious charges. "Listen to what I am saying. You are not telling us the truth about the car. You're not telling us the truth about your relationship with him [Mileski]. Okay? This is your chance to get out in front of this. This is your chance to tell us, 'I did not shoot those girls, I did not rape those girls, but I do know what happened.' "

"I *don't* know what happened, so how can I tell you I know what happened if I don't know what the fuck happened?" He was shouting now. "I am done with this, man! If you're gonna keep on accusing me of something, take me back to prison, charge me, prove me wrong."

"I'm done talking to you because I'm not convinced you are telling me the truth," said Chris. "I will give you the time of day if you're telling me the truth. If you wanna sit here and talk to Dave and tell him the truth, that's fine."

"I'm telling *you* the truth."

"I want to know what happened to those girls in the mall. I want to know what he did to them. I'm not saying you're involved, and I know you're scared, but I know you—"

"I don't know!"

"—know, and I know you're scared, but you need to tell us what he did to those girls."

"And I'm telling you for the last time. I do not know"—banging his hand on the table and shouting—"what happened to those girls! I do not know what he did to them girls!"

"Mr. Welch, I think you better pay attention to what this letter states, because—"

"I understand what that letter—"

"Because—"

"I'm done!" said Lloyd.

"If we find that you are not being truthful—"

"I'm done. I'm done."

"—then the next time we meet it's not gonna be a conversation like this."

"Okay, well, then, arrest me, because I'm done."

"You and I are done," said Chris, angrily. He stood and left the room.

Who Says "Burned Them"?

The room was silent after Chris's abrupt departure. Lloyd looked plaintively at Dave.

"All right, let's regroup and back up," the detective said. "Let's just relax for a minute."

"No," said Lloyd. "He's trying to get me to say that he [Mileski] abused me. Had sex with me. And what happened to the girls. I don't know what happened to them girls."

"Right, and I don't want you to make anything up. I think you've already done some good in this thing."

Lloyd calmed down.

"I apologize for blowing up on him like that," he said, "but he was trying to get me to say something that didn't happen, you know? He was trying to get me to say the man was abusing me because he abused other people. Maybe I'm one of the lucky people who he didn't abuse. Maybe I looked like his son or something. I don't know."

"Don't take it personal," Dave said. "Sometimes that has to be done to push to see if, in fact, you're telling the truth."

Lloyd kept insisting that he was not a violent person, that he had never hurt anyone.

"Did you ever beat on Helen at all?" asked Dave.

"Ah, yeah, I have when I was younger," Lloyd admitted. "Yes, I did and I feel bad about that. When I would get drunk and I wouldn't get my cigarettes or my dope, I'd smack her, you know? And I ain't gonna lie about that. I was an angry person when I was young."

It was now dark outside. They had been at it all day. Lloyd complained about the chair. They could at least get a cushion for it. Everyone was tired.

"All right, I think they're, we're pretty much done. But what I wanted to ask—your opinion only—what do you think he did to those girls?"

"Personally?"

"Yeah, I'm asking you for an opinion."

"Well, my opinion is that he killed 'em and raped 'em; he killed 'em and he probably burned 'em. I don't know."

In the adjacent room, Chris and Pete looked at each other.

"Who says 'burned them'?" asked Pete.

"If for any reason we wanted to come back and talk to you, would you be all right with that?" Dave asked.

"I have no problem talking to y'all and stuff like that," Lloyd said. "As long as I'm not implicated in, you know, doing something to them." He said he planned to contact a lawyer, "just to be on the safe side."

"No, I don't think we're even anywhere close to that," said Dave.

He left Lloyd with a copy of the immunity agreement.

"I don't know anything else," Lloyd assured him. "If I knew, believe me, I'd tell it."

As the detectives and the deputy state's attorney left for the long drive back to Gaithersburg, they talked over their impressions. Chris was convinced that Lloyd was holding out on them, particularly about his relationship with Mileski. The fact that they had both been in Wheaton Plaza that day was a coincidence too big to swallow.

All three of them were now more suspicious of Lloyd than they had been. This long dance had convinced them of three things:

First, Lloyd was a compulsive liar. His stories were all over the place. There was no way he could have forgotten completely about giving the 1975 statement to the police and being given a polygraph exam. When he chose to remember a thing, he could, to a remarkable level of detail. His memory was clearly fine, and these were things a person didn't forget. There was no way, living in the neighborhood in March of that year, that he would not have heard anything about the missing Lyon sisters. His explanation that "something wasn't right," seven days later, was ridiculous. Besides, anyone who asserts so often that he is telling the truth probably isn't. Again and again Lloyd protested, "Believe me," "Trust me," "I'm telling you the truth." He had invoked the words "honest" or "honestly" sixty-eight times, sworn to God and on imaginary stacks of Bibles, and once had tossed in his unknown "children's lives." Only liars work that hard to appear sincere.

Second, Lloyd knew more than he said he did. If the story he had told was all he knew—he had witnessed the girls leaving the mall with someone—then why was he so concerned about immunity? Why was he inventing stories? Chris was struck by how Lloyd, alone in the room reading over the agreement, had lamented to himself, "They got me." Albeit, Lloyd was distrustful of police, but what pure witness would be so worried that telling what he'd seen would get him charged with the crime?

Third, contrary to his oft-repeated and vehement denials, he had been directly involved. It was the best explanation for his continual lies, his implausible memory lapses, and his evident fright.

His comment at the end about the girls' likely fate was especially curious. Anyone asked to conjecture what had happened to the Lyon girls might have said rape and murder. But "burned them"?

Who says "burned them"?

4
The Test

Police search for the Lyon sisters around Wheaton Plaza on April 1, 1975

What Exactly Did He Do?

As far as Chris Homrock was concerned, they were closer than ever to proving Ray Mileski was the kidnapper and killer. There was still no concrete proof—there probably would never be any—but Lloyd Welch's testimony felt like real evidence.

Hadn't Lloyd recognized Mileski's photo instantly? He said he couldn't remember the man's name but admitted that he knew him. He'd said he was certain—although it was already apparent that "certainty" from Lloyd was anything but. To nail it down they needed to firm up a connection between the two.

After all, how likely was it, as Dave had said, that these two men who shared a sordid sexual appetite for children—*and who knew each other!*—would just happen to be in Wheaton Plaza on the same afternoon Sheila and Kate disappeared? As Chris had told Lloyd, he knew men whom Mileski had picked up hitchhiking as teenagers, and who had been victimized and then groomed to attract still younger victims.

Lloyd had plainly been one of the former. Even his vehement denial fit the pattern. Men denied such things. Chris wrote to his supervisors that Lloyd, although unreliable and less than fully cooperative, had handed them a breakthrough. As far as the lead detective was concerned, the Lyon case had gone from whodunit to *what exactly did he do?*

Dave was less sold. He did not have as much invested in the Mileski hypothesis, and his hours one-on-one with Lloyd had heightened his misgivings about him. But Chris was in charge, and his priority made sense. Together they set out to reinterview all of Mileski's relatives and his seedy old circle.

They got help. It was a sign of how nettling the unsolved crime remained for the department that its assistant chief, Russ Hamill, told Chris he could have as many detectives as he needed. For a case nearly four decades old, this was unprecedented. The first to join them, in November, was Mark Janney, a no-nonsense cop's cop, tall and athletic (a basketball player in college), the son of a Maryland state trooper—he carried his late father's badge with him. Mark was forty-six. His father had risen to the top ranks of the state police, but Mark had no passion for promotion. What he loved was the work itself. He had spent most of his twenty-two years with the department working undercover, making drug buys on the street in his mid-twenties, graduating to federal task force work against drug dealers. In more recent years he'd worked on homicides. He found the job thrilling. Off duty he consumed true crime books; the Lyon case was just the sort of stumper to grab him. At the time he joined the squad, his two daughters were about the same ages Sheila and Kate had been in 1975, which brought the outrage and tragedy of it home. He would return from work feeling guilty about his own good fortune and acutely aware of John and Mary's loss. Mark's size and stern mien made him the most physically intimidating member of the squad, and he would play that role comfortably. When it came time to lean on someone, it was generally Mark who did the leaning. He was briefed on Mileski and Welch, and in December rode out to Dover with Dave to meet Lloyd for himself. It was an informal visit—they did not even tell Pete Feeney about it, much to the prosecutor's later chagrin. Chris and Dave wanted Mark to size up Lloyd Welch for himself. To Mark, it was simple. He had watched some of the video of the first interview and was appalled foremost by the way Lloyd described (and excused) his crime. Mark reckoned him a sociopath, a man self-interested to the exclusion of feelings for others, not just without remorse but incapable of it.

All through the holidays at the end of 2013, the squad sought out and questioned face-to-face, one by one, Mileski's contacts. To each they described Lloyd and Helen and showed pictures, but no one recognized them. Mileski's surviving son, who was familiar with his father's illicit circle, said Lloyd looked familiar but could not be sure. The conversations, meanwhile, led them deeper into Mileski's furtive underworld, one that Chris believed had enlisted young Lloyd Welch and into which they feared Sheila and Kate had fallen.

Unable to confirm the link between Welch and Mileski independently, they were stuck with getting Lloyd to admit it. He had been adamant in that first session that there was no link, but the detectives had observed that his defenses weakened when he grew rattled and tired. It was after he'd been caught in a lie in his most recent witness statement that he'd admitted, eight hours into the session, that the man he had seen taking the girls from the mall was Mileski. So making him rattled and weary became a strategy. Mark took a step in this direction during the unofficial visit. He told Lloyd that the department was considering linking him publicly to the case, naming him a "person of interest." This would not identify him as a suspect, at least not formally, but would amount to the same thing. A press conference would broadcast his image and recap his criminal past. It would be a public shaming. Like most sex offenders, Lloyd had labored to keep the nature of his offense quiet. As the squad well knew, it would disturb his life on many levels, not least within the prison itself, where pedophiles were held in vicious contempt.

This was no idle threat. The department was eager. Lloyd's connection to the case seemed certain, and the FBI was curious enough about other children's disappearances to believe that shaking the tree—spreading word of his involvement—might scare up new leads not just in the Lyon case but in others. For their part, however, the squad members didn't like the timing. If they named Lloyd publicly, it would be hard to sustain the pretense that they wanted him as a witness—which remained Chris's primary goal. It would almost certainly shut Lloyd up for good. Chris was holding his superiors off. He wanted one more crack at him.

Lloyd had given them a pretext. He'd asked to be polygraphed. The detectives didn't believe the machine actually detected lies, and evidently neither did Lloyd, because he seemed confident it would get him off the hook. But the device didn't have to be foolproof to be useful. It scared those who believed in it, and it made even those who didn't anxious. Told they'd flunked the test, some suspects panicked and came clean. This is what the squad hoped would happen with Lloyd. But giving it could also backfire. If he passed, it would embolden his mendacity.

To conduct the test, Chris invited Katie Leggett, the department's premier polygrapher. She was a veteran detective, age thirty-nine, with long experience in the sex crimes unit. Funny, smart, and outgoing, she had set out to become a lawyer, until she realized she hated spending all her time in a law library. Her brother was a police officer, and she had an uncle and a cousin in uniform. Their work seemed more exciting, so after sampling some college classes in criminal justice, Katie went for it. She had endured the mandatory years of patrol duty. Wearing the bulky, manly uniform bugged her, and she found the work unsatisfying. Particularly discouraging was seeing so many of those she arrested go free. The system did not punish offenders the way she believed they ought to be punished. But the job changed for her when she made detective. The work was more consistently interesting. She could dress fashionably. Her colleagues teased her about being "prissy," but Katie felt like herself again. She had blond hair that fell to her shoulders, wore designer shoes, and carried her Glock in a Louis Vuitton handbag. There was nothing prissy beneath the gloss. Her appetite for harsh justice led her to specialize in child-abuse cases, where both the law and the societal mood were less tolerant. Those she busted went to jail. She did it for eleven years, during which time she had two children of her own. Eventually, the work began to wear on her. It says something about the awfulness of sex crimes that she sought refuge working on homicides.

This was where she was when the Lyon squad came calling. Katie did not know Chris, Dave, or Mark. She knew little about the case, even though she had grown up in the Washington area and, of course, had heard about the Lyon sisters. The squad wanted both her polygraph skills and her sex crimes experience. Accustomed as she was to the worst forms of sexual predation, she would hardly be unnerved by someone like Lloyd. Katie was a talker and was also attractive. Her conspicuously feminine style would also play well. She was perfect.

But she said no. The case seemed too difficult, and weak. The squad didn't have much to go on. She had other reasons. Her youngest was still a baby. Katie was looking to pull back from the ugliness, not dive in over her head.

But the squad persisted, enlisting one of her friends, Karen Carvajal, to plead on their behalf and to help with the polygraph session, and Katie gave in. She eventually came to believe it was fated, finding almost spooky connections with Sheila and Kate. She had been only eleven months old when the girls disappeared, but her birthday, March 30, was the same as Sheila's, and she shared Kate's name. Their child photos looked a lot like hers, and she had hung out in Wheaton Plaza herself as a girl. When she first introduced herself to John and Mary, they had been struck by these things. She was moved when they suggested that her involvement "was meant to be."

Her initial instructions concerning Lloyd were straightforward.

"We just want to know if he was involved in the actual abduction, the murder of the girls, basically," Chris told her. "Can you find that out on the polygraph?"

Katie thought she could. She believed in the test, which monitored a subject's blood pressure, pulse, breathing, and skin conductivity as he or she was asked carefully scripted questions. She had started off thinking it was hocus-pocus—its results were still not allowed as evidence in a criminal trial—but after years of practice she had become a believer, at least in its usefulness. People nearly always agreed to take it, even if they were guilty. Most thought they could outsmart it—she felt sure Lloyd Welch would fall into this category—but in the hands of a skilled operator, it could, she believed, expose deception.

The session was set to take place in Smyrna on the second Monday in February 2014.

February 10, 2014

The conditions were not ideal. Katie had brought an unfamiliar portable machine, and the prison had set them up in a basement room—more like a cell—that turned suffocating whenever the door was closed. They had to keep the door open, so anyone walking past could see in. Here was inmate Welch meeting with a whole battery of fuzz—Maryland cops and FBI. It made Lloyd anxious, understandably. Prisons are hothouses for rumor and suspicion. What was happening in that room looked like a big deal. Why was Welch cooperating with them? What was he saying? At one point a female guard wandered in uninvited. She was, Lloyd explained, in charge of hearing grievances filed by other inmates. "She's just nosy," he said.

Eventually Katie and Lloyd were left alone for the exam, but for much of the session her friend Karen Carvajal was also in the room. In contrast to the setup in Dover, there was no adjacent conference room or video link through which the others could observe. Katie had brought a small digital recorder, but there was no hidden camera or microphone. She struggled with the lie detector, which was outfitted with the necessary wires and sensors. She played it up a little. His eyes kept wandering to the open door, and she wanted his full attention, so she became the dumb buxom blonde struggling with modern technology. Men were unfailingly captivated by this.

She sighed heavily.

"All right, well, it looks like it's gonna be . . . I need an Internet connection to be able to pull up my files. Is there no Internet?"

"Well, they have it, but it's—"

"I have it, I mean, I'm afraid it's just gonna fade in and out."

She made ingratiating small talk with Lloyd while playing up her struggles. Her colleagues stepped in and out. Carvajal sat with Katie and Lloyd as Katie fiddled with the device.

"So we got that you had a shitty childhood," Katie said. "Your dad was physically, mentally, and sexually abusive."

Lloyd nodded and grunted assent.

"You never really had a mom. Your stepmom was decent to you, but you kind of at that point were already screwed up. Not good things."

"Right."

"I mean you didn't have half a chance to teach yourself, you know, to become street-smart, teach yourself survival skills. You did what you needed to do to survive but not any violent crimes."

"Right."

"Would you consider yourself a relatively honest person, especially now?"

"Yeah."

"You kind of get the error of your ways? You're done with all this crap? You just want to get out of here and live your life?"

"Yeah."

"Do you find yourself being pretty honest with people here, like the guards or inmates?"

"You can ask any guard, any of the guards that know me, and they'll tell you that I'm one of the quietest people."

"Okay," said Katie. She walked him through the course of his normal day, sleeping until two in the afternoon, working through most nights in the kitchen.

"You have to be minimum status in order to work in a place like that," he said.

"Meaning that you're relatively well-behaved."

"Right."

Lloyd told her about how he made his own pizza, which he shared with his friends and sometimes with the guards. The crust was fashioned from crushed soup crackers, which he coated with pizza sauce, cheese, pepperoni, and sausage.

"They take it down to their microwave, and we heat it up," he said. "They trust me enough because they know that I—"

"You're not going to poison them."

"No. I put the plastic gloves on and stuff like that. I show a lot of respect."

"Just a low-key guy tryin' to get by. Okay."

Lloyd explained his hopes of getting out of prison eventually and living out the remainder of his days in a "normal" way. He relaxed. He liked talking to Katie. At one point he swore and then quickly apologized.

Katie started to respond, "There's nothing you can say that—"

Carvajal laughed.

"Trust me," said Katie. "I'm the worst mouth you'll ever hear. Don't let my innocent look fool you."

Lloyd was warming up to her. He talked more about his life in the prison, about how inmates rarely asked one another to talk about the crimes that had gotten them locked up. Katie was still struggling with the machine, distracted, but encouraged Lloyd to keep talking.

"I think I have a pretty good idea about the kind of person you are, or that you're presenting to me at least. You're very laid-back. You seem very settled and calm. I mean, it is what it is, right?"

"Yeah."

"I mean, I guess there's gotta be a calmness that comes over you. You've atoned for what you've done. You've admitted to doing it, and in the event that you get out, you would even apologize to this girl, so you've made peace in some fashion. Maybe that's what makes you appear so peaceful to me, you know?"

Lloyd laughed. He was flattered. Katie assured him that she was professionally nonjudgmental—which was not true; she was the opposite and was revolted by his crimes. She said she had made mistakes in her life, and that he was really no different from her in a fundamental way. "We've all done things that could have really wound us up in bad situations."

"Right."

"Some people get caught, some people don't," Katie said. "I just don't really like judging other people, which is fascinating because of my line of work, but it's what keeps me healthy. I've actually had people write letters from prison thanking me for treating them the way that I do. I'm kind of like a social worker stuck in a cop's world. As I've grown up I've realized that I'm not perfect, so who am I to judge other people? So that means I do have to, we do have to, go into a little bit of what this situation is, if you don't mind."

Lloyd recounted his connection to the Lyon case, the most recent version. He and Helen had gone to the mall looking for jobs. They saw a man whom Lloyd recognized talking to two girls, a man who had given him "the heebie-jeebies," and whom he described in detail. Later, as they boarded a bus to leave (in his 1975 story, they had been in a car), they had seen the same man putting the two girls in an auto. The younger of the two looked as if she was crying. He described the car. A week later he went back to the mall to tell the police.

"You see something on TV?" Katie asked. "Did you have a radio?"

"See, that's what I'm saying, I honestly don't remember if we saw it on TV, or read it, or heard about it on the radio," he said, stepping back slightly from his implausible insistence that he had known nothing about the missing girls. Now he was saying, indirectly, that he *might have* known. "I guess after a few days it just started bugging me, and I talked to Helen about it, and I said, 'You know, it just don't feel that it was his kids,' or whatever, but I don't know if I saw a newspaper and it clicked or what, because I started to get high again."

He was working to make a good impression. He said he wanted "to do one good thing" in his life. "If I don't do nothing else, let me at least tell somebody, 'Hey, I saw this person.' I'm gonna be honest with you, if I had anything to do with them or any kind of involvement like that, it would tear me up inside so much that I would end up telling somebody, and I've never told anybody."

Lloyd kept returning to this. He said he had admitted all the crimes in his life. If he had been involved in this one, he would admit that, too.

Katie commiserated with him. Being a criminal, she said, "doesn't make you a liar."

He talked about his road years with Helen, about their breaking up when he got arrested and giving up their children. He said he had never thought about the Lyon case until recently.

"What, thirty-nine years, whatever it is?" he asked. "I'm surprised that I'm even involved in it. I thought I was doing a nice citizen thing. I didn't think they were going to try to involve me in something like this." He added that he was not a "monster."

"Well, let me ask you this," said Katie. "Why do you want to take a polygraph?"

"Because I'm not guilty of taking them girls or being involved in it, and I want to prove that to them and to prove to myself, too."

Katie screwed up her face.

"What do you mean, 'prove to yourself'?"

"Because they're trying to make me sound like I'm some kind of monster or something like that."

"But if you didn't do it, you *know* you didn't do it. Are you second-guessing yourself?"

"No."

"Okay."

All of this was preliminary. Their conversation, which had been free-form, was intended to build rapport and put Lloyd in the right frame of mind. He confirmed that he was taking the test voluntarily, indeed, that he was the one who had asked for it.

The Test

"There's no surprises," Katie told him after connecting the sensors. "We'll do something called a skin test. Basically, I want you to lie to me. It's about a number. It's a stupid thing. I'm gonna ask you to choose a number and then ask you to lie because I want to see what your lies look like. Does that make sense to you?"

"You want me to *lie*?" asked Lloyd, who sighed, as if insulted by the very suggestion.

Katie explained the test further. There were three charts. She would ask him the same questions and plot his responses to all three.

"They're just going to be in different order because I want to make sure you are paying attention, yes?"

Lloyd laughed. "I mean, I ain't gonna lie. I'm tired, but—"

"Do you still want to take it?"

"Oh, yeah! There's no ifs, ands, or buts about it. I mean, I'm tired, but I'm awake enough to where I can do it. I'm not on any drugs. I mean, I'm clean."

She asked him to pick his favorite number between one and ten. He chose six. She explained that she would ask him a question about this, and wanted him to "lie about the number six."

Katie then fussed some more with the machine, and Lloyd chortled; her act worked every time. She instructed him to keep his feet flat, his arms still, and to look straight ahead. "Don't get fixated and start making animals in your mind."

Lloyd laughed.

"Don't get trippy on me."

"No."

"Don't get fixated. Hold as still as possible." She told Lloyd that he was "probably the calmest person I've ever done this to." As she maneuvered him into the correct position, Lloyd made a joke about being put in an electric chair. Katie laughed.

"I don't think the person would be this nice," she said.

She inflated a cuff on his arm. Then she began asking him which number he had chosen.

"Is it the number four?"

"No."

"Is it the number five?"

"No."

"Is it the number six?"

"No."

"Is it the number seven?"

"No."

"Is it the number eight?"

"No."

"Is it the number nine?"

"No."

She spent a few more minutes reassuring him and positioning him.

"Are you comfortable like that?" she asked.

"I'm comfortable."

"All right."

"Did I lie on the number six?" he asked.

"Yep."

"Did it show?"

Katie said yes.

They then went through the careful regimen of the polygraph, short, direct questions and equally short, direct answers. One of the questions—emerging out of a list of ones that had nothing to do with the case—was, "Did you do anything to cause the disappearance of those girls?"

"No," he answered.

"Not connected with this case, have you ever lied to someone you loved or who trusted you?"

"No."

"Did you do anything to cause the disappearance of those girls in Wheaton in 1975?"

"No."

"Is there something else you were afraid I will ask you a question about on this test?"

"No."

After a few more questions, Katie said, "Okay, that's one in the record books."

"Oh, okay," he said. "How'd I do on it?"

"Oh, I don't know," she said. "You tell me. How did you do?"

"I believe I did good."

"It's not that easy," Katie said. "I can't just look. See, I'm watching you. I'm watching the charts. I won't know the results until after we add the score. It has to be scored."

Then Katie took him through a list of similar questions, differently ordered and phrased. One was, "Regarding the disappearance of those girls, do you intend to answer truthfully each question about that?"

"Yes."

"Not connected with this case, have you ever lied to get yourself out of trouble?"

"No."

"Did you do anything to cause the disappearance of those girls?"

"No."

And so on. It didn't take long. She gave him a chance to relax and scratch his nose—"It never fails," she said—and then she went through the list a third time. When it was over she deflated the cuff and took it off his arm. She told him to stay put and then left the room to score the test. Lloyd chatted with Dave and Karen. He worked to convince them he had been truthful.

"I've got nothing to hide," he said. "What I told you down in Dover is the same thing I told her in here, you know? My story is not going to change, because I know nothing about it except for what I told you. I mean, I was straightforward with her. That's why I said I'll take the test, you know? I told you I'd take hypnosis, truth serum, whatever you've got, you know?"

"This is all we've got to offer you," said Dave.

"I mean, I don't know nothin'. You know what I'm saying?"

When Katie returned, she asked again, "How do you think you did?"

"I think I did good. I'm hoping I did good, I mean."

"Okay."

"How did I do?"

"You didn't do real good," Katie said. "Which I'm a little bit disappointed about, because I thought we had, you know, something good going on here."

She laid the charts out on the table. She seemed genuinely disappointed, as if Lloyd had let her down personally.

"I can show you. I hand scored in here, and I also had the computer score it to give you the benefit of the doubt, and both—'deception indicated.' That's a really high number," she said, pointing to the computer score.

"'Deception indicated'?" Lloyd asked. "What does that mean?"

"That means that you are lying about the whole thing, the girls."

"Well, I'm not lying!" Lloyd said, now angry and confused. "Could it be that I'm so tired? I mean, I worked last night."

Katie said fatigue would not affect the results.

"The thing I'm worried about," she said, "is if you know something along the lines of trying to protect somebody else. I don't know enough about what's going on, because I think you're a decent guy. I mean, I don't want to be wrong. I feel like you're not really this violent, bad person, and I hate being wrong. I'm not saying that that's changed. We're kind of at a point where the damage is done. The situation is what it is."

"Right," said Lloyd, deflated. He had asked for the test in the hope of eliminating suspicion. At this point the wheels in his head must have been turning. If Lloyd believed the test was capable of detecting a lie—and this appeared to be his belief—then he must have been confident he could fool it. But he had not fooled it. The pattern he had shown in the first session, when caught in a lie, was to immediately spin a new story, one in which he incorporated the facts he had just been given without incriminating himself. It was his method, a reflex. It was apparent in the way he often would pick up on words and phrases spoken to him and use them himself minutes later. But the polygraph was a machine. It didn't contradict his story with evidence or logic, it didn't offer conflicting facts, it just said he was lying. What new story could he spin from that?

"We just want to know where these girls are, you know what I'm saying?" said Katie. "You're a dad. You know how that feels. You would want the same respect and peace. They deserve to be buried properly; they deserve to have their family be able to stand around and say, 'We loved you.' You can understand that. All of us can understand that as parents."

"And I do understand that, honestly. I just don't know where they are at. I had nothing to do with them. I mean, if it's locked up in my brain somewhere with all the drugs I've done, I wish somebody would help get it out."

Katie was struck by this comment. It wasn't the first time Lloyd had hinted that he *might* have some knowledge of what happened to the Lyon sisters, that it might be trapped somewhere in his memory. Innocent people didn't say things like that. She was reasonably confident of her ability to detect untruth with the machine, but not certain. If the flunked test made her strongly suspect that Lloyd was hiding something, this remark convinced her that he was.

"But you were pretty clear that you didn't use drugs that day," said Karen.

"That day! But that night I did."

"But you would not have forgotten being involved in the disappearance, right? I mean, that's not something you would have forgotten."

"No, that's not something I would have forgotten, but I didn't do it so I wasn't involved. I mean, I can't make it any clearer than it is. I'm not involved."

This was not going as Lloyd had hoped. Katie and Karen were no longer being friendly and cute. Karen, in particular, bore in. She told him he was in "a precarious situation."

"I think you probably feel like maybe you have something to lose with your family," she said, offering him an out. "I think Dave meant it when he said that they would spin this in a way that wouldn't hurt you with your family"—she was speaking of his scattered children.

"I understand that," said Lloyd. "I want it off my family."

"Well, Lloyd, the bottom line is, you don't trust the police," said Katie. "I pride myself on not making people's experience shittier." He had turned his life around in prison, she said, and was now trying to live differently. "In my heart of hearts, I believe there's some part of you that knows something more than you are giving us. I don't think you're a bad guy. I think you've made mistakes in your life."

"Yeah."

"I believe enough in my skills and I believe enough in this test to know there's something bothering you," she said.

Lloyd insisted this was not the case. Karen told him that the news of his involvement would come out, and that it would destroy any relationship he hoped to have with his children—this was the line that would later trouble Pete Feeney. It was a threat. They were offering him a chance to tell his side of the story to prevent a public shaming.

"I can't tell you something I don't know! Honestly!"

"There's two things, if you are honest with yourself," Karen said. "Like the fact that sometimes your statements have differed from one interview to the next, which is hard for us to reconcile, because it raises questions and it raises doubts in our minds."

"I've given you the same statement every time."

"Well, no. No, you haven't. I don't think you're being entirely truthful with us. And the other thing is—and maybe you can answer this—you were considering the immunity documents. You know, a person who wasn't involved in this wouldn't have considered it. Do you agree?"

"They offered it to me down there. I mean—"

"But you considered it. And you told Dave that you actually did have something significant to say, but then when they wouldn't give you the immunity you wanted, you didn't say it. So there's something you're not—"

"The only thing, the significant thing I said was, I saw two girls being put in a car."

"But you said that *before* the immunity documents," said Katie.

She was right. He had. He retreated again to blanket denial. He knew nothing. He was holding back nothing.

Katie tried a different tack. Maybe the girls had not been kidnapped, she suggested. Maybe they had gone off willingly.

Karen mused, "It's possible you were with the person who did it and maybe—"

"No," Lloyd said, abruptly.

But Karen continued with the thought: "—you didn't know that's what they were going to do?"

"No. I wasn't with nobody." He said he wanted a new immunity agreement, which had the effect of undermining what he'd just said—if he had been by himself and had nothing more to offer, then why seek broader immunity?

Katie shifted gears again. She commiserated with Lloyd, suggesting that Mark Janney's veiled threat to release Lloyd's name to the press had been heavy-handed.

"I thought he was a little strong," she said. "I didn't think that was fair." (This comment, too, would later haunt Pete Feeney, who had to guard against anyone overstepping the state's strict interrogation guidelines. Katie was admitting that Mark had threatened Lloyd.) Then she effectively repeated the same threat, only phrasing it as a show of sympathy: "If they do put that information out there to get leads, that might be detrimental to you. That's why I'm concerned. I don't want people to paint you as a monster."

"I've already been painted as a monster with my family."

"I don't think you're a monster," offered Karen.

"I mean with my mom and my niece and my sisters. I'm considered the monster of the family now."

Lloyd complained that his sister and niece had stopped visiting him.

"That's something that can be rectified," said Karen.

"I think there was a good person at the mall that day who saw something that he didn't like. Would you have stepped in?" Katie asked. "Because I'm wondering if maybe you tried to step in and that's how you got hemmed up in all this? Because I think you're a good guy."

"What did I tell you?" said Lloyd.

Katie ran with this. What if Lloyd saw something bad happening and tried to step in and save the girls?

"If that's the case," she said, "you need to tell us so we can fix the situation with your family. We're the two girls who can advocate for that." She rephrased this idea as Lloyd listened intently. "You're not shaking your head, so I know I'm onto something," she said.

Lloyd laughed.

"I'm listening to you," he said.

So Katie continued this line of reasoning. After all, Lloyd was just "a kid" back then. He lacked the confidence he would have today. Karen suggested that Lloyd might have found himself caught up in something bad and panicked.

"I want to believe the rapport you and I established," said Katie. "I want to believe that I am not a fool, that I should go back to Police 101 because I've just been had. I believe there's a reason and that it's in there somewhere. I believe wholeheartedly in that."

The women worked him every which way. They told him how smart he was. What a good guy he was. They said they understood his fears, and his need to protect himself. But both told him that they now *knew* he had been involved. As they went on, Lloyd grew increasingly irate, so Katie zeroed in on that.

"Prior to Karen coming in, you and I had a very pleasant exchange. Your whole demeanor and body language and eye contact has changed."

"Because I'm tired! I've been working all night long. I've had two hours of sleep."

"You're getting a little pissed off, which I get," said Katie. "I mean, I don't feel like this is the same person I've been in here talking to. So it's easy for you to change demeanor. I mean, am I an asshole for thinking you are a good guy?"

"No, I'm still a good guy," said Lloyd, calming down. "I'm just getting tired. I've been sitting here in the same spot for, what? Four hours?"

It went on. At one point Lloyd said "My mind's dropped down, whatever. You know? I'd be happy to tell you something I knew, but I don't. Maybe I ought to start seeing a psychiatrist here."

Then Lloyd accused Katie of fudging the test results. She got angry, or feigned anger. There was no separating the fake from the real; Katie was playing a role, and as with anyone good at it, the role had begun to play her.

"I believe you saw him take those girls away, and I know that you know him," she said, referring to Mileski. She told him she believed he panicked when he realized that what Mileski was doing was "fucked up" and left. "Maybe that's where the guilt comes from. Maybe that's where the test [result] comes from. If there's something locked in there—and you're not saying unequivocally no—something could be locked in. Is it possible you have seen them again since then?"

"I can't say yes or no on that," said Lloyd—a curious answer. "You can interpret it any way you want."

"I'm not interpreting," protested Katie.

"No, I'm saying you can interpret it any way you want with your college education, your background. All I can say is, I know nothing about it."

"No! What you just said is, you can't say yes or no."

"Yeah, but I can't!" Lloyd complained, loudly.

"Again, that's like being KIND OF PREGNANT!" Katie matched Lloyd's raised volume. "It's not an answer! It has nothing to do with my college education. You're probably smarter than me, to be honest with you, because you've lived a lot of life, okay? The bottom line is, it can't be both ways. I'm asking you is there a possibility that you have seen those girls?"

"Why are you raising your voice?" he asked.

"Because you're raising your voice at me, and you know why? Because I went out and I stuck up for you, and I look like a stupid fuck right now because I believed in you and I thought you were being honest!"

"I thought I *was* being honest, too! I think you all did something to that test, took it out and did something to it!"

"That's absurd," she said. "That's absurd!"

Lloyd said she could have falsified the results if she wanted to. "That's what you do. You can change anything on it."

"I don't even know how to sign on the damned thing. How am I going to switch something?"

"Well, that's my opinion," said Lloyd. "I thought we were having a good conversation and stuff like that, but when you started getting mad I started getting mad."

"No," said Katie. "You got mad first. I'm just defending myself." Katie stepped out of the room to cool off.

Karen tried to calm Lloyd and then offered him a way out of the standoff. He listened intently.

"I actually think you are still the nice person we thought you were," she said. "I don't think you are the person who would hurt those girls. I don't think that's what happened. I don't. I really don't. I don't think that you kidnapped those girls to do something bad. I think those girls went with you guys, whoever was involved, and I think something went wrong, and you got scared. And that's completely understandable, because you were a kid back then. The people that you were with should have done better by you and not gotten you involved with something like this to begin with. But here we are now. We know that you are involved. I just want to know how involved you were. That's it, Lloyd. You are not going to convince me that you were not involved. And it's not just a matter of the test. We can disregard that test."

He knew more than he was saying.

"You want to say," Karen continued, "but you're afraid [of] what is going to happen if you do. Were you just on the sidelines or did somebody make you do something you didn't want to do? It's not your fault that something happened that day."

"I can't tell you something that—"

"It's the person who orchestrated this whole thing. Right? Do you agree? They're the ones who should take the responsibility, right?"

"Whoever did something to them, yeah. But I didn't do anything."

"Let's say there were a couple of people involved. Do you think everybody is equally responsible?"

"I can't say."

But Lloyd seemed drawn to this line of reasoning. Karen was offering him a way to admit the crime without taking responsibility. Katie returned as Karen said, "My question is, you had the person who made the plan, and that person says, 'Hey, come on over.' Then this other person [Lloyd] shows up, and it's like, holy shit! They did something bad with those girls. Do you think that other person [Lloyd] is responsible?"

"Yeah! But I don't think it's his fault. And it wasn't me!"

"It's just that you know something that you're not telling us, and that's why we're having a conflict," she said. "I know Katie's pissed off and she's disappointed because she felt like she gave you the benefit of the doubt, and she feels like it's making her look bad, and I'm still here telling you that I'm still giving you the benefit of the doubt."

"And I'm sorry it's making you . . . that you're fighting with that, because I have been honest with you. I don't know why I didn't pass that test. I was relaxed, comfortable, and everything like that."

"Well, it's offensive for you to think that we are tricking you," said Katie.

"Well, you can change anything on a computer."

"Do you really, honestly—"

"I do! You're a cop!"

"Does that make me a bad person?"

"No! No! But I'm just saying."

"You've never had a good experience with a cop?"

"No."

"No?"

"No. I've never had an officer offer to help me on anything. Even when I asked."

"Well, I'm sorry about that."

"It's not y'all's fault."

"Have I been obnoxious or rude or tried to trick you in any way?"

"No."

"This test wasn't a trick."

"It's my opinion, that's all," he said. "I apologize and all that, but that's just my opinion."

Karen said the state's attorney would be disbarred if he lied to him. She defended Dave's trustworthiness—they could all see that Lloyd liked Dave and trusted him. Katie defended herself.

"You don't trust police," she said. "I get it. I don't care. I mean, I don't take it personally. Honestly, Lloyd, if I were in your same situation, I'd be doing the same thing. If I had a life of shit with cops—and Karen and I have seen enough shit cops in our career, and they exist—so I can completely believe you. Cops that make me disgraced to be a part of the same fraternal order as them because they suck. I get it. I'm not a sucky person. Karen is not a sucky person."

"And I don't think you are," said Lloyd.

"And I wouldn't be a part of anything that would make me lose sleep. Tricking somebody. This is a cat-and-mouse game. Let's be honest. But you've got to play clean, and you've got to play fair, and telling somebody that they are bullshit is not in my DNA."

Katie made a plea. She said she had formed a high opinion of Lloyd, and that it would be dashed if he didn't help them. "As a mom, and I would certainly hope you would feel the same, as a father, those girls, they deserve to be commemorated and properly buried. Their parents deserve to have some peace, and for their girls to finally rest in peace. The bottom line is, that's what we want. That's what I want. I don't care, even if you did it, you've done your time in here. You've been in hell. I don't care about that stuff. I care for me, as a mom, as a cop near the end of my career, that those girls get what they deserve. What happened happened, and we can't go back. We can only move forward and change how we're gonna handle the situation. I don't know how I would feel if I find out that later, once this thing erupts and the information's out there, if you don't take advantage of this opportunity."

"If I could give it to them, I would!" said Lloyd, exasperated. "I'm sorry!

But then, after all these hours of denial, after all the back-and-forth without an inch given, abruptly there came a break. Lloyd suggested that if he were given some further assurance of immunity, his answers might be different.

Katie asked, "If they got a public defender for you that sat at this table with our state's attorney, and one of these guys made you a deal that was happy to you, do you think you would remember something? Tell me the truth."

"Honestly, I can't say yes or not to that," said Lloyd.

If they set all that up and came back tomorrow, Katie asked, would he have something helpful?

"I can't say yes and I can't say no."

"But it's possible?"

"Anything is possible."

I'm Going to Give You Something

And that appeared to be that. After hours of grilling, the pretest chatter, the test itself, the hammering at Lloyd after he'd failed, all of it had brought them back around to the beginning. The detectives felt played.

Katie apologized for losing her temper. She said it was the Irish in her. Karen reassured Lloyd, "We're still cool."

Dave entered and said he had been listening outside the door. He endorsed the idea of arranging a meeting for Lloyd with a lawyer. He thought they could hold off releasing Lloyd's name to the press.

"I'm going to have to dig really deep down and ask for some favors," he said. He would find Lloyd a Delaware public defender, who could meet with him privately before they spoke again. It might take time. "But the flip side of that is, I don't want to go through all that hassle and make this work if we're not going to gain anything additional."

Lloyd suddenly turned to Katie and Karen. "Could you two step out for a minute?"

"Absolutely," said Katie. She and Karen left and closed the door behind them.

"I'm going to give you something, Dave, and you think about this," he said. "Okay? I wasn't involved."

"Okay."

"With the grabbing of the girls. The picture you showed me was the guy that did, that took the girls, and, yes, I used to get high with them and stuff like that. We took them to his house. I went over to the house. When I was getting ready to pull in I heard screams, a kid. I got scared, and I looked in and everything like that. I seen men there. I ran. That's why I went back to the mall."

"Right," said Dave. He didn't show it, but he was startled. He didn't know what to make of this. Lloyd had just changed his story in a very significant way. He was now admitting that he was involved with Mileski *and* with the kidnapping. Mileski was no longer just a man who had given him a few rides; they had hung out, smoked dope together. Then there was this: "We took them to his house." This may have been a slip, but it was a revealing one. He had placed himself with the kidnappers. Then he had backtracked—"I went over to the house," retreating quickly to his position as witness. Had he helped take the girls to the house, or had he gone back later, heard screams, and run? Which was it? Dave held off asking.

"What happened after that I can't tell you," said Lloyd. "This is between you and me right now."

"Yes, but I have to be able to know that's the truth, between me and you."

"It is."

Dave asked what the man's name was, the one who took the girls.

"I want to go with Manny," said Lloyd. "Manning or something like that."

"Okay. Do you remember where it was that he lived?"

"See, that's the thing, I can't."

Dave asked him to describe what he remembered.

"It had a fence around it, one of those small little wire fences."

"Okay."

"It had a basement in the bottom."

"Okay. What was in the basement?"

Lloyd said that there was a mattress. He said he and others used to party in that basement.

"Helen would go over once in a while with me, and she wasn't involved in anything. She just sat around. She had a couple of drinks, and that's it. We'd leave."

"Do you remember where the house is located?"

"I want to say that it was in Wheaton," said Lloyd. He said he would recognize the house if he was driven past it. He described a house with a basement that opened to a backyard. They had to go around the house to let themselves in. He described a small bar in the basement, a couch, some chairs, the mattress in a separate back room, a TV, and a stereo.

Dave pressed for more. Lloyd described the cars he saw at the house in general terms. "Like I said, it's been a long time. I mean, she [Katie] kind of got me angry and shit."

"Oh yeah," said Dave, sympathizing.

"You know, I apologize for yelling and shit."

"You need not apologize."

They talked further. Lloyd tossed out several vaguely remembered first names, then he added something more. He spoke hurriedly, as if he were in a rush to get the memory out.

"When I went over there the next day, the girls were still there, and they were . . . it looked like they were grown up, you know? And I heard her scream, and I looked in and I got scared. I wasn't going in there. I wasn't getting involved. I saw the girl. I knew that was the girls that he picked up at the mall, and I took—"

"Do you remember what they looked like? What they were wearing or anything?"

"They were wearing nothing."

"Nothing?"

"Nothing. They were drugged up. You could tell they were drugged up because they were lying there like that, you know? I mean, I looked in. When I heard the scream, I did look in, and it was him and two other people in there."

"You can't remember who they were?"

"I didn't see their faces. I just saw them body parts, you know. I know there was two males because they were screwing the girls, and I didn't see her face. That's why I got scared and ran but can't tell you more."

Lloyd refused to say more. He pleaded memory loss. He said he had run back to Helen's house afterward and hadn't even told her what he'd seen. "It just scared me," he said. "I got high. I went back to the mall and told a security guard of what I saw in the mall, and that was it. I didn't tell anybody. I wasn't protecting anybody or anything. I was a scared kid."

"Right."

"You know? And I'm still scared. I'm fifty-seven years old and I'm still scared. I'm scared that I'm gonna get charged with something."

Dave had not been in the room when Karen had spun her alternative scenario for Lloyd, suggesting that he had, perhaps, gotten drawn into something by older men without realizing what they intended. He was running with it now. "Something went wrong, and you got scared," she had said. Clearly, flunking the lie detector test had shaken him. The detectives now had something on him. If he were searching for an escape route, he had seized upon exactly the one Karen had offered—only to steer himself straight into a kidnapping charge.

Dave pushed him harder. He went over the impossible coincidence of his just happening to be in the mall when the girls were abducted and then just happening to visit the very house where the girls had been taken.

"See, that looks bad," he said.

"Yeah. Oh, I understand, but I didn't go to the house until the next day." Then he said that he was afraid that the men who had taken the girls, and who had seen him at the window, were going to come after him and Helen and kill them and their baby—which had not yet been born. He repeated that he couldn't remember who they were.

He had nothing more. The session had lasted all afternoon. Lloyd once more had held out until exhausted and then had abruptly, voluntarily, thrown out something new, something that contradicted much of what he'd said before, and something that far more directly implicated him. And the weird thing? He didn't seem to realize it.

Those final five minutes were huge. They now had a case against Lloyd Welch, and, again, it was from his own mouth.

5
Teddy

At a February 11, 2014, press conference, the Montgomery County Police named Lloyd as a person of interest

The Goblin

Hours of bullshit, then five minutes of half-truth. The pattern was as clear as it was vexing. As Chris Homrock's wife, Amy, put it, "Lloyd was blowing smoke up their butts; he knew it, and they knew it."

The surprise "something" that Lloyd gave Dave at the end of the polygraph session briefly threw the squad off stride. Dave, Katie, and Karen stopped at a pizza joint in Dover afterward to regroup. What Lloyd had just admitted was big. Despite his previous adamant denials, he had completely reversed himself. Several people, including him, had participated in the crime. He was a friend of the kidnapper—who, they believed, was Ray Mileski. He "used to get high" with this man. The girls had been taken to the basement of a house in Wheaton—one with which Lloyd was familiar—where they had been drugged and sexually abused by several men. He had witnessed this before getting scared and running away.

This was the third significant departure for Lloyd and a striking one. Discounting his 1975 statement, he had gone from seeing a strange man with two girls miles away from Wheaton Plaza, to just happening to see a man he recognized leading them from the mall and putting them in a car, to now placing himself with the kidnappers. All three versions were dubious, but were parts of them correct? Were the detectives zeroing in on the truth, or was Lloyd just desperately inventing? Was there any reason to continue viewing him mostly as a link to Mileski? Given how freely he altered his story, even his recognition of Mileski—the thing that had most excited Chris—was suspect. The sheer industry of Lloyd's mendacity raised his own profile. When someone lies that persistently, you stop listening to what he says and start wondering what he's up to. If Lloyd was trying to point the squad somewhere else, he was achieving the opposite.

Dave assumed that this startling admission had not been recorded. Katie had brought a tape recorder, which she had used for the test, but she had left the room when Lloyd asked to speak to Dave alone.

They phoned Pete Feeney, and he urged them to turn around, return to the prison, no matter what the hour, and get Lloyd to repeat, on the record, what he had just said. Pete didn't want Lloyd to sleep on it or talk to his fellow inmates or have any time to reconsider. But turning around was the last thing the detectives felt like doing at the end of a long day. Besides, who knew what Lloyd would say now? The comment, "We took them to his house," appeared less than fully considered. If they drew attention to it, how likely was he to repeat it?

"Wait," said Katie.

She had left her recorder in the room. In wrestling with the polygraph machine, she said, she might have forgotten to turn the recorder off. She retrieved it, fast-forwarded it to the end, and, much to their relief, Lloyd's final comments were there.

When they got back to Gaithersburg, they were so excited they felt like popping champagne. They believed there was now sufficient evidence to charge Lloyd. For thirty-nine years the department had been stymied by this case, and now, at last, they had broken it. No matter

Lloyd's steadfast denials, they could prove he had been at Wheaton Plaza that day—he admitted it, he had given a statement to the police to that effect in 1975, and the drawing on file was a clear match for him. He now said he had known the kidnappers and in an unguarded moment had admitted being with them. He had witnessed at least one of the girls being sexually abused. It wouldn't hurt that he was a convicted child molester. Even if he hadn't taken the girls himself, he had stayed silent through those critical days in 1975 and had even tried to mislead investigators. At the very least he had obstructed justice. He looked guilty as hell. In fact, he seemed, suddenly, a lot more likely a suspect than Mileski.

But Pete demurred. He had a team poring over every transcribed line of the interviews and saw problems. He was still concerned about the immunity agreement they had signed in October, which he considered compromised by Dave's reassurances to Lloyd. It had hinged on Lloyd telling the whole truth, which he admitted he had not done, so that would make a strong argument in favor of using his words against him, but the whole thing seemed more vulnerable to challenge than Pete would have liked. He had been dumbfounded to learn that Mark and Dave had visited Lloyd without informing him, had not recorded the session, and had—according to Katie's apology in the polygraph interview—effectively threatened Lloyd. A defense lawyer could make much of these things. And in Lloyd's newest gift to Dave, while he had initially said, "*We* took them to his house," he had immediately backtracked. It might be considered a slip of the tongue. Conviction would be no slam dunk. Lloyd could claim that he'd been coerced and had, on that one occasion, simply misspoken, using the wrong pronoun. Pete advised the detectives that unless Lloyd admitted that he had been present when the girls were taken from the mall, they did not have enough to charge him. The champagne mood fizzled.

For its part, the Montgomery County Police Department had heard enough. Tired of being led in circles by a convicted child molester, the chiefs wanted to go public. Here was a potential solution to the most stubborn mystery on the department's books, not to mention, possibly, the rarest of criminal justice finds: a serial killer of children. They scheduled a press conference for Tuesday, February 11, to name Lloyd as a person of interest. Posters were prepared showing enlarged images of Sheila and Kate and of Lloyd as a young man, the old police sketch, and an old photograph of him with Helen.

Chris pushed for more time. Maddening as Lloyd was—he was like a fairy-tale goblin guarding a treasure, speaking in riddles—they needed to keep him engaged. There was still so much they didn't know. They wanted to find the girls' remains and to be able to explain exactly what had happened to them and who had been involved. With Lloyd in the room, those answers had seemed close. Pete, reviewing the most recent session with Lloyd, noted that he had offered to point out the house where the girls had been taken if he were driven around Wheaton. Shouldn't they try that before permanently alienating him? In-house, the debate abruptly ended when Dan Morse, a *Washington Post* reporter, called with a scoop. He had gotten wind of Welch's connection to the case and had confirmed with members of the Welch family that the detectives had been asking about Lloyd. His story would run the next day. So, late that morning, the show went on. The squad made sure that the nightly news programs would be shown on cellblock monitors in Smyrna. If they were going to hit Lloyd, they might as well hit him where it hurt.

That morning, at the department's headquarters in Gaithersburg, the dais decorated with the poster-size images and surrounded by the flags of the United States, Maryland, and Montgomery County, the press conference opened with a prepared statement from John and Mary Lyon, who were present but who did not wish to face the cameras and reporters. They stood nearby behind a screen. Their comments were read by a department spokesperson: "Throughout these years our hopes for a resolution to the mystery have been sustained by the support and efforts of countless members of law enforcement, the news media, and the community. The fact that so many people still care means a great deal to us."

Chief J. Thomas Manger, a man with a stern white crew cut, dressed in the department's black uniform and black tie, announced the tentative breakthrough to a packed room of journalists—the Lyon case was still a big draw.

"Our cold case team has been able to identify a man, currently incarcerated, and we have been able to establish that this man was at the Wheaton Plaza mall that day [and] might have had contact with the Lyon girls," he said. "The person of interest is Lloyd Lee Welch." He gestured toward the photo of Lloyd and summarized his carnival travels from 1974 through 1977. He pointed to the picture of Lloyd with Helen, noting that she had been with him during those years. "We are looking for the public's help. Anyone who has any information [from] during that time . . . we ask for them to contact law enforcement. Mr. Welch was at the scene, and looking at his criminal history has made him an important person of interest in this case."

Then he took questions.

One reporter asked, "What led you to him?"

Manger praised the hard work of his special squad, noting the value of fresh eyes on old files, and this was partly true. The right answer—which perhaps the chief didn't fully realize—was that the discovery had been fortuitous. Hard work was behind it, for certain, but it had started with Lloyd's old description of a man with a limp. Convinced he had seen Ray Mileski, they'd gone looking for Lloyd. Now Mileski seemed a peripheral figure at best. His name didn't even come up in the press conference.

As anticipated, the announcement generated a flood of coverage in Washington, DC; Baltimore; northern Virginia; and well beyond. It prompted a detailed, two-minute national report on CNN, complete with pictures of the girls from 1975 and of plain memorial stones over two empty graves, and an old interview with John and Mary, from after the twentieth anniversary of the girls' disappearance. Both had white hair but still looked hale. Beyond the tragedy of losing their daughters, Mary tried to itemize the enduring nature of their sadness: "The brides that he didn't walk down the aisle," her voice breaking as she nodded toward John, seated next to her on a couch. "The grandchildren we didn't have. The sons-in-law we didn't have."

As hoped, the reports prompted many new tips. Lloyd, it seemed, had left a string of abandoned, abused, angry women and discarded children. Katie and Mark set out to talk to each, one by one, which sent them on a tour of the squalid reaches of rural tenancy. Outside a trailer home in the hills of western North Carolina, dressed in her best wool coat and expensive shoes, Katie balked when confronted with a muddy yard replete with grazing donkeys.

"I am not going to step in donkey shit with these shoes," she said. Mark refused to give her a piggyback ride, so she had to give in, muddying her heels on the walk to the front door. Inside, as she started to sit down on a sofa, her host shouted, "Not there! The dog just peed there!" She slid over to a dry spot. She would never wear the coat or shoes again. They collected horror stories from Lloyd's domestic past. One man who had known Lloyd years earlier said flatly that he "hated women." All described his overriding attraction to the very young. He had once taken up with a girl of fifteen, telling his furious twenty-two-year-old companion, "You're too old for me."

None of these angry personal stories shed light on the Lyon mystery, but they did bring Lloyd into better focus. His own accounts of his past were uniformly unreliable, even about how old he was. Over the years he had given various birthdates to authorities, all of them in December but in the years 1952, 1955, 1956, and 1957. The rest of his story was equally slippery. The memories of these old girlfriends and acquaintances helped color in the tale told by his criminal record, and in some instances corroborated what Lloyd had said about himself. Also helpful was a handwritten life summary that would be found in his prison cell. From all these things, in the weeks after the press conference, a fuller picture of Lloyd Welch emerged.

A Failure and an Embarrassment

Lloyd's true birthdate was December 30, 1956. His childhood went wrong early. As Lloyd told it, "My father killed my mother when I was two." His father, Lee Welch, driving drunk, had crashed their car, killing Lloyd's mother, Margaret Ann, who at the time was pregnant with twins. Lee was convicted of manslaughter and went to prison. Young Lloyd had some broken bones and lacerations that sent him to the hospital—including that broken nose. From there he was cycled through a series of foster homes until he was seven, when Lee and his new wife showed up.

"They came and got me," he had told Dave in their first session. "They introduced themselves, 'I'm your father; I'm your stepmother.' That was Edna. That's the woman. I love her like a mom. She treated me with respect. She loved me. We went to Maryland and there was a house . . . Buchanan Street."

But whatever hopes he had at that tender age of recouping his family were short-lived.

"Me and my father just kept bickering with each other. He pulled a shotgun on me. Put it up to my head. Said I looked like my mother a lot. He sexually raped, sexually assaulted me a few times when he was drinking. Slapped me around whenever he'd come back from work and shit like that, and I would always run away from home. The cops would bring me back."

Lloyd said he began drinking at a very early age, and when he was a young teenager he started using drugs—marijuana, cocaine, uppers, downers, acid, whatever he could find. Street drugs were plentiful in those years, a big part of the teenage scene. In the late 1960s and early '70s, cities like Washington had teenagers squatting in abandoned buildings and hanging out on the street, living the dream. Lloyd was savvier than most about fending for himself, and he preferred being on his own. Whenever he was placed in a home or shelter, he ran away. By sixteen he was already a confirmed grifter, living from score to score. He was nothing like the hippies around him; there was no flower power ethos behind Lloyd's lifestyle. He was so out of step with the youthful antiwar fervor of the period that he enlisted in the army at the height of the Vietnam War, only to be thrown out for lying about his age, education, and criminal past.

Lloyd had written the summary of his life for one of his correspondents. Like many prisoners serving long sentences, Lloyd carried on epistolary friendships, sometimes convincing people to wire money to his prison account. He had not told any of these correspondents why he was locked up. After the press conference, he had a lot of explaining to do, so he'd set about the task.

"My life was already screwed up," he wrote of his teenage years. "I was a failure in life and an embarrassment. My dad had told this to me many times."

He would often hitchhike out to Hyattsville, another edge city northeast of Washington, in the district's other Maryland suburban county, Prince Georges. His father, Lee, and stepmother, Edna, and many other members of Lloyd's large extended family lived there, clustered around his grandmother's house. They were part of what has become known as the Hillbilly Highway, the migration of largely Scotch Irish Appalachian families to northern cities after World War II. Many of these families retained the insularity, habits, and dialect of their native region. Lloyd's large extended family was typically close-knit, but he had always existed only on its margins. By his late teens, he was only half-heartedly welcomed when he showed up at Lee and Edna's home. By that point they had a houseful of their own children. He tried to avoid his father, who was perpetually drunk.

Lloyd met Helen in 1973. He approached her on a street corner in Takoma Park and started talking. They walked together to her house.

"I stayed that night . . . in the backyard. They actually put up a tent for me. I ate dinner with them. I got to liking her a lot, and every day I would come back to see her and stuff like that."

Rootless, impulsive, and up for a good time, Helen fell in with Lloyd, leaving home to stay with him at a boys' shelter in DC. When she was discovered and asked to leave, Lloyd went with her. After that they fended for themselves on the streets, together everywhere. As Edna would later put it, "You seen Lloyd, you seen Helen." They spent almost four years this way, hitchhiking, working for the carnival, doing odd jobs, drinking, and taking drugs. Helen and Lloyd even shared a few run-ins with the law.

"We were all wild, I guess you could say," he had told Dave in the October interview. "Drugs and everything like that. I lived that life. I always wandered. I just couldn't stand to be locked down, and she went with me. I wanted to travel. She wanted to travel with me, so I would do an odd job for six or seven months and make enough money, and we'd travel, we'd go to Texas, we'd go to Florida. We finally decided to go back to Maryland and live. First we lived in Takoma Park, Maryland, for a while, close to her mom, her brothers and sisters."

Helen lost one child before term and was carrying another child when they returned to Maryland sometime in 1974 or early '75. They camped out some of the time or stayed with Helen's mother or with Edna and Lee, whose address was then 4714 Baltimore Avenue, Hyattsville, across busy Route 1 (Baltimore Avenue) from the head of Buchanan Street. This was the address Lloyd gave when he made his original statement about the Lyon kidnapping. Soon after that sit-down with Montgomery County police the couple departed again and were gone for years.

"I was not a hard criminal," Lloyd wrote. "I just did stupid shit to people I knew."

When released from the prison stretch that split him from Helen and their children, Lloyd went back to wandering, drugs, drinking, and petty crimes. He was in and out of jail. In 1985, during one of his periods of freedom, he got married, in South Carolina—he was then using the name Mike. He started his own landscaping business in Myrtle Beach in 1989, by then living with a different woman from the one he had married. Then came his three child-molestation arrests, the last of which had earned him his current lengthy term.

In his letters and his talks with the detectives, Lloyd repeated that he always owned up to his crimes—by way of arguing that his denials about the Lyon girls should be believed. But his past demonstrated something else. Lloyd would admit a thing only when he had to, after he'd been caught, and only those parts that he couldn't refute. All his admissions had been calculated to mitigate his punishment. They were grudging, limited, and laced with denial. In every instance, Lloyd portrayed himself as an innocent victim. He'd pleaded guilty after molesting one little girl in Virginia, arguing, as he put it in his life summary: "She used to get in bed with her mom before I came along. One night I guess she could not get next to her mother so she got in bed next to me. I guess I thought it was my wife cuddled next to me in my sleep. I guess in my sleep I put my arm around her. She told her mom that my hand had touch her private area. I cannot say it did or did not happen because I was asleep." Lloyd owned up to nothing if he could help it.

Concerning the Lyon case, it was the same pattern. Each alteration in his story addressed a contradiction he could not escape. And each, in ways he did not anticipate, drew him closer to the very thing he sought to evade. It was a good bet that he would never accept any blame for the fate of the Lyon sisters. There are some things too terrible to admit, especially to yourself.

March 25, 2014

On the thirty-ninth anniversary of the girls' disappearance, Katie and Mark confronted Lloyd again in Smyrna. *Confronted* is the right word, because this session was not like the others.

The press conference had turned Lloyd's life upside down. Overnight, he had become a pariah in the prison. He was depressed and irate, and the detectives met him head-on. With Lloyd thrown off balance, it made sense to hit him hard. Sympathy and flattery had gotten them only so far. The pretext for this visit was the need to collect his palm prints—the FBI wanted to compare them with evidence of another crime—but the real reason was to see whether they could get him to cave in. Katie came armed with the bitterness of all the women he'd impregnated, abused, and left.

Lloyd was clad now in bright orange, the color for inmates in lockdown or, in his case, protective custody. His days were spent in isolation. He had lost his kitchen job. He looked ill. He had noticeably lost weight. He looked mad enough to spit. He started complaining as soon as he saw Mark and Katie.

"You all put out there that two children are missing, so the first thing that goes through their minds is, 'Let's kill him,'" he said. "I mean, there's judgment all the way around. I didn't kill nobody. I wasn't involved in anything like that!"

Katie ignored his outburst. She told him, in so many words, that she didn't feel sorry for him, and was done giving him the benefit of the doubt.

"Let's just cut out all the shit," she said. "We talked to people. I just met a woman who had a kid with you. You failed that [polygraph] because there is something that you are not telling the truth about. Period. Let's just cut all of the shit out, there is a lot of stuff you told me that's not true. I have been all over this country, we have been all over this country. Do you know that you had a child that died, a female child? Does that ring a bell? Charlene? You knew she was pregnant when you left her and went to Baltimore with some fifteen-year-old chick. You knew she was pregnant."

"I went to Baltimore with some fifteen-year-old chick?"

"Yeah. Pam or some chick that was living in the trailer park. She [Charlene] walked in and found you sleeping with her. I mean this woman, you left her pregnant, she had a kid and suffered her whole life with this child that was ill, and with no help from you. No nothing. The kid died."

"I didn't know she was pregnant! How could I have known she was pregnant?"

"I mean, you have kids all over the place."

"I do?"

"Yeah. I probably know more of your kids than you do at this point."

"Wow! How many I got?"

"A lot, a lot."

"Yeah?" Lloyd looked proud.

"Do you remember Charlene? Cici? She was very visibly pregnant when you left her. She was twenty. You told her she was too old and you were looking for somebody younger."

He denied it. Mark mentioned the name of a local pastor in South Carolina who had known him and had corroborated Charlene's story.

"I didn't leave with no fifteen-year-old girl; they can make [up] all the lies that they want."

"Why would they?" asked Katie. "Everybody can't be wrong. Everybody can't be lying. These are people that haven't spoken with anybody. They saw the report on the news, and they thought, 'Oh gosh, let me tell them about my experience.' I thought you were a decent guy. Every single female I talked to said you beat the shit out of her. And every dude I met told me that you like to beat up girls. Why would everybody lie?"

"Wow, maybe because I did something to them and they didn't like it," Lloyd offered, lamely.

"But there are a million things they can make up. They can say you are a dirtbag. Or they can say you are a thief. They can say you are a cheater."

Katie asked him about a pickup line he used on a woman in Myrtle Beach in the mid-1980s: "You want to go halves on a baby?"

Lloyd loosed his favorite exclamation—"Wow!"—then, "That was a good one!"

"Charming," said Katie.

"You were with Keelie then, weren't you?" Mark asked.

"No."

"Well, that's not true," said Mark. "This is where we get into trouble. Because you lie about everything. You got married to Keelie on January third, nineteen eighty-five. You were married to her; she was pregnant when you got married."

Mark then walked Lloyd through a list of women and places.

"Believe whatever you want," said Lloyd. "I don't care."

"It's not a matter of believing," said Mark. "It's what the evidence tells me."

"Let's cut the bull," said Lloyd, repeating Katie's directive in spirit if not word for word. "Charge me, or let me go back to my cell. It's as simple as that."

Let the Lies Catch Up

But Lloyd made no move to leave. If the squad had worried that shaming him publicly might shut him up, it had the opposite effect.

With the heat turned up, he now had no choice. As he neared the home stretch of his long prison term, freedom was something he could taste. Prior to this collision with the Lyon squad, the path had seemed clear. His prison mental-health report had all but pronounced him rehabilitated. "Mr. Welch took advantage of the treatment opportunities available within the prison to come to an understanding of the problems that led to [his] offense," it read, its author either asleep or completely taken in. "Mr. Welch seems to have developed deep insight, empathy, and remorse for his victim's pain and suffering." The report recommended that he be placed in a "transitional setting" in order to begin preparation "for a gradual release into society." Any tie to this terrible old crime would scotch that plan. So Lloyd was stuck. In order to maintain his position as a witness, not a *doer,* he had to stay on top of this investigation, and the only way to do that was to keep meeting with the detectives. Knowledge gave him leverage. As long as he could sell the detectives a narrative they liked, one that gave them what they were looking for, he had a chance. It was a delicate balancing act. If he admitted too much—being in any way involved with the kidnapping, being around when the girls were being abused—he was done. If he admitted too little, as with his earlier claim to have never been in Wheaton Plaza, and they found something to contradict him, he was done. The sessions were perilous but vital.

Mark, in particular, seemed to get this. He showed no sympathy for Lloyd whatsoever. He badgered him with the falsehoods and inconsistencies in his stories. He also liberally exaggerated the evidence against him.

"We found a lot of cases that are all across Maryland, South Carolina, Florida. All these cases around Wheaton, Takoma Park, that look like they've got your name on them. Rapes. Girls have disappeared. Girls that have been found murdered."

"Hold. Hold. Hold," Lloyd protested, raising his hand.

"No, this is the truth, Lloyd. We have all the old evidence. All the old fingerprints, DNA samples, stuff that was never analyzed. Because back in the seventies they didn't have DNA analysis. But we kept all that evidence. Now it is all getting compared. And it's not just going to be us saying that you did it. That's evidence, Lloyd."

Mark was bluffing. None of this was true. The detectives had taken a stab at locating old physical evidence of crimes committed in Montgomery County in the 1970s. They had found nothing more than heaps of moldy boxes the police department had stored in an old garage. None of it had been catalogued or kept in order—no one at the time foresaw much use for doing so. A further effort would be made to find, sort, and mine this material, but it hadn't even gotten under way, and the chances of its yielding anything useful were small.

"Okay, show me the evidence," said Lloyd. "I am tired. I only got two sex charges."

"It's not a matter of what you got charged with, Lloyd. That's not how you keep track. It's what you actually did. You got away with a lot, but it is catching up to you now."

Katie reminded him that when Dave and Chris had come to him in October, they had not been trying to build a case against him. They had just been looking for information.

"If I knew I would have told you."

"Lloyd, you know," she said.

"No, I don't."

"You may not have been the one that did it, but you know, and you know we know," she said. "That polygraph shows you know. The truth is, I don't even think *you* can keep up with your lies anymore. It's got to be exhausting; it has to be. And at some point, you have to break down and give yourself a chance to show some humanity. To these old people who have never been able to bury their kids, who'd like to die in peace knowing that these kids got proper burying. And that's all I asked you that day, 'Tell me where they are, and let's get this done.' And this shit storm has started because of that. That's all we wanted to know when we came in here. They were willing to give you a deal;

they were willing to cut you out and say, 'Okay, he is a changed man. He came forward he did the right thing.' Thirty-nine years today. And instead you tied our hands. Now the shit storm has started. And the bottom line is, you still have a chance to do the right thing and tell us where these girls are. Or where you think they are, because there is nothing in this world that's going to convince anybody that you don't know."

She said she had no interest in trying to charge him with past crimes against women.

"I don't want to be their victims' rights advocate. I want to know where those girls are buried. That's what I want out of this whole situation. And instead, because you want to play games, because you know, Lloyd, you know, you know. The polygraph says you know, your body language says you know. Your lies are catching up with you."

"Let the lies catch up," he said. "I don't know where they are. I am going to keep on telling you that. And I would love for them [the Lyon family] to know. I would, I really honestly would."

Katie said, "Let me ask you, when I sat here and said to you, 'What's it going to take? What is it going to take for you to just tell us?' And I gave you some options in terms of the deals they were giving you. And you were into that. You wanted to hear more about it, you said, 'Okay, if this is what we do, then I might go back to my cell and have a memory.' What was that?"

Lloyd pleaded again that long years of drinking and drugs had eroded his memory. Katie scoffed. Why, if he couldn't remember anything, did he keep angling for a deal? How was he able to come up with such detailed recollections of the things he did admit? Why had he confided something new to Dave at the end of their last session?

"Just be real with us for five minutes," she said.

"I am being real! I don't know where. I don't know. I don't know."

Katie tried flattery again. She told Lloyd she considered him an extremely intelligent man: "People who have PhDs probably aren't as street-smart as you are. This is a game of chess to you, and you are just waiting to see our move."

She walked him through some of his past, the women who said he had abused them, his history of arrests. Mark reiterated how assiduously the FBI and his own department were now gathering evidence against him.

"Because that's the choice you made," he said. "Now, I can put the skids on that. I have the power to do that. But it has to start with you. And it doesn't start with you continuing to lie to us. It's time for the truth, Lloyd. Beyond any doubt, we know you were there that day. And you had something to do with the girls' disappearance. There is no doubt about that with any of us."

Lloyd asked, why, if he had been involved in kidnapping two little girls, would he have brought Helen with him?

"There is nothing to say that you did, other than your word," said Mark. "And you have lied about everything. Why would we believe that? And the witnesses at the mall never saw Helen. They saw only you."

"I ain't sayin' nothing else. I am done saying things. You all are not believing anything I am saying."

But, again, he stayed put.

Mark reminded him of the option Karen Carvajal had presented him a month earlier. Maybe he wasn't fully culpable. Perhaps he had been used to help lure the girls without knowing what was in store.

"If there was somebody else who was there, you need to tell us who it was," he said. He said he was amazed that Lloyd had carried this secret for so long. "There's some reason this is weighing very heavily on you. I can try and move you to a facility where no one knows you and doesn't know [i.e., and no one knows] all of this shit. I am willing to go forward. But you have to give me something, man, this has to be a two-way street."

Lloyd wouldn't budge—yet.

He Is a Motherfucker

"Can we clarify the last time when Dave talked to you, and you said you saw them the following day at that house naked in the basement?" asked Mark.

"Yeah, I did say that."

"Is that the truth?"

Lloyd paused for a moment, then said, "Yeah."

"You had to think about that."

"It's the truth. I seen two girls. I don't know if it was them two girls or not. I told him that."

"And whose house was that?"

"I don't remember the guy's name."

"But how did you know that guy?"

"We used to party all the time. I used to party with a lot of people up in Maryland. I had a cousin named Billy. I don't know if you all know him or not. He is probably dead. He introduced me to a lot of people. He lived near, in Prince Georges County. He lived near Uncle Dickie and them. Did you meet Uncle Dickie?"

"Yes, we talked to Uncle Dickie."

"I am sure he has a lot of good stuff for you," said Lloyd, balefully. This was the first hint that he now believed his extended family was working against him. His manner had changed. The threat of a broader FBI investigation and of new charges, Mark's bluffs, had apparently got him thinking. Was there some new, safer ground he could find? If he had seen something important—this was what he'd suggested to Dave at the end of the polygraph session—he would once again become a valuable witness, not a target.

Katie noticed the change. She said Lloyd's body language showed he was being deceptive and suggested that he was scared. Both suppositions were clearly true.

"Is it, you are afraid to tell us?" suggested Mark. "Is that what it is?"

"It could be."

"Okay, that's fair," said Mark. He was getting somewhere. "I can understand that. That's reasonable. So let's deal with that."

"I've dealt with some pretty nasty cops."

"What are you afraid of?" asked Katie. "Let's start with that. Tell us. Are you afraid it's going to hang you up in something, or are you afraid that whoever is involved is going to do something? Let's just start with what you are afraid of."

"I don't know if the person is still alive or not," he said.

"And are you afraid of the person?" she asked.

"Yeah."

"How in the hell are they going to hurt you in here?"

"It's not me I'm worried about."

"Okay, tell us so we can fix that," said Katie.

"My kids."

"How would they know about your kids?" Mark asked. "You don't even know where your kids are."

"He is a motherfucker."

Mark pointed out that Lloyd's children all went by different last names. The detectives had great difficulty finding them, even with all the tools available to the police. "Some average Joe out there on the street is not going to find your kids."

"It's not so much my kids," said Lloyd. "It's my family and stuff like that."

"Lloyd, the thing is, I think this is the first time you said something that I actually one hundred percent believe," said Katie. "I believe that. That's a legitimate concern of yours. But that person does not know, especially if that person has seen this on media, they do not know what you have told us."

"I don't even know if the person is alive or not," said Lloyd.

"All right," said Mark. "Then there's a good chance it's not even an issue."

"Why don't you tell us the person's name, and we can figure it out?" suggested Katie. "We can make a phone call now and see if that person is alive. We will have Dave figure it out in minutes. He's a computer whiz, unlike myself."

"My cousin Teddy still alive?" he asked.

"What's his last name?" asked Katie.

"It would be Teddy Welch, the same as mine."

"I don't think so," said Mark. His mind was racing. Did they know anything about Teddy? "Did he live in PG [Prince Georges] County?"

"He used to," said Lloyd. "I don't know if he does anymore or not."

Lloyd explained that Teddy was his uncle Dick's son, or he thought so. He wasn't sure. He hadn't seen him or most other members of his family in decades, and they had never been close. "Find out if he is still alive or not."

"I am pretty sure he is alive," said Mark. "We haven't talked to him, but I am sure he is alive because when we talked to Dickie and Patty [Dick's wife], they mentioned him."

"Is he the one you are worried about?" asked Katie.

"Uh-huh."

"So he's the key to this whole situation?" she asked.

"He's one of 'em," Lloyd said.

"So what was his role?" asked Mark.

"Him and the other guy was the ones who grabbed them."

Here was his new safe ground. He knew the kidnappers and had seen them take the girls but had not himself been with them or involved. Lloyd again insisted that he had gone to the mall with Helen to look for work.

"Helen wasn't there; we know that," said Mark.

"She was."

"I mean, again, we are making progress with the honesty—"

"I am being honest," said Lloyd. "She was there."

"Her sister doesn't think she was," said Mark, "and your stepmother doesn't think she was."

Lloyd held fast. But he was willing to talk more about his cousin Teddy, offering yet another version of what he saw that day.

"I saw them leaving with two girls. I don't know if it was them two [Sheila and Kate] or not, because I wasn't really close to them. But I did see them leave with two girls. A couple of days later the girls were missing."

"How were they walking off?" asked Mark. "Did they look like they were forcibly walking off?"

"Teddy had his arm around one of them, and the other guy had his arm pulled in close to her. I don't know who the guy was."

"Like around her head, like a headlock type of deal?" asked Mark.

"More like her shoulders, pulling her in close."

"Okay," said Mark.

"How old do you think Teddy was back then?" asked Katie.

"I don't know, maybe eighteen or twenty."

"Okay, so he wasn't their age," said Katie. "He was older?"

"He was older."

"Is he a bad dude?" Katie asked.

"He was."

Lloyd insisted that he had just happened to be at the mall that day. They asked why he was afraid of Teddy.

"Because I seen him beat the crap out of somebody before. He has threatened my family a couple of times."

"What family?" asked Mark.

"My sisters, my brothers, my kids. He said he will find them and he will kill them. Because I did see two girls at a home, like I said. That was true. I ran. I was scared. He knew I saw them."

"How did he know?"

"Because he saw me."

Lloyd said Teddy had come to his stepmother's house that day, the day he had seen the girls drugged and being raped. He had threatened him.

"He called me out to the backyard," said Lloyd. "Told me, 'I know you saw me walk off with those girls. Don't worry about it. You say anything, you can be hurt and your family can be hurt and your kids.'" (At that point, Lloyd had no children).

His story had taken a substantial turn. Teddy Welch and "the other guy" were the kidnappers. He did not know who the other guy was. Ray Mileski had been erased. Forget about what he had said earlier.

"Here is what I think," said Mark. "If that is true—and I have a lot of concerns about it being true—but if that were true, I think you were there at the mall with them that day. Okay? And I think what I said a while ago about you knowing something more is that I think what happened is you got into something that day you didn't realize was going to be as serious as it turns out. And maybe you broke off at some point when you realized that this is not where I need to be or want to be. And whatever happened to them after that happened. But there are big concerns that I have about it. And I have every version of your story so far. They don't logically make sense. And I will tell you why. Why would you, if he pulled you out in the backyard and had this conversation and all, why would you go back to the mall and report whatever it is you reported you saw?"

"I was scared."

"If you are so scared, why would you? You would stay as far away from that mall as you possibly could."

"Because I thought that, even though he threatened me at that time, he wouldn't know that I said anything."

Lloyd said that at the time he wasn't thinking straight.

"Think straight now, Lloyd," Mark said.

"Well, I am thinking straight. I want to know if he is alive or not."

Two Naked Girls

"So, if I have this straight, you are at the mall, you see Teddy and this other guy grab these girls," said Mark. "The next day you go to this other guy's house to party, and these two naked little girls are there. And you get scared and you run."

"Yeah."

"What guy's house?"

"The one that Teddy was living at."

"So it's not the guy whose picture we showed you. That was all bullshit. Was that to just steer us in the wrong direction?"

"No, that guy looked familiar."

"You just latched onto that guy because we gave him to you."

"No, I am saying he did look familiar. I can't say I knew him."

"So, let me ask you, why would you go to that house that day if he threatened you?" asked Katie.

"No, he didn't threaten me that day. It was the next day that he threatened me. I didn't say that day." Lloyd repeated that he had run away after seeing Teddy with the two girls. "I left," he said. "I went to my mom's house."

"What was it you saw?" asked Mark. "You say you saw something."

"Two girls in the house naked."

"What were they doing?"

"Laying on the bed."

"What part of the house was this?"

"It was in the basement part."

"Who else was in the basement?"

"Teddy and another guy, and then there was another guy I don't know. I had never seen him before. I left. Teddy saw me; he actually saw me. I went back to my mom's house. I was scared. Later on that day he came over, and he said, 'I know you saw something. Leave it alone, don't worry about it. Or you are going to be hurt.' "

"So you were looking just to party, so you went to the house?" asked Katie. "To get high, drink, whatever?"

"Yeah."

"Did you walk in the house without being invited? Is that kind of what you guys did?"

"Yeah."

"So you walk in, and you saw these two girls. Were they tied up? Were they laying down?"

"No, they were laying down. They looked like they were drugged. They looked like they were high. They looked like they were partying all night long."

"But they were little?"

"Well, I couldn't see the entire face, body, and everything like that. I mean I saw one girl's face. She didn't look young-young. But I left. I got scared."

To sell his new story, Lloyd was offering lurid new details, all of which deepened his credibility problem. If he knew these things, things he could no longer claim to have forgotten, why hadn't he told the detectives earlier? They had *begged* him for the truth.

"What you told us before, was it true? About seeing them pushed in the car or something?" asked Mark. It was hard to keep track of all the versions.

"Yeah."

"And the little one was crying?"

"Yeah."

"You remember that?"

"Yeah."

"Was the taller one crying?"

"I can't say if she was or not. All I saw, like I said before about the car, it was a Camaro and it was Teddy's, and I think it was blue. I don't remember the color."

"I think that's what you told me last time," said Katie—actually, up until now, the car had always been maroon.

"Yeah. I think it was blue. I am not sure. I am not good on remembering colors. I saw two girls getting into the car. We were getting on the bus. I don't know. We left on the bus, that was it. The girl getting in the back seat looked like she was crying. You know, she had her head down, [but] you can hear it. You know, it wasn't that far away. I mean the bus was right there; you can tell that she has been crying. We left."

"Was he doing anything? Trying to shut her up?" asked Mark.

"Just pushing her in the car. Not literally push. But putting her head in there. I didn't think about it at that time. I mean I was eighteen years old. I was stupid. I mean I didn't do anything about it. That's what I am talking about being stupid. If I was smart enough I would have done something. But I didn't do anything. I went to the house the next day, I saw the girls there."

This story didn't make sense, so Mark went back to his original strategy, trying to give Lloyd an excuse to say what happened without implicating himself.

"I think what you just said lines up totally with my theory here," said Mark. "That you were out with those guys that day, probably at the mall trying to pick up chicks, because that's what people did back then. And this shit went sideways, and you got out. You bailed out of it. That makes more sense to me. You know, because here is the thing. Think of it this way: Three guys go to rob a bank. Okay, it sounds like a good idea. They are down on their luck, they need some money. 'All right, let's go rob a bank.' One guy has the gun, the other guy puts his finger in his pocket, pretends he has a gun. And the third guy is just driving the getaway car. He never even goes in the bank. All right? And he is thinking to himself, 'I am just along for the ride. I will get a little money out of this. I am not going to hurt anybody, I am not going to confront anybody. I am just driving the car.' You know, all of a sudden these guys go into the bank and wind up shooting somebody. Well, the guy driving the car never expected that; he didn't sign up for that. You know what I mean? So he gets the hell out of there. Leaves them, leaves them with the mess they created. Is that what happened here?"

Lloyd was briefly silent, weighing it. He was taking extreme care not to link himself with the kidnappers.

"No, that's not what happened," he said. "I wasn't there with them. I went to the house to party. Like I always did."

"You thought really hard about that."

"No, I listened to everything you said."

"I know."

"I mean, I was taking in everything that you were saying."

"No, but after I was done it seemed like you were really contemplating that. You know what I mean?"

"So, you want me to say?"

"I just want the truth, Lloyd."

"No, you want me to say that I went to the mall with them and I picked up chicks and everything like that. Sounds like a good theory, but it's not the way it went. I am sorry. I can't say anything else because I don't know anything else."

It was, of course, another lie—except for the parts that were true.

6

One Hundred and One Percent the God's Honest Truth

Leonard Kraisel (left) and Teddy (right)

UNCLE LENNY

Who was Teddy? It had taken Mark a few seconds to process the name. He was Thomas Welch Jr., not Dick's son but the son of Dick's, and Lee's, brother Thomas. The fact that Lloyd didn't know shows how removed he had been from his extended family all his life. Teddy was most definitely still alive. He also went by "Tommy" and "Junior." He now lived with his wife and two children in Lusby, Maryland. He was seven years younger than Lloyd. This meant, of course, that in March 1975, Teddy would have been eleven years old.

This made Lloyd's characterization of him—"He is a motherfucker"—ludicrous. How likely was it that a boy of eleven would kidnap two girls roughly his own age? How likely was it that Lloyd had seen him having sex with the girls or that he would subsequently have been so intimidated by him? Or that Lloyd was still afraid of him?

It was comical.

Two days after that session with Lloyd, Dave and Chris paid a surprise visit to Teddy. They found him at his workplace, a fuel equipment and service company in Laurel. A tall, tan, handsome man with an engaging manner, well spoken and forthcoming, he was the most polished Welch they had encountered. He was also completely candid about the intimate details of his life, surprisingly so. He told the detectives once that he had infected sores on his buttocks, pointing to the place with two fingers, after which they dubbed him "Teddy Two-Fingers." As a child, he had known Lloyd only as a slightly scary older cousin who had been around from time to time. Lloyd had built a tree house that Teddy remembered; they had smoked dope in it once, something that would make a lasting impression on a boy. He said he had no personal memory associated with the Lyon sisters and had never heard them spoken of in his family, but he was aware of the case and how terrible it was and said he was willing to help in any way he could. In short, Teddy sparked no suspicion whatsoever. The detectives called Mark and Katie from the car on the drive back to Gaithersburg and told them that Teddy had nothing to do with the case. Lloyd had thrown them another curveball.

Except . . . the more they learned about Teddy, the more they had to wonder. His story was remarkable. Like Lloyd, he had been abused as a child and had spent much of his life on the outs with his family, but his path had been very different. He was more than just a survivor, something Lloyd proudly called himself. The abuses in Lloyd's past had shaped him into a sexual predator and landed him behind bars. In Teddy's case, sexual molestation had led him into a long-term, peculiar, and materially advantageous relationship with his abuser. Lloyd's math may have been off, but the decision to name this cousin, of all people, as the kidnapper showed cunning.

You had to know Teddy's story to understand this decision. As a boy, he had been, in essence, adopted by a wealthy, middle-aged pederast named Leonard Kraisel. Teddy had had an ugly early upbringing. His father was an abusive drunk. His mother left when he was still little. Teddy was beaten regularly by his father until, at age thirteen, he fought back. That episode sparked the intervention of county social workers, who placed him in a boys' home. On a field trip with other children to a horse show at the Capital Centre, he noticed signs for Andrews Air Force Base, which are very visible along the northeastern portion of the Capital Beltway. He didn't know exactly where his mother was living—she had remarried and started another family—but he'd heard it was in Clinton, Maryland, which he had been told was near the air base. So, once inside the center, he excused himself to go to the bathroom and exited the arena. He scaled a fence to reach the beltway and stuck out his thumb.

He was picked up by a middle-aged man who treated him with exceptional kindness. Adults who took a caring interest were rare in Teddy Welch's world. The man, Kraisel, helped him find his mother's house, something Teddy could not have done easily on his own, and after dropping him off, gave him a business card and said, "In case you ever need anything or want to talk or to hang out."

Teddy's attempt to blend in with his mother's new family didn't take. She didn't return him to the boys' home, but he soon felt like an intruder and a burden in the crowded household—his mother and stepfather had six children of their own. So Teddy dialed the number of the nice man who had picked him up on the beltway. They met a few times. The older man listened to him intently, advised him, took him to nice places, and bought him things. Kraisel's home was enormous, a palace compared with any place Teddy had previously seen. He had a live-in maid. Together, Kraisel and Teddy talked openly about things the boy had never discussed before. When they were not together, they spoke on the phone. At first Kraisel made no sexual demands. He was affectionate, generous, and genuinely concerned. So when he suggested that Teddy move in with him, the boy agreed without hesitation. Technically, he was still a ward of the county, but Kraisel avoided any clash with social services by offering Teddy's mother free remodeling for her home. "She sold me for carpet and tile, more or less," was how Teddy later explained it to me.

His life changed dramatically. Kraisel was an abused, abandoned boy's dream of an adoptive father—except the deal had a price tag. Kraisel began asking Teddy to masturbate him. Teddy was less shocked than some boys might have been. He had demonstrated some sexual fluidity as a younger child, sometimes dressing as a girl, and he came from a family—the detectives would learn—where engaging in sex acts with children was common. As Teddy later explained—insisting he was not gay (then or now)—at age fifteen he regarded Kraisel's requests as a reasonable bargain. The older man was caring, gentle, and indulgent with him. In most ways it was a situation any teenage boy would relish. Kraisel taught Teddy to drive as soon as he was old enough to get a learner's permit and then gave him a Corvette. There were nice clothes, spending money, and travel, and Teddy no longer had to attend school. He saw the world—twenty different countries over the next five years. Kraisel introduced the boy to his family as his adoptive son—although Teddy insisted that Lenny, as he called him, tell the truth about their relationship when they stayed with Kraisel's mother in Florida. She accepted him as her son's younger lover. It was she who suggested that Lenny send the boy to modeling school, which launched a brief career of photo shoots and runway shows. Teddy had come a long way from Hyattsville.

And the relationship endured. Teddy lived with Kraisel for ten years. As an older teenager he led a double life, keeping a girlfriend on the side and enjoying the party scene in Florida. When Lenny discovered that Teddy was using cocaine, he checked him into a rehab center in Pennsylvania. During treatment there, Teddy explained to counselors the bargain he had struck with Lenny and his discomfort with it. He was encouraged to confront Lenny, which he did. Teddy said their sexual relationship ended at that point, but Lenny promised to continue treating him as his son, a promise he kept.

The fuel company where the Lyon squad found Teddy in 2014 was owned primarily by Lenny—Teddy had a small share. His comfortable house was also Lenny's. Teddy and his wife and twin sons enjoyed a lifestyle well beyond anything they could afford on their own, and "Uncle Lenny" was still very much a part of their lives. There was a big framed family photo atop their stairwell showing the attractive couple and their boys, with Lenny standing over them, his hands on the shoulders of husband and wife. From time to time Lenny stayed with them. This cozy arrangement continued until one of Teddy's twin boys confessed to a school counselor that his uncle Lenny had been playing sexual games with him. Teddy said he was shocked and felt angry and betrayed. He cooperated with the police in building a criminal case against his old partner, who was eventually sentenced and imprisoned. Still, it was hard not to notice in Teddy and his wife's relationship to Kraisel an echo of the deal Teddy's mother had struck years earlier, trading him for home improvements.

What all this meant was that Lloyd had chosen with great care whom to name next as the Lyon girls' kidnapper. Locked in isolation, with little to do but stew over his predicament, he had come up with the most notoriously aberrant member of his family—which was saying something. He had talked to the detectives about "the older man" with whom Teddy had been living, certainly Leonard Kraisel. This unseemly pairing was well known to the Welch family. His relatives knew all about Teddy's work as a teenage model, and his "adoption" by Kraisel. They called Teddy "gay," disparagingly, as if it were a catchall term for sexual depravity. Lloyd had heard all the stories and had sized Kraisel up as a perfect new suspect for the Lyon squad. Teddy fit perfectly into the scenario they'd suggested about himself and Mileski, an older pederast seducing a boy and then using him to lure additional victims. And Teddy, handsome enough to find work as a model, was well suited for the role. Lloyd correctly surmised that Teddy and Uncle Lenny, with their creepy sexual arrangement, would be like red meat to these hungry detectives.

The problem was that both Lloyd's math and his family history were off. Teddy had not met Kraisel until he was fifteen, four years after the Lyon kidnapping. This completely blew the premise of Lloyd's story, but, just as he'd likely imagined, the detectives found Teddy's past irresistibly suggestive. And interest in Teddy had an unintended and ultimately more significant consequence. It drew the squad's attention to the entire Welch clan.

All families had secrets, but few had ones like these.

Becalmed

After the Montgomery County Police Department's press conference about Lloyd Welch, the most important evidence to surface was a two-year-old report that the squad had not seen. A woman named Dee Danner, after sitting on a memory for many years, had phoned the National Center for Missing and Exploited Children in 2012 to report that she had observed a suspicious man in Wheaton Plaza on the day the Lyon sisters had disappeared. When Danner saw Lloyd's photo on TV in 2014, she recognized him. She phoned the Montgomery County police to repeat her story, which was all the more credible because she had initially reported it long before Lloyd was publicly linked to the mystery.

"This has been bothering me for years," she had told the man who took her call in 2012. She described seeing that day a young white man with long brown hair and a mustache who had scared her. He looked to be in his twenties, she said. The man was staring so intently at her and at other girls that she and her companion had been frightened. They noticed that he seemed particularly fixated on girls with blond hair, which reassured them—both Dee and her friend had dark hair. She said the man was "creepy." When he saw them watching him he had stared back menacingly, spooking them enough that they went to look for a security guard. They found one but shrank from talking to him. "What would we say," she asked later—that someone was staring at girls and had made a face at them? So they said nothing but kept watching the creepy man.

"We were scared of this guy, really scared of him," she said. When Mark interviewed her, Dee said he had definitely been alone, which jibed with the story told years ago by Danette Shea, who had provided the description for the police artist. Dee also remembered seeing Sheila and Kate—she knew Sheila from school—and the notorious tape recorder man, who had been such a focus of the investigation years ago. She said this man had been a big center of attention, with a crowd around him, children and parents. In such circumstances it was hard to imagine him walking off with Sheila and Kate without being noticed. When the girls were missing, Dee and her friend immediately thought of the creepy man, but neither had contacted the police. They were children, she explained. All the news reports were focused on the tape recorder man. They felt what they had seen wasn't important. But it had bothered her enough that she never forgot it.

Dee's memory was detailed and in parts verifiable. She had definitely been in Wheaton Plaza that day. Her identification of Lloyd was solid. She also remembered seeing the Lyon girls talking with a boy who was about their age, maybe slightly older. The previous investigation had confirmed that Jay, their older brother, had briefly been with them in the mall. But what if, the detectives wondered, the boy she had seen was Teddy?

The effect of Dee's memory was to intensify the focus on Lloyd, but the squad had little else to go on. Despite what Mark and Katie had told him, that the press conference had generated significant new leads, it had not directly advanced the case. In the first months of 2014, the probe was becalmed.

But the conference had had a huge impact on Lloyd. He was miserable. It had not only affected his prison relationships; the publicity had outed him to his regular correspondents, who were horrified to have befriended a child molester. Lloyd's carefully cultivated epistolary support system crumbled.

He wrote a peevish lament to Edna in April: "I am an embarrassment to my family. I will send family pictures back to you that you sent me. I cannot believe that my brothers and sisters would turn on me like they have." In another letter written in the same period, he apologized at length to a former cell mate's mother-in-law, with whom he had corresponded regularly—she had encouraged him to become religious—and whom he had misled about his offense.

> I know you are upset, and hurt by me. I can understand this. As I said, I am a shame of my life. I wish I was never born, that way people would never have been hurt by me. I told you I always hurt people I know and love. Yes, I did lie to you and that hurt me

> more than you will ever know, but everything I told you about me in here [in prison], what I was doing and how I was trying to change my life around was true. I have had people all my life do judgment on me and walk away. It hurts like hell but you get use to it. I am not a monster. I might be stupid and a screwed up life. But I could never hurt anyone like that. I lie to you because, yes, I was very a shame of my life. . . . I wanted to tell you face to face about my life and show you that I was a good person in life. I am not going to lie to you anymore. I ask for your forgiveness in this matter. Only you can decide this. I thank you for all you have done for me. If you feel in some way that I have use you in any way to get money from you then I am sorry for that. It was not why I wrote.

He told her he would understand if she stopped writing. He denied any connection to the Lyon sisters and noted that he had not been charged.

> I am being question about this, yes, because I made a stupid mistake 39 years ago and said I saw something when I did not see anything. I am not guilty of this. There is know [no] evidence on me, just that, yes, I was there that day and I made a false statements back then. I could never in my life kidnap anyone or hurt them. I've done a lot of stupid things in my life but not this. . . . I made mistakes in my life but I am still a decent person. I should not be treated like some kind of a animal, people will always judge me. May God be with you and your family.

He signed off with "God bless."

Despite this seemingly heartfelt plea, Lloyd had eclipsed Ray Mileski as the squad's prime suspect. Mark and Katie had done what they could to batter him into admitting his role, only to elicit more misdirection.

It was painful to admit, but Lloyd was all they had—and they had now surely alienated him. When Dave went to see him again a month later, it was all about damage repair.

The detective had lain awake the night before, wondering how to handle the interview. The truth was that they had never adequately prepared for these sessions with Lloyd. They needed to be smarter. For the first session they had prepped long and hard, but then they had seen Lloyd as a witness. The second meeting had been about introducing Lloyd to Mark, and in the third, which included Katie's polygraph test, they had hoped to sort out which version of his story to believe and perhaps shake him up enough to extract the truth. The fourth had been designed to take advantage of the blow struck by the press conference, to pressure him, but had only backed him deeper into his corner and produced the dubious story about Teddy. It had one positive outcome; they no longer needed to worry about Lloyd's refusing to see them. The press conference had hurt him badly. If he were going to shut down, it would have happened then. The FBI's estimation that Lloyd would clam up had clearly been off base. Now the squad needed to rebuild rapport, and for that they needed a sound strategy. What had they learned about him? What could they use?

Nobody ever tells you when you go into police work that it will require dishonesty. The objective, it would seem, is the opposite, utter honesty. But once you get into the really interesting stuff, you descend, by necessity, a moral ladder onto slippery ground where the truth is a liability. This was one of the reasons Katie had felt the need to escape the sex crimes unit. To catch the child molester or the possible child killer, she'd had to play along, to pretend—convincingly—sympathy and even amity. This sometimes made her skin crawl.

Dave knew that was where he was headed. It was the basis of his approach to all the suspects he had interrogated, and it came naturally to him. The armored-car robber who had confessed and then led him and Chris to the buried loot had done so because Dave had won him over, had convinced him that he was on his side. He had reasoned with him, had talked him into believing that cooperation was the only thing that might help him. This was a standard tactic, one that most seasoned criminals saw through; but fewer did so with Dave, because he was able to summon something like real empathy for the accused. In his years of detective work he had seen disadvantaged defendants get creamed by the justice system for crimes that warranted leniency, and also the opposite. He remembered in particular a well-spoken, white, presentable high school teacher who had gone on an armed-robbery spree to support a drug habit, and who got off in court with a slap on the wrist. Dave felt the educated criminal with the good job was, if anything, *more* culpable than someone who committed a crime out of desperation or stupidity. His default posture was to try to understand the poor sucker in deep trouble. And yet, on another level, Dave knew that empathy itself was a ploy. Earning trust was nearly always a ruse. Cooperation rarely worked to a suspect's benefit. The armored-car robber got a life sentence—so much for coming clean to his good buddy, Dave! The detective coped with this duplicity by narrowing his vision. He focused only on the relationship he developed with a suspect inside the interview room, looking neither back nor forward. The simplicity of the room helped. Small, windowless, and bare, it constricted the world to the conversation. But the work required more, he knew. It meant donning moral blinders to the terrible things his subject might have done, to the consequences that might await the subject, and to his own behavior. In that confined space, Dave became a suspect's last best friend.

His determination not to dwell on the crime itself was why Dave had never met John and Mary Lyon. To feel their pain and to obsess about their daughters' fate would make it harder to act chummy with Lloyd. Unless he could summon some genuine empathy for Lloyd, his act would be all pretense—and unconvincing. It was easier to adopt this approach because Lloyd, Dave understood, was also playing false. It was a game. Each man was trying to get over on the other. It was something Dave enjoyed as much as Lloyd seemed to enjoy it—although the stakes were clearly higher for Lloyd. So far, as Dave saw it, he, Dave, was losing. But he had clearly established himself as the "good cop." Now he would play it to the hilt. Mark and Katie soon would be calling him Lloyd's "Wubbie."

April 24, 2014

They met again in the same interview room upstairs at Dover Police Headquarters. Lloyd, in his bright orange denim, with his hands shackled in his lap, looked dejected. He was seated on one side of the desk and Dave on the other. The detective slid across a large cup of coffee. Lloyd hardly stirred. He looked thinner still, his white goatee longer, the patches of hair left on his scalp straggly.

"Does he have to be hooked up?" Dave asked the two guards at the door, pointing to the chains attached to Lloyd's handcuffs.

"We can take the travel gear off, but the cuffs will stay on," said one.

"Do you mind?" he asked.

The chains were removed.

"What's happening, brother?" he asked Lloyd cheerfully.

Lloyd rubbed his eyes with his cuffed hands and sighed heavily.

"Nothin'," he said, glumly.

"Long morning again?"

"I've been in these things since six this morning."

"I know there's been a lot of undue pressure put on you," began Dave. "It's been a lot of pressure put on the community and on this police department to try to get this thing to come to a head. And one of the reasons I wanted to sit down with you is because I think I've come up with some different things."

He said he wanted them to start over.

"It's going to be very laid-back, very informal. I wanted to start off by saying I apologize for the last six or eight months, the way that this unfolded on you, as well as how it's obviously affected you, how it's displaced you in the prison—"

"Yeah, look at me," Lloyd said. He was feeling sorry for himself. In his life summary, written at about this time, he complained, "I am treated like a piece of shit now. Maybe that is what I am now. I have been the black sheep of a family that has never loved me or cared about me. I guess I will die that way."

Lloyd referred back to their first meeting, laughing bitterly: "That's when my life went to hell. Seventeen years of work, trying to do good in this penitentiary and change my life around, and all in three months' time it went downhill. I mean, I can't even go into population now. They got me on lockdown. Pure, pure lockdown."

"I think a lot of that's for your safety, just based on the media release."

"Yeah, that's what it was. Then I hear the people that I've known for years have been telling all kinds of bull crap about me."

"They have," said Dave. "I have been talking to several of them. I don't know that I believe them, but I had to talk to them. I mean they're all reaching out to us."

"Well, that's what I don't understand. What they're talking to y'all about. They don't know nothing about me, what's put me in jail, you know? Because I didn't share nothing with nobody. I didn't share my life with nobody."

"I can tell you're a little upset, but I think after today—"

"I'm a little discouraged about a lot of things. I got officers treatin' me like shit, talkin' shit about me. I've had a few of them threaten me."

"Officers?"

"Yep, calling me a child killer, child rapist, all of that and then telling people on the tier that I'm on now the same thing. I tried to ask for something, and they act like they don't know me. Officers that I have known for years don't know me all the sudden. Oh yeah, I'm a little discouraged by a lot of things. That's why I'm going to be taking the Fifth on a lot of things and asking for a lawyer all the time."

Lloyd now believed that the whole Mileski angle Dave had presented in October, showing him pictures, asking him to be a witness, had been a setup. It had not been, and Dave told him so. He said the squad in fact had been focused on Mileski but had since found evidence that completely exonerated him. "That was a mistake," he explained. "Everything you were told about that guy was accurate. But he was in jail at the time." This was not true, but he wanted to dismiss Mileski from their conversation.

He reiterated that Lloyd had the right to stop talking and to consult with an attorney, and that he would understand if Lloyd went that way, but then tried to carve out an exception for himself.

"You've heard me, and I've never come up with anything shady," he said. "I've never lied to you."

They talked a little more, and then Lloyd, without further complaint, once more agreed to waive his rights.

"All of the times we've sat down and talked, there's been a variation," Dave said. "Different events. Different people. Kind of a variation in stories. What I mean by that is not lies—"

"No, a lot of them was lies," Lloyd admitted.

"I'm trying to sit back and take an absolute point of view of it and not base it on opinion," said the detective. "Because I like you. And part of this is hard, because when you gain some sort of trust after being with someone for a while, it's hard to understand how you could have done something like this. But you have to look at it objectively. You have to do your job, and you have to take your opinion out of it. Does that make sense?"

"Uh-huh."

"I can't come in here and judge you just based on how I feel about you. I have to look at all the facts as a whole. So that's what I did. I broke them all apart. And there's some factual things that I think that you'll agree upon. That in nineteen seventy-five, March twenty-fifth, you were inside Wheaton Plaza."

"Uh-huh."

Dave proceeded to outline the other things they could agree were fact. Lloyd had paid enough attention to a group of girls that they had heckled him, and they had later given the police a description that produced a composite sketch.

"And that doesn't make you a criminal," Dave hastily added. "That makes you a man, because they were a good-looking set of girls, and anybody—no matter how old they were—would have looked at them. And that's a fact. So much that one of the girls approached you."

"Uh-huh."

"That's things that we can't dispute," said Dave. "That physically happened."

"And I agree with you on that," said Lloyd. "I told you from day one that I was in the mall."

In fact, he had not, but Dave was not here to quarrel. He was trying to reset their relationship. He wanted a clean slate. He continued to outline the facts upon which they could both agree: Lloyd went back to the mall to say he had witnessed something. He took a polygraph. Lloyd acknowledged these things were true.

"Remember talking about the bus?" Dave asked.

"Uh-huh."

"Hopefully you are going to enlighten me. Maybe you got into a car. Maybe they got into a car. Maybe you got on a bus, and they got on the same bus. But at some point in time, you, my friend, were the last person that saw those girls. You might have been the last person to have a conversation with them. And when you were questioned by the police in seventy-five, if you would have told them, what would the police have thought?"

"Arrest him. He did it."

"Exactly, and that's what's been bugging you for the last thirty-nine years."

Lloyd chuckled. "I'm laughing because ain't nothin' been buggin' me. I'm being honest with you. I did not—"

"I'm not saying you did it."

"No, no, no, no, I did not even think about this in all these years, until my sister and my stepmother sent me a letter stating that the cops were askin' about two girls missin' in Wheaton. Do I know anything about it? I *didn't* know anything about it, and I told them I don't know anything about it. I went and made a lie up to get a reward." This was new. Lloyd had never mentioned reward money before. "I'm bein' honest with you," he said. "I lied, back then. I lied now. Because I wanted to feel important. I wanted to make myself look important."

Lloyd admitted that recently he had been "down on" himself. He blamed himself for his current predicament. He had lied in their first conversation because Chris Homrock had intimated that Lloyd had been raped by Mileski. "That really pissed me off," he said. "So I said, 'Well, let me fuck with them some.' I lied. The last time I saw those girls or anybody was inside that mall. That was the last time."

Never mind the story he had confided to Dave at the end of the third session, and then reiterated in the fourth about seeing the girls nude, drugged, and being raped in a basement room. He was either forgetting this or discarding it. Dave chose to ignore it. Instead he pressed Lloyd about the new reason for going back to the mall.

"How much money were they offering?" he asked.

"At the time, I don't even remember how much it was. I thought it was enough to get me and Helen a place and maybe for her to apply for doctor care and stuff like that. You know what I'm sayin'? And my stepmom told me not to go and say anything, and Helen said the same thing. Dumb ass me had to go. Dumb ass me had to lie, and I've been lying ever since. You know? And now it's done screwed me so bad that I can't show my face in no institution. I done screwed myself over so bad it's pathetic. I should have never said anything. I should have never gotten myself involved, and I apologize to all of you."

Dave asked if they might go "off the record," a completely hollow offer, because he had every intention of using everything Lloyd told him, not to mention that the session was being videotaped and observed by his colleagues.

Lloyd talked about Teddy and the older man he was living with at the time the girls disappeared. Dave knew, of course, that this was a red herring.

"Teddy introduced me to this guy. Teddy had disappeared for a while. He came back with a Camaro. He said he was a fashion model or something like that, and this guy was giving him a place to live and money and stuff like that. But we used to go to his house and party all the time. I went to the house one day—we were partying and shit like that—and he had two girls, and I left. I don't know if it was them or not. I mean, in all honestly, I don't know if it was the twenty-fifth, twenty-eighth, or what it was."

Lloyd now admitted that he had known about the Lyon sisters' disappearance at the time. He had gone back to the mall to tell his story, over his stepmother's and Helen's protests, "because stubborn ass me had to say, 'I want that money.' I was eighteen years old. I was ignorant. I was dumb. I'm still ignorant, and I'm dumb."

"But you're awfully sharp," said, Dave, laying it on thick. "I mean, you're as sharp as a tack."

"*You* think I am."

"You are!"

Lloyd laughed.

Dave said, "You're an intelligent dude."

One Hundred and One Percent the God's Honest Truth

It was time to puncture the story about Teddy.

"Are we talking about the same Teddy Junior?" Dave asked.

"Teddy Junior."

"He was twelve back then," said Dave. Actually, Teddy had been eleven. He turned twelve in July of that year.

"Nah, he was—"

"He was twelve. I know when he was born."

"He was thirteen years old. Yeah, Teddy. Teddy was a scary little fucker back then."

"How old were you, though?"

"I was eighteen, but I was a snotty little—"

"You could have handed him his ass in two minutes!"

"No, I was a scrawny little kid. I was scrawny. What's he say? Is he alive?"

"Oh yeah. We talked to him. He says you're nuts."

Lloyd chuckled to himself and said softly, "*I'm* nuts."

They went back over the events at the mall, and Lloyd then correctly described the clothing that the Lyon sisters were wearing, which had never been made public—Sheila in a dark blue sweatshirt, jeans, brown shoes; Kate in a red jacket, flowery blue denim shirt, jeans. Lloyd seemed not to realize the significance of this. He was digging himself in deeper.

They talked for a while about Teddy and other members of the Welch family. The squad had decided to develop further the notion that Lloyd's entire family had turned on him. This was not true. Few of his relatives had anything nice to say about him, and they were all ready to believe he had done it, but none were actively trying to get him convicted. What was important was that Lloyd *believed* they were. It made him feel vulnerable, which was something the detectives could exploit.

"I've got a fucked-up family," he said. "They say they're my family, but I don't know what they are anymore."

"There's something that you're trying to explain to me without coming out and telling me," said Dave.

"I want this to end," said Lloyd. "Let's go with this."

He then launched back into his story of looking for work at the mall with Helen, seeing Teddy and another man—he was not giving up easily on his newest culprit.

"Teddy had his arm around the girl with the glasses, and the other one had his arm around the smaller one," he said. He had watched as the girls were led from the mall. After looking at pictures of Sheila and Kate again, he said for the first time that they were definitely the ones taken. He repeated his story that, on the following day, he had seen them in the basement of the house where Teddy was staying. As for whose house it was, he was quite plainly thinking of Kraisel, although he didn't know the man's name. He now said that the person who had threatened and frightened him was not Teddy but this older man—he had clearly absorbed how ridiculous it was to claim he'd been terrorized by an eleven-year-old.

"I'm scared to this day," he said. "My hands are sweating right now."

"Now, is this the truth?"

"Yeah."

"I mean, this is no more fabrication?"

"On Helen's life, on my mother's, on my kids'."

"This is finally it?"

"This is it, and that's all I can tell you."

But Lloyd, as always, had more. He described the condition of Sheila and Kate one day after their kidnapping in shockingly casual terms.

"I wouldn't say they looked like they were in stress. I'd say more like they were getting high for the first time, you know? You're like, 'Wow, man.' They were kind of like rocking back and forth on the couch there, and the guy was sitting on one side, and Teddy was sitting on the other side with the other girl. I seen 'em lean over to kiss or whatever, and turned around and walked away. They looked like they were high. Looked like they were having a good time. They weren't screaming or hollerin' or anything like that."

It was chilling, not the least because nothing about the scene he described seemed exceptionable to him.

"I have no idea what they did to them. I left. I'm still scared."

"But he [Kraisel] is, like, eighty-some years old," said Dave.

"Yeah, but money talks. I'm still scared it's gonna come back and bite me in the ass, you know."

"Yeah, but you had to come clean, because it wasn't right."

"Well, like I said, I've been back in the SHU [Special Housing Unit] there and locked down by myself and not being able to work and shit. I've had a lot to think about, and it's been on my mind a lot. It's been eating me up. I haven't been sleeping as good as I used to."

"Right. You look like a totally different person from the first time we met."

"I look like a bum."

"Things may change."

"I'm not going to be able to go on the compound no more, so that means I'm gonna be sitting in that cell. I got thirteen years left, you know."

"Things may change, my friend."

"Everything I told you today is the God's honest truth," said Lloyd. "I'm tired of this shit . . . getting' tired of it. . . . I brought it on my own self. On the day I met you, I brought it all on my own self. I did because y'all warned me that if I didn't, you know, come clean with everything, it was gonna have to go out into the media. Like I've always said, I've always hurt the people that I know and that I love, you know? I either know you and I hurt you or love you and I hurt you. I mean, it's always . . . don't ask me why. Maybe it's because [of] the way that I was hurt so much when I was growin' up."

"By people that loved you."

"You know? Yeah. Or I thought they loved me. . . . I mean my niece comes. My niece and my sister came to see me when I ended up in the back. Three weeks later, detectives are coming up to me again and telling me word for word what I said to them. To my nieces, you know? Now they've turned. Everything that I told you in this room today is one hundred and one percent the God's honest truth." He held his right hand high, as if pledging. "On my children's life, on Helen's life—even though she's passed—and my stepmom's life, you know? Everything that I told you. The rest of it was all bull. You know? It was me trying to be important, me trying to make a name for myself, and I found out that didn't work. I backfired on me. I was a bullshitter. And it backfired on me one hundred and one percent."

After four hours, Dave was back in Lloyd's good graces, but the goblin was still speaking in riddles. His knowledge of the girls' clothing was real evidence. But the rest? They needed to create leverage, and for that they were going to take a long hard look at the Welches.

7
The Clan

Dick Welch

Pat Welch

Two Branches

Teddy Welch made little sense as the kidnapper, but his story afforded a glimpse into the curious Welch family. What the detectives found shocked them. The abuse that Lloyd had suffered in his father's house and Teddy had suffered in his was not an aberration. It was the norm. Few family members had escaped it. Fathers beat and raped their children, brothers terrorized and raped their sisters and cousins. Alcohol, drugs, and violence colored every relationship. It was not much of a stretch to see teenage Lloyd and perhaps even Teddy as pawns enlisted by the older, more practiced predators in their family.

The clan had two branches, one in Hyattsville, Maryland, and the other five hours south on a secluded hilltop in Thaxton, Virginia, a place the locals called Taylor's Mountain. Here the family's Appalachian roots were extant, even though some of its members had gradually moved into more modern communities in and around Bedford, the nearest town. The Maryland branch, while its environs were markedly different, clearly belonged to the same tree. Hyattsville sprawled on both sides of Route 1, America's oldest highway, which between Washington and Baltimore was so cluttered with commercial excess that H. L. Mencken had once called it "a monument to America's lust for the hideous." It was called Baltimore Avenue within Hyattsville's limits. Abutting the District of Columbia of which, for all practical purposes, it had become a part, the city's border existed only on maps. Isolated remnants of the county's bucolic past remained in blocks of older wood-frame houses stranded between acres of parking lots, strip malls, and big retail outlets. Its population was mixed in every way. The Welch family, with its country ways, lived shoulder to shoulder with city dwellers seeking affordable housing close to jobs inside the beltway. The clan had sunk its roots here wide and deep, with enough Welches, Overstreets, Dooleys, Esteps, and Parkers to fill Magruder Park when they gathered for a reunion. If they had a look, it was generally pale and blue-eyed, with small pinched features in a broad face. Their men were scrawny and their women wide. There was a marked downturn to their thin-lipped mouths, as if a frown had been imprinted in their DNA. Taylor's Mountain and Hyattsville may have been radically different places, but the family was the same in both. Its mountain-hollow ways—suspicion of outsiders, an unruly contempt for authority of any kind, stubborn poverty, a knee-jerk resort to violence—set it perpetually at odds with mainstream suburbia. Most shocking were its sexual practices. Incest was notorious in the families of the hollers (hollows) of Appalachia, where social isolation and privation eroded social taboos. The practice came north with the family to Hyattsville. Here, where suburban families had turned child-rearing into a fetish, some adults in Lloyd's immediate family exploited their offspring and ignored barriers to incest. It was not uncommon for Welch children to experiment sexually with siblings and cousins.

The family hid all this. Its business was no one else's. Criminal behavior rarely warranted family censure, much less a report to the police. Indeed, the more shocking the conduct, the stronger the impulse to hide it. Protecting the family from outsiders was more important than protecting its members, including children, from each other. And the

Welch women, often victims, were its fiercest guardians. In Virginia the rule was, What happens on Taylor's Mountain *stays* on Taylor's Mountain. If the Lyon sisters had fallen into this cesspool, as Lloyd claimed and the detectives now suspected, then some of the family might have known—and even helped.

Lloyd had emerged from this culture as both victim and predator. After years of wandering and imprisonment, he had strayed far from the family's grip, but the peculiar values and behavior he learned (and endured) had not played well in society at large. Locked away now in Delaware, he felt isolated and shunned, his letters to kinfolk rarely answered. Still, the family had a hold on him.

Two of the relatives he had mentioned, besides Teddy, were Uncle Dick and Aunt Pat. Just a week after the fifth session with Lloyd, the squad invited both to police headquarters in Hyattsville, where they still lived. Dick was Lloyd's only surviving paternal uncle. Mark interviewed him while Dave and Katie sat down in a separate room with Pat.

Dick was a pale, skinny man in wire-framed glasses who looked lost inside an oversize blue work shirt and baggy khakis. He had thin white hair combed across his head; a stern, pinched face with a wide, crooked nose; a distinct underbite; and an unusually broad, slack neck. His grown children now called him "Poppy." Fighting a chronic heart ailment, he looked older than his sixty-nine years and frail, nothing like the rough customer with long sideburns and a sneer in old family photos. Mark found him amiable and sharp-witted. Like Pat, he had little affection for Lloyd.

Nothing in Lloyd's storytelling had linked either Dick or Pat to the crime, but the squad had grown suspicious of them because of Teddy's phone records. On February 11, the day of the press conference, Teddy had phoned Dick, someone he called rarely, and talked with him for more than twenty minutes. That same day he had then driven an hour and a half in rush-hour traffic to Hyattsville to speak to Dick in person—his cell-phone use showed his location and time in transit. There was something important and urgent for them to discuss that day. Dick said that Teddy had wanted to talk about his sons.

The detectives doubted that. The trip had prompted them to rethink Teddy's role. The more they considered it, the more they reasoned that Lloyd's scenario might make sense. What if Teddy had been the boy Dee Danner had seen talking to the Lyon sisters? This had long been assumed to have been their brother Jay, who confirmed that he'd seen them there, but what if it had been someone else?

Dick said he knew nothing about the Lyon girls. He had never seen them and had long wondered, like everyone else, what had happened to them.

Pat—Patricia Jean—was clever. She was a pale, squat woman, so fat that she walked with a pronounced waddle. Her hair was thin and white, although she occasionally dyed it a light brown. Farsighted, she wore oversize reading glasses that she kept propped on top of her head. For years she had worked at a Giant supermarket. Pat had nothing for the detectives. She was cordial and presented herself as slightly befuddled—which, in time they would learn, she was not. She had been born an Engleking and did not see herself as a Welch. Indeed, she held the clan in some contempt. "That's *his* [Dick's] family, not mine," she said. She had particular disdain for Lloyd. Pat portrayed him, in so many words, as a black sheep even by Welch standards. She had a hard time even untangling his parentage; she was unsure whether the woman killed in the auto accident, Margaret, had been his mother. She said her most vivid memory of his father, Lee, was of him passed out drunk on his living room couch.

Dave did nothing to discourage her attitude toward Lloyd. The man he now cheerily greeted as "my brother" in the interview room he described to Pat as "an animal."

Both Dick and Pat said they believed Lloyd was entirely capable of kidnapping, raping, and killing two little girls, but neither knew the first thing about it.

Those first interviews produced little but did nothing to dampen the squad's growing suspicions. After the April session in Dover, Lloyd's prison cell had been searched and all his personal papers seized—this was when they had obtained his recent, handwritten life summary. In this and in his letters, Lloyd made it clear that he believed his relatives were conspiring against him, which both stung him and also seemed to *scare* him. What did his family know that he was afraid they might tell?

In their next session, scheduled for July, Dave would play on those fears. At the same time the squad was gearing up for a full-court press on the Welches, in both Maryland and Virginia.

July 14, 2014

"What's happening, man?" Dave said in greeting, as he sauntered into the interview room at Dover.

Three months had elapsed since their last visit. Lloyd again sat slumped in his orange jumpsuit, hands cuffed and chained in his lap. He grunted sullenly.

The detective set a big cup of coffee on the table before him. "It was kind of a mess getting over here; I don't know how warm that is."

Lloyd didn't drink it.

"It has been a couple of weeks because we had to run down all that stuff you told us."

Lloyd squinted at him.

"And it's good. It's good for both of us. There's some things we want to clear up, and I think now we're closer with you in being together on this thing."

It wasn't true, and Lloyd was not buying it. As they again went through the ritual of legal consent, he was more than usually suspicious. He pointed to a paragraph, one he had seen several times now, which outlined the steps that would follow his being charged with a crime. In the past Dave had always made a point of x-ing that out to emphasize that they were not planning to charge him.

"You didn't cross it out like you did the last time," Lloyd said.

"Oh shit. We can cross it out."

"I'm just sayin'."

Lloyd was still angry. He was smarting over the seizure of his papers. To justify it, prison authorities had alleged that he had broken their rules, a charge which appeared to have been trumped up.

"What's the deal [with the seizure]?" he asked.

"That's a good place to start, because I'm sure in your mind—"

Lloyd laughed. How else would anyone take it? The seizure of his property and search of his cell meant that he was a target.

"I mean, I can totally see it from your perspective," said Dave. "It looks bad. But look at it from this perspective. If we're going to try and build anything against you . . . How long have we known each other? Damn near over a year, right?"

"Since October of last year."

Lloyd knew exactly. He was not in the mood to be snowed. He complained bitterly about "the charge that was put on me," referring to the justification on the search warrant, which claimed that he had abused his letter-writing privileges. He said it was a "fabrication," a "lie," and "threatening."

"I'll explain it to you," said Dave. "When we left here, you said, 'Hey, you need to talk to my cousin.' So we went out and explored the cousin [Teddy], we explored the family. The family is not in your corner."

"Yeah, I know they're not."

"The family is against you, and they're lying to us," said Dave. He said that Welch family members had told them that there was relevant information in Lloyd's letters. That's why they had been seized.

"There ain't nothing in it," Lloyd said.

"There's nothing there," Dave agreed. "Which is good. It's good for both of us."

Dave was trying to find his footing, to cut through Lloyd's sourness and skepticism. He decided to be straight with him about Teddy. The accusation didn't add up. He also pointed out that Lloyd's claim to have traveled to and from the mall with Helen on a bus also could not be true, because there had been no such bus service in 1975.

"It's time for you to kick back and say, 'Look, I got a vested interest in myself,'" Dave reasoned. "You've got a vested interest in not getting any more time."

He still viewed Lloyd sympathetically, he said, but it was becoming a minority view. Dave was Lloyd's resolute defender. He had figured something out, he said. It was one thing to react with disgust to a fifty-seven-year-old man's interest in girls aged twelve and ten, but if Lloyd had been attracted to girls that age in 1975, it was no big deal.

"You were nineteen! [He had actually been eighteen.] Any nineteen-year-old kid, there's nothing wrong there. And that's the thing. You gotta say, 'Okay, wait a minute now, he wasn't fifty-seven doing this, he was nineteen.' Any nineteen-year-old kid that went to a mall, the whole purpose of going to a mall back then when you were a kid was to hang out, to find girls and find people to party with. That was it."

"But I already had a lot of people to party with," said Lloyd. "You already know that."

"Right. But it's always fun to have different people."

"And I was involved with Helen."

"All right."

"I was."

Dave altered course. Noting again Lloyd's youth, he suggested that he might have been roped into the crime by his family.

"You've got a vested interest in protecting your family, but they're not protecting you," he said. "I've been here to see you more than your entire family, which is sad."

Lloyd shrugged his shoulders. This was true.

Dave got him talking along these lines. He asked about Lloyd's father, Lee. "He liked girls and boys. It didn't matter, right?"

"Who, my dad?"

"Right."

"Yeah."

"And that seems to be the running theory about your uncles, too. It didn't matter."

Lloyd nodded emphatically. He said, "Now, me, I like women."

He was warming to the conversation again. It was hard to overestimate the desire of a man living in isolation to talk. After his initial petulance, he began to relax. He peeled the lid off the coffee Dave had brought in and took a sip. The detective persuaded the guards to come in and remove both Lloyd's chains *and* his handcuffs, a first. Then he commiserated with Lloyd about his eyes, which were puffy and red.

"They keep saying I have hay fever," said Lloyd. "Or some kind of allergy. I keep telling them, I'm fifty-seven years old. I've never had an allergy in my life. I've never had hay fever."

"Could it be a detergent they clean that shit with?" Dave suggested, gesturing toward his bright orange prison uniform.

Dave returned to Lloyd's relatives. So far the detectives had talked to Dick, Pat, and Teddy.

"Every time that you sit down and talk, we learn a little bit more about your family."

Lloyd sighed and shook his head sadly.

"And then you talk to them and you find out about all the craziness and weird activities that they've been doing, and all the lying that they've been doing, you have to take a step back and say, 'Wait a minute, there's more to this story.' Why you are not telling us what the hell happened, I don't know. They trashed the shit out of you."

"Oh, I'm sure they did. 'He's a sex offender. He's in jail.'"

"Right! 'Look at him.'"

"Yeah, 'Look at him and look at all he's done.'"

"I'm trying to figure out when you are going to kick back and say, 'I'm in this for myself,' and say, 'Look, this is what happened.' This is where I step in and say, 'Wait a minute!'" Dave banged the table for emphasis. "'Look at what he's done.' So what? Has he ever done anything to a stranger? His DNA's in the system, right? It has been there since 2003. That's eleven years. And have you caught any additional charges?"

Lloyd shook his head no.

"Your background is not the best because you're sitting here, but we can't change that."

"Right."

"The only thing we can do is, you do the time and get out. How many years you got left in you, you do the right thing?"

"This Friday it will be eighteen years for me being incarcerated. Seventeen years ago, I told myself that I was gonna turn around and bring myself to the Lord, and I was gonna change my life and everything like that, and if I ever get a chance to get out, that I was gonna help people, and I meant it. I still mean it, even though I have all this bitterness in me of what's going on here about this whole incident thing with the two girls. I didn't do it. I would never walk up and take two strangers. How am I going to get them out of a mall to begin with? You know what I'm saying?"

"Right. And I think that's the thing we need to clear up, because I think there was a casual nineteen-year-old male who was interested, and I think after the party and whatever happened that day, I think someone else got involved, and I think you said, 'That's not what they're here for,' and I think you decided, 'You do what you need to do, and I'm gone.' So, my thing here today is to pull that shit out of you."

Lloyd said he had nothing more to tell. "Think about this," he explained. "Every crime I've ever done has been to somebody I know. Never been to a stranger. The two sexual charges that I have has been with the girls that have lived in my own house. Never been outside of my house or anything like that or doing any sexual things to anybody."

"Why would the family paint you to be this horrible person when to me, looking at it from the outside, you're damn near normal," said Dave. "Is that why they don't like you? They're just not telling the truth about what happened. They know."

"If you find out what happened, as to why they pushed me away, I sure would like to know."

"There's something there," said Dave.

"But this ain't about me telling you about Teddy at the mall that day. He was there that day, you know? I don't care what he says, he was there. Him and some other person was there. I don't even know who that person was."

Lloyd was still pushing his allegation about Teddy and Kraisel. The squad knew Kraisel had not been involved, but what about Lloyd's father and uncles?

Dave said, "Is it at all likely that those two girls, however they went away from that mall, whether it was willing, whether it was drugged, whether it was somebody forced them, however they went away from that mall, and I'd like to think that it was willing—the reason is because it's a lot of people [watching]. It was a holiday week and in the middle of the day. If somebody had forced them away, somebody had to see or hear."

"That's what I've been saying."

"But if they went with another twelve-year-old, and another guy who was, say, just nineteen," it wouldn't have attracted as much notice, Dave hypothesized. "And then they went to wherever and somebody else got involved, and the shit went sideways. And at that point you and Teddy went like this," he put his hands together on the desk and slid them wide apart. "And the person responsible for doing harm to those two little girls—"

Lloyd nodded. "I see what you're saying."

"And as hard as it might be, I think you are gonna have to dig down inside and say, 'You know what? It's time for me to stop. People are painting me as a monster because of my background.' And you're still dug in, saying, 'Man, if I say some shit like that, I'm gonna be stuck here forever.' That's not what we're trying to do."

One of Dave's methods was to "admit" that he wasn't revealing all that he knew. He pretended that Lloyd's relatives had fed them all sorts of damaging things about Lloyd. "I'm not giving it all to you," he said, "because if you give it back to me, then I know it's the truth," he said.

"Well, see, that's the thing. I can't give you something that I don't have. And I'm not going to sit here and say I have something that I don't have, you know? I've been racking my brain. Trust me."

The Driver

Lloyd had invoked his drugged-addled brain so often it no longer even registered. His memory was fine. The problem was to convince him that it was in his best interest to reveal what he knew, even though it manifestly *was not*.

Dave took a creative leap. He supposed Lloyd had been at the mall with Teddy. His story of riding there with Helen on a bus had been shown to be false. If he and Teddy had made the trip together, who drove them? Teddy was too young to drive, and Lloyd didn't have a car. And if someone had driven them there, that same person most likely had brought them back, which meant that this person, an adult, had helped them kidnap the girls. Dave now pretended he *knew* who the driver was. By not naming him, he said, Lloyd was hurting himself. He was obstructing justice. He was protecting someone guiltier than himself. As Lloyd's buddy, his champion, Dave urged him to help himself.

"I can't get you to come around and say, 'Look, man, this is what happened,'" said the detective. "If you truly had nothing to do with them disappearing, then you need to say *what the fuck happened!"*—banging the desk again—"Because, it changes. All of the sudden you're this huge person that everybody has painted. You're wearing orange. They put you in solitary. To a person that's simply a witness. And we need to unfuck this thing. If it is coming around and saying, 'Look, I'm gonna have to tell on my family,' then that's what you fucking need to do. You can't keep eating this shit over and over and over again!"

"But I've already said Teddy," Lloyd protested.

"Who else? Teddy was twelve [he was actually eleven]. He couldn't drive a car."

"I know he couldn't drive a car. I don't know who the other person was. I told you that."

"But I need you to tell me who it is."

"His fuckin' dad. That's who I believe it was."

"It wasn't your dad?"

"No. Not my dad, I said *his*. I don't know who the other person was. That's what I'm trying to tell you. I don't know the person's name. If I knew the person's name, I'd be happy to say his name."

"You're in a car with your uncle, and you didn't know who was driving?"

Lloyd was silent.

"You need to take that step," said Dave.

"Let me ask you this, hypothetical," said Lloyd. "If I do say who it was, what's going to happen to me?"

This was an emerging pattern. Whenever Lloyd was about to give in, he asked this question, and Dave expertly ducked it. He said, "That's a tough question, and the reason I tell you that is because I don't know what role you played in it."

"No," said Lloyd. "I was gone. I left. There's no ifs, ands, or buts about it. I left, and if you ever find those bodies, you'll never find my DNA on them."

"Did you do anything wrong?"

"Nope."

"Then what the hell would we charge you with?"

"I'm the one that's in jail."

"You're a witness! You're in jail for something different. I've never worked harder on this fucking job, after I left you, trying to corroborate the things that you've told me when we sit in this room, and every single time I come back, have I ever presented you with a charge?"

Lloyd shook his head no.

"Have I ever said, Lloyd, it's time for me to sit down and charge you?"

"No."

"Every time I sit down and talk to you, we get a little closer to pushing you away from this thing." The opposite was true. "So you have answered your own question. If you tell me, then my job is to go back out there and figure it out. And if you tell me who did it—which I already know—then it's my job to take what you've told me and turn it into something to make it work, whether it be charging, whether it be to find them bodies, to make it actually work. There's a reason you told us Teddy. It's time, Lloyd."

"What if I tell you who the other person is, and you go and talk to him, and all of a sudden it's, 'No, I didn't have anything to do with it'?"

"We've got other things. We've already talked to that person. The person's an asshole."

"I've said his name a few times in here, haven't I?" Lloyd asked.

"Yeah . . . he's an asshole."

"Yeah. Uncle Dickie."

"Right."

All of this Dave had orchestrated. He had taken Lloyd's own story and thought it through more carefully. Neither Lloyd nor Teddy would have had a car. So somebody else had to have been the driver. Dave's hunch was Dick, so he had led Lloyd into naming him. It was an iffy interrogation practice, but, technically, he had gotten Lloyd to volunteer Dick's name.

"Tell me what happened that night," said Dave.

"All I know is that we were at the mall that day, and the girl came up to me and said, 'Take a picture,' and I said, 'If I had a camera, I would.' Teddy got talking to these two girls. I don't know where he came out of. We were actually walking around. Uncle Dick stayed in the car. He [Teddy] got 'em to go outside. We all left. We did go back to the house. I had him drop me off at the store there on Route 1, right where the bridge was at. There used to be a little store. Helen had asked me to pick up something for her, and I told her I'd get it on the way back. They dropped me off. They left. That was the last time I saw the four of them that day, and I went back to the house [Lee's]. Me and Helen sat there. We ate dinner and stuff. We talked. That was the last I seen those girls was when they dropped me off at the store."

"Fill in the blanks for me, because we've come a long way," said Dave. What Lloyd had done was substitute his uncle Dick for Leonard Kraisel. Dave wanted a narrative that would flesh out this shift. "And you are now a witness. I'm not saying that I am going to put you up on the stand and [i.e., to] testify against your uncle and Teddy, but there's some things that we need to clean up. Were they [Dick and Pat] babysitting Teddy that day?"

"Yeah. I don't know if you'd even call it babysitting or what. He was stayin' there. I mean, he was with him."

Lloyd described the car that had driven the three of them to the mall, an old Ford station wagon. He couldn't remember the color.

"Y'all went up to the mall. Ted gets these . . . recruits these two girls. Tell me what happens then."

"We got in the car."

"Were they willing to go?"

"Yeah."

"What was the conversation like?"

"One girl sat up in the front with Teddy. I sat in the back with one of them."

"Do you remember which one?"

"No, I don't. I don't honestly. They were talking, and I didn't really even say anything to the girl. I asked her, 'What y'all doing?' and they said they were going to party, and I had them drop me off at the store. And that was the last that I saw them."

Lloyd admitted he'd been scoping out preteen girls in the mall. He was high, he said. In the days after they took the girls, he said his uncle Dick had turned against him.

Dave asked why.

"I would think that it would be because he was afraid we were going to say something."

"That's exactly why," said Dave.

"You know?"

"Or maybe because you weren't in for it, that's why he hates you. Had you gone back and participated in whatever happened, you'd have been one of the boys."

"Yeah. Believe it or not, I was not into hurting people. At the time I had no sexual thoughts in my mind. Don't ask me what happened in the nineties [when he did molest children], because I don't know. I don't know if shit finally caught up with me, all the drugs and alcohol."

"Was your uncle Dick into things like that?"

"As the years went on I heard that he was, that he was into younger girls and guys, younger kids and stuff like that. I can't say that he was and I can't say that he wasn't, because I wasn't around that much."

Lloyd now said that the story he had told about seeing the girls with Teddy and the other man in a basement was "bogus." He reverted again to his account of being dropped off at the convenience store; he said it was to buy ice cream for Helen. He walked home with it.

"I think Teddy was thinking something different than what actually happened," said Dave. "I think Uncle Dick joined in, and then I think Uncle Dick finished it."

Lloyd nodded.

"And then that's the demon that's been in this family for thirty-nine years, and that's the reason you and Teddy were punished like this, because y'all didn't agree with it. It's not what you sat in for."

But when Dave suggested that Dick had planned the whole thing with him and Teddy, Lloyd shook his head no.

"I went to that mall to look for work," he said.

Coming Clean

Having placed himself with the girls as they left the mall, in the car with those he now identified as his uncle and cousin, Lloyd was now officially a co-kidnapper. To keep him talking, Dave told him the opposite.

"Your involvement in this thing went from solo to high priority to very low priority to, hey, maybe you're just a witness," he said. "You're providing information. And with that being said, you are in a whole lot better spot than you were. But I don't know that you totally get it. And do I think you are still holding back on me? Yeah, and I understand why."

"I can't be holding back any more than what I've already said!" Lloyd protested. "I mean, what Teddy and Dick did that day, I can't say."

He had found what he considered safe new ground. He had been at the mall looking for work. He had innocently ridden away in the car with Teddy, Dick, and the girls, taking a ride to pick up ice cream. He'd gotten out of the car and left. He was in love with Helen. She was having a baby. He wanted nothing to do with "partying" with these girls. Now that he had admitted knowing something of what happened to Sheila and Kate, he claimed to be haunted by it—a thing he'd denied for months. Lloyd made these shifts with no apparent sense of how false they sounded. He had no ear for it.

"It's gonna bug the shit out of me until the day I die," he said, a comment so hollow it echoed. "You know? Why didn't I do anything? I mean, there's always going to be that question there. Why didn't I step in and do something?"

Lloyd had completely dropped his tale of going back the next day and witnessing rape. Dave was not going to let him drop it.

He said, "My thoughts on this were, when you separated yourself, at some point you went back over, not necessarily to know anything about the girls, just went back over. It's your family. You went back to the house, and you saw something and you left. That's been consistent in every time we talk"—Dave was exaggerating here—"whether it has been at that house or, whatever that guy's name was . . . and it was probably around that time frame that you said, 'I'm going to do something about this, but I don't know how to do it,' so you went back to the mall, you got cold feet when security picked you up, because what were you going to do, tell on your uncle? What the hell did you see"—Dave banged on the desk—"that drove you to that?"

"Saw 'em in the basement fucking."

"Who was fucking them?"

"Dickie."

"Was Teddy?"

"Teddy was there. I don't know if he was fucking them or what."

Dave asked if he knew which girl Dick was assaulting.

"No. She was underneath. I don't know which one it was. I don't know if it was the younger one or the older one. I saw one. That was all. I don't know if Teddy had already done something to them or not. I saw that. I didn't want nothing to do with it, and I just left. I didn't even tell Teddy that I was there. I don't know if he saw me or not. That was when Helen and I had left there again. We went back to South Carolina. We liked it down there. A couple of years later I came back."

"Did he say anything to you?"

"I didn't say nothing to them. They didn't say nothing to me. Then I got myself in trouble and ended up in jail."

"So, who would have killed them?"

"That I can't say, but if it was me in the house that day, I would say Dickie would do it because he has that much anger in him."

Dave pushed for more. Did Dick have guns? He had. What else had Lloyd seen?

"Nobody was screaming," he said. "You know what I'm saying? I don't know if they were drugged or not."

"Who would have drugged them? Was Dick into drugs back then? Teddy? Was he into drugs at that age?"

"I can't say if he was or wasn't. I knew he was drinking. I know he was a drinker. That was Lee's [Lloyd's father's] best buddy on drinking."

"A twelve-year-old?"

"Could he have gotten drugs?" said Lloyd. "Most definitely. There was drugs all over that area, you know?"

Lloyd speculated that Dick had kept the girls locked for a week in his basement room, a finished room with a worn old carpet, a built-in bar, couch, chair, a mattress, black-and-white TV on a stand. His "sanctuary" he called it. It could be entered only from the backyard. His wife and children lived upstairs, but no one was allowed into his space. Whenever he left, he locked it.

"If they stayed down there for a week, probably nobody would know, because that door was always locked," Lloyd said. "Two weeks. No."

"Is he that sick?"

"He was when I was a kid."

Dave asked him to describe his uncle Dick. Lloyd recalled an angry, violent, drunken man.

"I've wondered where he'd taken them," Lloyd said. "I've wondered what he did to them, you know, how he got rid of them."

"Do you think they are in Maryland or Virginia?"

"Good question. I never thought of that. I mean, Virginia ain't that far away. We got relatives that live in Virginia."

"I gotta ask you, just out of curiosity. I mean, I get the first couple of times that we talked it was difficult to get you to come full circle. How come you waited until this long?"

"Scared shitless."

"But—"

"Scared shitless. Plain, simple admission."

"You've given us subtle hints, but it has taken damn near a year to get this far."

Lloyd laughed.

"Well, you're comforting," he said, and threw his hands up in the air. "It got me out of my cell." He said he thought his stepmom, Edna, was the only one in his family who believed he did not kidnap and kill the girls. She still wrote to him.

"Who all in the family other than you, Teddy, and Dick?" Dave asked. "Who all definitely knows?"

"I can't say. I don't know who they talk—"

"Do you think your aunt knows?"

"Which aunt?"

"Pat."

"I don't know. I honestly don't."

Bullshitting

They took a long break for lunch. Katie came in with pasta and a sandwich for Lloyd. After he ate, she and Mark entered and sat down to talk with him further.

"Dave says you guys have come a long way today," Mark said. He said Dave would be back in a while.

Katie tried to patch up her relationship with Lloyd. She offered a benign explanation for why he had failed the lie detector test and said she no longer blamed him for it. It was hot. He was tired. He reached over and shook her hand.

"So, let's just forget it," he said.

"We were both tired," she said. "We were both hot. It had been a long day."

"I thought you were gonna come over and body slam me there," said Lloyd, laughing.

"I'm actually a nice person that makes pasta salad and sandwiches, see?"

"*I'm* a nice person," said Lloyd.

She asked him what he thought Sheila and Kate had been thinking when they left with him and Teddy.

"I believe they thought they were going to hang out, listen to music. I believe they came with that in mind. Thought they were going to hang out with this cute boy. I remember the girl in the front seat asked Teddy where we were going, and he said we were going to go party. I do remember that."

"Do you think that those girls at that point meant, like, hanging out, listening to music?" She told him that a twelve-year-old's idea of "partying" was likely to have been different from his at age eighteen.

"I really believe they thought they were going to hang out and listen to music."

"Just hanging out, being kids?"

"Right."

Lloyd said the girls had not been distressed in the car at all.

Katie asked him why, after years in prison, after working to be a model prisoner, after finding the Lord, had he never thought to write a letter to anyone explaining what he knew about what had happened to the Lyon girls.

"For the simple reason that I had totally forgot about it completely," he said. "I mean, totally forgot it."

"How do you forget something like that?

Mark made a pitch for Lloyd to tell more, to do "one good thing."

"I've done everything I can possibly think of," he said. "I've come clean today, telling who was involved."

Mark explained that they would be going to Teddy and Dick to hear their versions of all this. "Now it is going to be three people's versions, and we've got to set your version apart. Because you have credibility now, you know? They're going to come in and tell us various lies that have some truth mixed in. What parts of the truth are they likely to tell us that you're afraid to tell us?"

"Exactly what I told him [Dave]. That's just as far as it went with me. I was not involved with them two girls. I didn't have sex with them two girls."

Mark reminded Lloyd of an earlier detail from his stories that he had now changed: that the younger of the two girls had been crying. "Where did that come from?" he asked.

"Don't know where that come from, in all honestly," said Lloyd. "I don't."

"But you see what I'm saying? Like, that's sort of an odd detail to put in consistently."

"I guess I kind of bullshitted my way through a lot of stuff."

"Well, you did; you absolutely do bullshit a lot," Mark laughed. "But that's something that there's no reason to bullshit, you know? That's something that would stick out. If it were me, and I was in your shoes back then, if I see one of those girls crying, the human side of me, that's going to make an impression in my mind and stay there."

"Like I said, she was sitting over in the corner there. I mean, she didn't say nothing to me." He shrugged. "Maybe I thought she was crying. I don't know, you know?"

"You'd know if she was crying or not."

"She wasn't saying nothing to me, and I wasn't saying nothing to her. I mean, her face was turned."

"It stands to reason, if she's the younger one, that she's not as emotionally or socially advanced as her older sister, who is probably the one that's leading this train. The little one is more out of her element and might be, like, 'Well, where are we going? I thought we were going home.'"

Lloyd was not offering further insight. Mark returned to the idea that his family was trying to pin it all on him.

"We've kind of opened this door now, and we're going through it with you," he said. "You can't go through it halfway. You've got one foot through. You've got to get all the way through it, and, honestly, I don't know where this ball is gonna go when we leave here today." He said the more details Lloyd provided, the more leverage they would have with Teddy and Dick.

"I've known all along that you were bullshitting us, that you knew the answer to this, and it's frustrating. Dave and I have different personalities. Dave is the kind of guy . . . he's much more patient than I am."

But Lloyd had nothing more to add, for now.

8
The Duffel Bag

Investigators survey the Welch property on Taylor's Mountain

Poking the Beehive

Within weeks of the July visit, the Lyon investigation exploded. Over the next six months it would engage scores of police in Maryland and Virginia, prosecutors from both states, contractors, and FBI specialists. There would be wiretaps, search warrants, and surveillance, audio and video. The old case would be worked on harder through the remainder of 2014 and into 2015 than it had been since those frantic spring days four decades ago. There would be extensive searching by air and on foot, excavations, soil analyses, lab tests, all seeking some scrap of physical evidence. There would be monthly grand jury proceedings and subpoenas from the Commonwealth of Virginia to compel testimony under oath. There would be intensive and repeated interviews, formal and informal, with nearly every living member of the Welch family. After nine months of parsing Lloyd's subterfuge, the squad now turned on the clan with a vengeance. The detectives imagined the Lyon sisters as the guarded clan's most deeply buried secret, running through its shared memory like a subterranean third rail, known to all but too hot to touch.

It was a siege. Bedford, a sleepy rural town of six thousand in the Appalachian foothills, was overrun by police and press. Spurred by Lloyd's naming of his uncle and cousin in July, the squad hustled to secure authorization for surveillance. Much to his wife's chagrin, Dave left a Labor Day picnic with several beers under his belt to visit the judge and county prosecutor to secure a court order. The wiretaps went up on September 2, and in the first week they revealed that the case was already a hot topic of conversation on the clan's phones and social media accounts. The active interest of the Virginia branch was, in particular, enticing. If others in the family had been involved in the crime itself, as Lloyd claimed, or had helped cover it up, there was a chance there were answers on Taylor's Mountain.

Dave, Mark, and Katie had driven down to Bedford on Friday, August 29, stopping first at the mountain. They had a time of it on the backcountry roads. At one point Katie, who was driving with the boldness and sense of privilege of a onetime patrolwoman, bounced so violently over a railroad crossing that she upset a cooler filled with ice water (and cans of beer) in the back seat. It sloshed over Mark. His partners' mirth didn't improve his temper. Katie relinquished the wheel.

Taylor's Mountain felt like a place stuck in time. They found the house and property owned by the late Lizzie Parker, Lloyd's aunt, sister to his father and Dick, where they stopped to talk with a friendly man, Paul Amos, who was sitting on his front porch across the road. On a later visit they caught Amos eating his dinner straight out of a skillet and two saucepans, leading the detectives to dub him "Paulie Pots-and-Pans." He knew the family well, and when he asked what the detectives were looking for, they told him about the Lyon sisters. He pointed up the road.

"Well, there's a graveyard up that hill," he said.

What they found did, indeed, look like an old graveyard, with plain stone markers spaced regularly around a weedy field. It was the kind of place where you might bury someone without attracting notice. There were local rumors that it had been a Native American burial site, but it was more likely just an old family cemetery. Like many in these hills, the clan had a long history of private interment.

Next they drove into Bedford itself, a spacious redbrick small town bisected by an Amtrak rail line, with expansive vistas in all directions. To the west were the blue-green foothills of the Appalachian Mountains. On Main Street the largest structure was a colonial-style courthouse with an impressive gray-columned portico, its roof topped by a cupola with a copper dome. Dave and Katie walked into the town's police headquarters a few blocks away, while Mark, still drying out after his dousing, stayed in the car with his laptop, putting the finishing touches on a PowerPoint presentation that laid out the case from its beginning to the newly discovered Virginia connections. The squad wanted to interview them all, for starters.

Dave and Katie learned they had come to the wrong place. Taylor's Mountain was in Thaxton, just to the west. The right constabulary was the nearby Bedford County Sheriff's Office, a larger operation. It was late afternoon on the cusp of a long Labor Day weekend when the squad showed up there with Mark's laptop. Folks were heading home. There was some grumbling, and the office brass were less than enthusiastic at first, but the PowerPoint got a hearing, and help was promised. There would be some friction over the coming months, but from that day forward the investigation was an interstate project.

The wiretaps in Maryland targeted the cell phones of Dick, Pat, and Teddy. A small camera was placed high on a telephone pole outside Dick and Pat's house, a conventional 1960s-era suburban ranch house with a white-shingled second story over a redbrick base. On the front lawn was a two-person swinging chair. Comings and goings were observed and charted. Up until then the elderly couple had been cordial, if not particularly helpful. The full-court press would soon turn them sharply adversarial.

Some in the clan had been cautious ever since Lloyd had been named at the press conference—the police saw Teddy's long drive that day to visit Dick in person as evidence of this. The squad had anticipated monitoring calls for a month, but they ended up listening for three months. It was costly. Supervised by veteran Montgomery County detective Rich Armagost, the bugs had to be monitored twenty-four hours a day, seven days a week, occupying four or five officers at a time. Many of the things overheard were redolent of deeper knowledge. For instance, after seeing news reports about the digging on Taylor's Mountain, Pat Welch told one caller, knowingly, "They are going to find something on that mountain." When told where the police were digging, she remarked, categorically, "Those aren't their graves" and "They are on the wrong side of the mountain," even though she had insisted to the squad that she knew nothing whatsoever about the Lyon girls. Occasionally the conversations were amusing, as callers wrestled with the fine points of jurisprudence, logic, and the English language. One described making "chicken salad" from turkey scraps. An affidavit was "an afro-davis"; asserting the right to avoid self-incrimination was "taking the Fourth"; a pedophile was a "pedifier"; and someone with proverbial skeletons in the closet had "a lot of shelves in his closet." Mostly the cops heard the clan comparing notes, complaining about the police, and warning and encouraging one another to shut up. There were no breakthroughs.

Working with their new Bedford partners, the squad began knocking on family doors. One of the first belonged to Artie Overstreet, Lloyd's oldest aunt. She was a friendly, white-haired, churchgoing widow, stooped now in her eighties, who still lived with other family members in Thaxton. On a target list of family names, one of the detectives had scrawled in the margin—referring to the old TV series *The Beverly Hillbillies*—"Looked like the Clampetts to me; quiet weird people."

Artie told them that Dick and Pat, whom she heard from rarely, had called her in August—at the same time the police effort was gearing up—to ask if they might visit. She had refused them. Having just returned from a vacation, Artie did not want guests, even her younger brother and his wife. But they had come anyway. They wanted to know if she had been contacted by the police. The couple stopped in on other Virginia relatives with the same question, circling the family wagons. They spread the word, in person, that phones were tapped and that the police were out to get Dick.

It was fascinating to overhear the family's take on the squad's efforts. Dave, Mark, and Katie became its chief tormenters. Dave was "the little one," Mark "the big one with glasses," Katie "the girl" or "the psychic," because, as Dick Welch put it, "she can read people's body language and setch." Each new visit by the detectives stirred up more urgent intrafamily chatter, which in turn fed the squad's suspicions. Family members had begun scouring the Internet for reports and speculation about the probe (in addition to mainstream media coverage, there had long been online sleuths obsessed with the mystery). Pat and her daughter went to the local library to use the computers there. On phones, by text, and in posts on social media, they commiserated and conjectured about who knew what, who was talking, what the police knew, and what the detectives were being told. If there had been no family conspiracy in 1975, there was one now. Each new interview poked the beehive, and afterward the wires buzzed, beginning with Artie, who called Pat immediately after being questioned. Through that summer and into fall the investigators consciously "tickled the wire," sometimes planting false information just to stir things up, always pretending to know more than they did, sowing discord and division, hoping that in the anger and confusion somebody would slip up.

They even enlisted Lloyd to draft a letter to his uncle Dick, urging Dick to visit him at the prison: "We need to talk about what happened forty years ago," Lloyd wrote, at their behest. "You remember, don't you? I don't think you want me to talk about those two little girls, the ones you and Ted got at the Wheaton Plaza. You know I have been taking this shit long enough."

Dick didn't respond. Unlike his nephew, he was smart enough to say nothing. Once he apprehended that he had become a target—the department would hold a press conference in October to name him as another person of interest in the case—he stopped speaking on the phone altogether. Pat fielded all the calls to their house. She became, with mounting indignation, a hub for much of the chatter. Well after she had stopped talking to the police, she was chatting cautiously on the phone with relatives. She asked many questions. Pat was keeping tabs on the squad just as they were keeping tabs on her.

Dick and Pat

In truth, Artie's call to Pat was instigated by the police.

"Were they at your house long?" Pat asked, and then lamented: "It's out of control, Artie. Did they say anything about me and Dick? I've heard so much stuff in the last month. It's made Dick sick. It's made me sick. So much gossip going on. If I could talk to everybody in Bedford, I'll tell them not to talk to them. They have connived, twisted things around, said things that can't be true, just to make the person they are talking to confused. Oh my goodness! It's horrible!"

"They are nice people," said Artie.

"*They have to be nice!* But how many times do you have to tell them no? It's gossip. People blowing things out of proportion. It's horrible! If they say it [the Lyon case] has anything to do with any of us, it ain't true!"

Pat was surprisingly savvy about surveillance. The sixty-five-year-old grandmother was more prudent than some professional drug dealers the detectives had monitored. She was vigilant and fierce. She viewed protecting her husband as an essential wifely duty. Her daughter, Kim Pettas, told police that no matter how badly she had been treated by her father while she was growing up—and the treatment had been, she said, horrific—her mother always took his side. Dick had once beaten Kim so badly when she was a child that she lost control of her bladder and was left too swollen and bruised to attend school for three days. When she was a teenager her father routinely called her "whore" and "slut." She remembered one warm conversation with her mother in the family kitchen ruined when Dick entered the room and began insulting her, calling her "cunt" and "whore." When Kim looked to her mother for help, Pat's maternal mood turned on a dime. She snapped at Kim, "He is my husband, and I will protect him until the day that I die, do you understand me?" She was still at it.

To shake something loose, the detectives encouraged old resentments. There were plenty of them. Joann Green, Pat's middle-aged younger sister, said she had been sexually molested by Dick when she was nine. She often spent time at her sister's apartment, where she had nieces close to her own age. She was terrified of her uncle Dick. She said she once watched in horror as he savagely beat the family dog for peeing indoors, repeatedly slamming its head into the floor. In later years, when he worked as a security guard, he had a dog that would snarl and attack on command. He would get it to growl and bare its teeth at Joann until she screamed in fear, and then he would laugh. She said Dick had molested her in his and Pat's house on Emerson Street in central Hyattsville. She said Dick, who was then in his twenties, had pulled off her pants and underwear, draped her leg over the back of a couch, and performed oral sex. "I'll make you so hot you'll piss your pants," she said he told her. "I didn't know what that meant," she told me. "I didn't know what he had did. I kind of knew it was wrong, but I didn't know what it was called. I didn't know why he did it, so I just tried to block it out." Joann said she had been too ashamed and frightened to tell anyone.

This sexual aggression lasted for years, Joann said, until she was old enough to understand and to complain. When she was a teenager, playing pool with her cousins in his house, she said Dick kept suggestively thrusting his pool cue between her legs until she fled downstairs and complained to Pat. "Just stay away from him," Pat advised. When Joann gave birth to her first child at Prince George's Hospital in May 1975, she came home to her sister's house in Hyattsville and then had to wait until Pat sobered up for a ride home to Virginia. Dick, now thirty, also drunk, kept coming into her room that night and touching her. She would squirm away from him. He left her room in anger, bellowing through the house, "I want a piece of pussy!" Joann said this continued until she complained to her sister.

This picture of a young, wolfish Dick Welch made it easier to imagine him in Lloyd's latest scenario. Joann was recruited to confront Dick directly, something she had never dared to do. She was crying when Pat picked up the phone.

"I just wanted to talk to him," Joann said. "Ask him why he did what he did to me. He never apologized! I thought I was the only one he did it to, but I'm learning otherwise. Pat, I'm putting two and two together. He was a security guard at the Wheaton Plaza when those Lyon girls went missing."

"He was not," said Pat.

"My God, did he have something to do with that?"

"He didn't."

"How do you know?"

"I know."

"How? If you didn't know he was messing with your own kids?"

"Because I know that."

"Is he ever going to apologize for having sex with me?"

"I'll talk to you later," said Pat, and hung up.

Joann dialed her back. She said the detective, Katie Leggett, had asked her about the sexual assault. She said she couldn't fathom how the police knew about it.

"Let me tell you something," said Pat. "They make lies up. Let me tell you. They are trying to catch anything or anybody, and they will make things up. They will lie that they heard it from somebody else or whatever."

"But it's the *truth*," Joann said. She reminded Pat that she had confronted her repeatedly in those years about her husband's behavior.

Pat said she had no memory of it. She said, "If you told them that's what happened then they'd arrest him."

"But I *denied* it." She said she was now worried about what might happen to her because she had lied to the police.

"You don't have to talk to them," said Pat. "You know that, don't you?"

"But if I don't talk to them maybe I'll get in trouble. I don't know."

"No. You don't have to talk to them."

"You want me to keep lying to them, or do you want me to tell the truth?" she asked. This was a key question. If Pat counseled her to keep lying, she would be obstructing justice. She was much too canny for that.

"Just don't talk to them," she said. "These people are very persuading. They tell lies."

Nothing rattled Pat. Late in September, Dollie Estep, her niece, who lived in Bedford, called with an urgent message. Lloyd, she said, had confessed to kidnapping, raping, and killing the Lyon girls, and had named Dick and Teddy as accomplices. She said Teddy had also named Dick. This, of course, was not true. Mark and Katie were sitting with Dollie as she made the call. They had misled her in an effort to stir things up, and suggested the warning call to Pat. Dollie urged her aunt to make a deal with the detectives to save herself and Dick.

"Don't say anything to me," Dollie told Pat immediately. "I'm going to do the talking; you're not. They took me to the police station today. They took my picture. The death penalty is on the line. Teddy is putting Lloyd there. Rapings, beatings. He's gonna make a plea deal. You need to start talking. Patricia Ann [another of Pat's daughters] is in danger. Teddy wants to silence her. They're saying they have evidence. The death sentence is on the line. If you and Dick don't talk first, Dick is going to get the death penalty. You need to talk because Tommy Junior [Teddy] is throwing you under the bus. You need to talk to them. Do it now! Don't let Tommy Junior do this to you."

"We don't know anything," said Pat, calmly.

"Junior is throwing you under the bus big-time. Call your lawyer and take him with you to see them. I'm worried to death about Dick."

Pat was unmoved.

In poking around on Taylor's Mountain, the detectives found much to interest them. There was that old cemetery with unmarked gravestones and the remains of a large fire pit used to dispose of brush and trash by the Parker family (Lizzie Welch had married Allen Parker). "They burned everything," their daughter had said. It was not an uncommon practice in rural areas. Sometimes the bonfire burned for days at a time. Suspecting it might have been used to incinerate the Lyon girls' bodies, investigators had begun marking off places to excavate. Part of the land was still owned by Dick and Pat. Dollie called them again at the end of September.

"They have marked your property up here as a crime scene," Dollie said.

"As what?"

"As a crime scene. They're gonna dig it up."

"Okay, that's cool."

Dollie said, "I told them, 'The person that killed those girls is dead.'"

"I'll call you back," said Pat, and hung up.

Despite Pat's seeming calm, she was worried, and even though she was cagey on the phone, there were plenty of hints that she knew more than she let on. Her daughter Kim Pettas called her as more reports were aired of the digging on Taylor's Mountain, prompting another of the exchanges that the squad found so suggestive.

"You better look at the news," Kim told her.

"I've been looking at the news. We're going to jail," Pat said.

"You ain't goin' to jail."

"Oh yeah? I ain't got time to look at the news 'cause I've got to get ready to go away."

"Mother, they [the Lyon girls' remains] was found up on Lizzie's property."

"What was found?"

"The grave site."

"That's not their grave site. They're still looking."

Pat's worry that she and Dick were about to be arrested suggested that there was incriminating evidence to be found.

In order to avoid polluting these conversations, the detectives had told no one the details of Lloyd's ever-changing account. So they were especially interested when comments by family members seemed to corroborate it. In his most recent version, he and Teddy had left Wheaton Plaza with the girls and got into a car waiting in the parking lot. The detectives were startled to hear Pat, discussing the case with Dollie, present virtually the same scenario.

"Didn't you say that the detectives said they know it was Lloyd and Junior [Teddy]?" Pat asked.

"No. He said Lloyd admitted to it and that Tommy [Teddy] was involved. Lloyd admitted to the girls, and Tommy Junior was involved with him. It was him and Tommy."

"Well, who was the other guy?"

"They didn't mention the other guy."

"The way I understood it was, there was two men out in the parking lot with Lloyd," said Pat.

"I don't think they are pressed about Dick; I think they know it's Thomas Junior," Dollie said.

"I heard there was somebody else there, you know? They have to know who it was."

The day after this call, Pat and Dick lost whatever self-possession they had, when the squad and the FBI searched their house. This was September 19. Pat was not home when the teams swarmed in with the warrant. Mark Janney cornered Dick in the front yard, sharply questioning and accusing him.

"Here's the thing, Dick," said Mark. "I think you have kind of been expecting this day, you know what I mean. You've probably been carrying around a lot of weight on your shoulders the last few months, wondering what's going on with us. We've been investigating this thing very thoroughly. It's over. It's time to put this thing to rest."

"What did I do?" Dick asked.

"You know what your role was."

"I don't know. What did I do? I didn't do anything."

"Our objective is to mainly find those girls."

"I don't know where they are at! I had nothing to do with it!"

"It's time for you to tell us the truth."

"I had nothing to do with it. On my mother's grave, I had nothing to do with it."

"Well, Dick, we've got a lot of evidence. We've talked to a lot of people. Put people's stories together, including Ted and including Lloyd, and the main thing I want is to hear your version of things."

"I didn't do anything. I wasn't there. I didn't do anything. I was accused of doing it, but I did not do it. I didn't even know the boy [Lloyd]; he was off from the family. I did not do it."

"There's no point in going down this road right now."

"It's the honest road. It's the honest road. It's all I can say; it's the honest road. I had nothing to do with it."

"It's time. It's time, Dick."

Mark said that not everyone involved shared the full weight of the blame, and they needed to hear from him what his role was.

"I didn't have no role," said Dick. "I didn't do anything. I did not do nothing."

"It could very well be a case where people were drunk, their judgment was screwed up, they got into something that they didn't expect to get into, and it just went the wrong way. And if that's the case, and if something accidental happened to those girls, and people got scared and freaked out, then that's what we're here to clear up."

"I don't even know the girls you're talking about. I never seen 'em. Of course, I know the girls you're talking about. I seen their picture. I didn't *know* 'em. I have not done nothin'."

"It's time," said Mark. "You've been carrying this a long time."

"I ain't been carrying nothing!"

"It's time to tell the truth."

"I AM telling the truth!"

"It's time to clear this up."

"This is clearing it up! Right here! I have done nothin'!"

Mark kept at him hard, but Dick didn't budge. He had not been running from this case. He had not been hiding anything. He didn't know anything. His distress made him unsteady, and at one point he keeled over. They placed him on a bench and brought him water. Dick kept insisting he had nothing to do with the crime.

"I am so sorry you think I do," he said, "but I don't."

"Our evidence says you do, Dick. That's the problem. Dick, you've done things."

"I have not. I don't know what evidence you got, but it's not on me. Am I under arrest?"

"No, you are not under arrest."

"Can I call my wife?"

"No, you can't."

"If I'm not under arrest, why can't I call my wife?'

"Because I said you can't."

Dick laughed with astonishment. "So you're the Man, and I'm the dummy, right?"

"You're not dumb. We're serving a search warrant at your house, and we don't want you calling your wife right now. We'll let you call her in due time."

Dick kept repeating over and over that he had never been to Wheaton Plaza. "I have not been there. I have not been there."

Mark said that their evidence indicated otherwise. "The bottom line is this isn't going to go away."

"The bottom line is I didn't do anything. I didn't do it, sir."

Dick demanded to talk to a lawyer. He broke down.

"Everybody has made mistakes in their life," said Mark.

"I didn't make no mistakes."

When Pat came they wouldn't let her near her husband. She threw a fit, screaming for all the neighborhood to hear, "Somebody call an ambulance! Everybody, remember this! They're denying help to a dying man!"

In the middle of it, Pat phoned Dollie.

"They're tearing my house up," she said.

"Where's Dick?"

"He's been on the ground a couple of times."

"He's gonna have a heart attack," Dollie said.

"I don't think it's fair that nobody knows what's going on," said Pat. "They say people in Bedford are giving them information. There must be twenty-five or thirty of them. They lie so fucking much. I want the people in Bedford to know."

A day later, sounding drunk and crying, she called Dollie again.

"I'm not a bad person. I told that detective I'm gonna call down to Bedford and tell them what's going on. I have caught them in lies several times. I told them I'm gonna talk to everyone down there who is feeding them information."

"I believe Lloyd implicated Dick," Dollie said.

"Junior too. I don't think they know what they're talking about."

"I guess they think I'm hiding secrets for your family," said Dollie.

"They implicated you as one of the people talking about Dick, saying he did something like that," said Pat.

"They ask me a hundred million questions a day. They ask me if I'm loyal to my family, and 'Do you have family secrets?' "

"They tell me you implicated Dick."

"How could I implicate anybody? I was twelve years old!"

"They said Junior implicated Dick. There are other people down there saying things." Pat said the police kept hammering at Dick, telling him that they knew he was the driver. "Over and over and over," she said. "They did take him a bottle of water."

The search found nothing incriminating. And despite Dick's assertions of complete innocence, the Montgomery County police went ahead with the press conference that named him another person of interest. Called before a grand jury in Virginia months later, under oath, Pat denied having urged others to be uncooperative. Recordings of her doing just that were then played. She was indicted for perjury, and cameras caught a glimpse of her with her hands over her face as a sheriff drove her away.

Teddy

Teddy felt the heat, too. The darkly handsome cousin with the curious past was summoned repeatedly for interviews and a polygraph, and he cooperated doggedly, appearing, as always, candid to a fault. He detailed his long relationship with Leonard Kraisel, an association the detectives found hard to comprehend; he acknowledged youthful sex play with siblings; and he continued to insist that he had nothing to do with the Lyon kidnapping. Lloyd, he said, he hardly knew.

Teddy was under tremendous stress at the time. His third wife, Stacy—his first had died of cancer, and the second had left him—had been diagnosed with a fatal malignancy. He and their two boys were still dealing with emotional, financial, and legal fallout from Kraisel's conviction; the fuel equipment and services company, largely owned by Uncle Lenny, was going under; and Teddy was shepherding a civil lawsuit on behalf of his sons against the old man (which they would eventually win). Now, for reasons he could not comprehend, his cousin had named him as a kidnapper, rapist, and killer.

Looking for ways to lean on him, the squad enlisted a male relative who said that as a boy he had been sexually assaulted by Teddy. Teddy had deduced early on that his cell phone was tapped. His landline at home was not—the squad had been unable to show a pattern of calls to the landline to warrant a tap—but on the theory that Teddy might trust that line more, they had this relative call him on it.

"The police asked me some questions about what happened to me as a child," he told Teddy. "What you and Michael did to me as a child. With the butter. Sexual."

"I didn't do anything to you," said Teddy.

"You don't remember what you did to me? Dad and Mom confronting you on the street?" He said Teddy had driven up to his house in a red car. "You came in drunk? Got butter out of the refrigerator?"

"I never had a red car," said Teddy. "I had a burgundy car."

They quibbled, and then Teddy said, "If you're sitting there with the police right now recording this phone call [he was], you can tell them to kiss my ass. Tell them to leave you alone. Lloyd is fucking dragging me into it!"

His cousin Dollie, who had her own grievance, was also enlisted.

"One time at Dick's house," she said, "they [Dick and his brothers] were all drunk on the front porch. Your dad [Tommy Senior] told me to get on his lap. I tried to get up, and Tommy pulled me back down." She said that Teddy had intervened on her behalf, yelling at his father and pulling her off him. "Me and you went around the side of the house, and you pulled your winky out." She said Teddy, having rescued her, had then pushed her to her knees and tried to put his penis in her mouth.

Teddy said he didn't remember it, but if it had happened, he was sorry.

Dollie said, "Patty Ann [their cousin, Dick and Pat's daughter] called me last night drunk off her butt. She called me and cussed me out. She called me drunk, drunk, drunk. Next thing I know, she's hysterical crying. Said you told the police that her daddy was the driver [in the Lyon kidnapping]. Lloyd is cooperating with the police. Said you were on the scene, raped those girls."

"Come on, Dollie," said Teddy. "I was eleven years old!"

"Not by yourself. Were you and Daddy and Lloyd involved?"

"I can't imagine anything like that."

"When people get drunk things happen that don't ordinarily happen," Dollie said.

"There's so much stuff going around," said Teddy. "They took me to the sheriff's office yesterday, put me on a recorder. I'm not going to worry about it."

The same tactic was tried with Teddy's younger half brother, Michael. He phoned Teddy (calling him "Tommy") in mid-October—two of the detectives were with him.

"Two detectives were here, Tommy. Going through everything, talking about everything. Things that happened in our family, those two little girls—"

"Do you know anything about those two girls?" Teddy snapped at him, cutting him off. He practically hissed the question through the phone, a warning as much as a question. Then he added, "I don't know anything."

"They were talking all kinds of crazy shit that went on in your family. Sexual things. They're just investigating, trying to figure out who killed those Lyon girls. I have a strange feeling that they still think you know something. Let me explain it to you, they can put you in jail for conspiracy. I haven't a—"

"Are you an *idiot*?" Teddy asked sharply, cutting him off. His tone suggested that his brother was stupid for even talking about such a thing. "I'm telling you I had nothing to do with it."

"They come at me with all this other bullshit," said Michael. "Our family is totally fucked up. Goddammit, I don't like these two strange motherfucking assholes coming in my house and talking to me about this shit! Cover your fucking ass!"

"I don't need to cover my ass. I didn't do anything."

But Teddy was worried. After the police searched his house late that summer, he set out to prove his innocence. As a boy he had climbed to the icy roof of a local school to retrieve a ball, slipped, and fallen off, shattering both arms. He believed this had happened when he was eleven. After a stay at Washington Adventist Hospital, he had come home with casts on both arms, which were elevated by straps. "I couldn't even wipe my own ass!" he told the detectives. It had taken many months and repeated surgeries to fully repair his bones. He wasn't sure exactly when it had happened, but he was sure it was in 1975. After his interview at police headquarters that summer, he went looking for his old medical records—and succeeded in finding them. The tap on his phone recorded him battling hard with hospital bureaucracy.

Teddy was able to show that his fall had happened on February 15, 1975, and he had spent a week in the hospital. He even found an old photo of him taken there, his cast-encased arms in traction. This was more than a month before the Lyon girls had disappeared, but he'd worn the casts for months. Two broken arms made him an even less likely kidnapper, even if you believed he was somehow involved at age eleven. It certainly would have been hard to miss him in Wheaton Plaza that day. None of the witnesses remembered a boy with two broken arms. Dee Danner, the woman who remembered seeing the Lyon girls talking to a boy, was asked specifically if he "had anything wrong with him." She said no. Teddy had even kept the casts, which were taken when his house was searched. They were tested for signs of blood—on the theory that Teddy might have been present at the girls' murder—and none were found.

He went further still to prove himself to the squad. He agreed to wear a wire for a surprise visit to his uncle Dick. The detectives instructed him to get Dick talking about the crime. Teddy drove over to his uncle's house on the afternoon of September 16. He sat with him on the swing chair in the front yard and for nearly an hour commiserated with him and Pat about the ongoing investigation. Dick kept reminding Teddy that his lawyer had advised him not to talk about it, but to the extent that he did, he repeated the same denials he had made to the police.

Even after this effort, the squad's doubts about Teddy lingered. His disappointing conversation with Dick and Pat didn't convince them that any of the three were innocent; instead they wondered whether Teddy had tipped Dick and Pat off to the wire.

Lloyd had known exactly what he was doing when he named his cousin. Chris, Dave, Mark, and Katie were, at heart, conventional cops. To them, Teddy lay so far outside their concept of normal that they were willing to believe almost anything about him. The sexual bargain Teddy had struck as a boy, the way his story had played out in recent years with Uncle Lenny, and his odd sexual history with cousins and siblings—it all made Teddy *smell* complicit.

Ultimately, the wiretaps produced more questions than answers. They were useful in fleshing out the tawdry context of Lloyd's family, and some of what was learned, as we shall see, would help move the case forward, but the keen anticipation at their launching went unfulfilled. By the end of 2014, the bistate siege of the Welches was looking like a great dollar- and time-consuming dead end.

Edna

If there was a moment that captured the exasperation of these months, it was the appearance of Edna Ayline Welch, Lloyd's ailing and obese stepmother, before the Bedford grand jury on November 7. Edna was a deceptively simple, mean country woman in her eighties, sharp as the cut rim of a tin can and prone to didactic and random biblical quotations. Her letters to Lloyd in prison were full of them—like textual glossolalia. These missives were written in her hand, although she said she was illiterate. Edna lived in Tennessee in a filthy, cluttered house littered with dog droppings. Her soft, full, lined face had sprouted gray whiskers, which were a source of family amusement. Her daughter had posted to Facebook a video of herself plucking hairs from her mother's chin to the sound of banjo music.

Edna was of particular interest for several reasons. She had been living with Lee Welch in the Hyattsville house at 4714 Baltimore Avenue, where Lloyd and Helen had sometimes stayed during March and April 1975. Edna had told of cops knocking on her door there looking for Lloyd in the weeks after the girls disappeared, something which the detectives had not known and for which there was no record. She said Lloyd and Helen had gone off by then; she did not know where. Even if she knew nothing about the Lyon girls, as she claimed, she at least might be able to corroborate or debunk bits of information Lloyd had dropped about those days. And there was reason to believe she knew much more than she let on. Soon after Dave had first phoned her in the summer of 2013, searching for Lloyd without mentioning why, hard-of-hearing Edna had apparently written to Lloyd to tell him that the Maryland police wanted to talk to him about the Lyon girls. She had made the connection immediately. Her letter to Lloyd was never recovered, but a search of her Tennessee home revealed one he had written to her in response, five months before the first police interview.

"I don't know about 2 girls missing from Wheaton, MD," he had written. "Tell me who called and what they say I did or think I did because I've never done anything to 2 girls to make them come up missing. So write me back and let me know what is going on on this."

So Lloyd, whom Chris and Dave and Pete had hoped to surprise, had been prepping mentally for the encounter for months. In the same letter, he had asked Edna a surprising question: "Mom, have you ever heard from Helen or from any of the girls? I don't know where Helen is."

Why, out of the blue, a question about Helen? Lloyd had neither seen nor heard from her in more than thirty years. He didn't even know that she had died of cancer some years earlier. But it was Helen who sprang to mind. The detectives could imagine a good reason for this. Helen had been with him when the kidnapping occurred. If she were still alive, her memories of those days might be very damaging to him. When Dave saw this letter, and realized that Edna had never written Lloyd an answer, he kicked himself for having told Lloyd that Helen was dead. If Lloyd were worried about what she might say, this would have given the squad useful leverage.

Edna was in the last year of her life. She was not happy about the summons to Virginia. She arrived weary and in a snit, a backwoods matriarch beset by the powers that be. Leaning heavily on a cane, she worked her way to the witness chair, disheveled, her curly gray hair cut short and jutting out untidily. She had, as the detectives had already learned, a hearing problem that fluctuated with her mood—a disorder common in the ornery elderly. She heard what she cared to hear. There was much to be learned from her if she chose to be helpful, which she did not.

"Ms. Welch, can you hear me?" asked Virginia prosecutor Randy Krantz. When there was no response he asked again, "Can you hear me?"

"I can hear you right—I might miss some words," said Edna.

"All right. If I—if anybody—asks you a question that you can't hear—"

"Would you come closer?"

"I'd be happy to," said Krantz.

She started out fine, answering questions expansively. When Lloyd was still a boy, she had agreed to take him in briefly, because her husband "kept whining about wanting his kids." Lee, as she put it, "drinked a lot." She obliged him, hoping it might mellow and sober him, "which it did not," she said, emphatically. He showed no affection for Lloyd. Instead, the boy seemed to make him angry and abusive, so Edna's kindly gesture only heaped new hardship on her already strained home life. She had not had it easy, as she put it, "with a drunk husband fussing and carrying on." She said she had to intercept Lee's pay every week, "or else he would go drink it up."

Edna had trouble remembering the names of all her children and stepchildren. She described as "difficult" those early days with Lloyd, then a boy, in her house. After being retrieved from foster care, "he didn't listen to me, for one thing. And I don't even remember what kind of trouble he got into or what. We had to go to court with him, or I did. My husband wouldn't have a thing to do with him, with nothing, PTA, children. 'No,' [he'd say], 'that's you,' you know? I had my hands full. And so, I told the judge I just couldn't handle it. And he put Lloyd in some kind of house or something. And that's the last I seen of him there, for years."

Edna's hearing began to falter as the detectives, Mark, Dave, and Katie, took their turns.

"Do you remember when you learned that Lloyd was being investigated about the disappearance of these two girls?" asked Mark.

"When you called me."

In that first phone call, since Dave had been careful not to mention it, they wondered how she had so quickly surmised they were working on the Lyon case.

"Did you relay that information to Lloyd?" Mark asked.

"What? Now, wait. Run that by me again."

"Do you remember when those two girls disappeared, the Lyon sisters?"

"Do I?"

"Yes."

"I didn't until you-ins brought it up."

"And what did you remember about it when we brought it up?"

Edna asked for a drink of water.

"I told them I hadn't even got my coffee this morning."

"Oh, I can relate," said Mark.

"We drove all night. We drove. We just got here."

She got her drink and then, with Mark's prompting, recalled Lloyd and Helen discussing the missing girls on a couch in her living room after seeing a report on TV.

"I don't remember what they said or anything, but Lloyd is kind of—I always thought he wanted to be noticed. A little wanting, wanting something. I don't know how to explain what I'm trying to say."

"Attention?" Mark suggested. "He wanted attention?"

"Yeah. I understood there was going to be a reward or something, maybe, you know? I don't know. But, anyway, Lloyd was after money, I guess. I guess that's the way you'd put it. But he called and said he knew something. But he was just an eighteen-year-old boy, never had a car."

When detectives came to her door a few weeks later, she said, she told them that Lloyd had gone and she didn't know where.

"He was a foolish kid," she said. "Well, I shouldn't say that, should I?"

"You can say whatever is the truth," said Mark.

"I don't mean to mean-mouth him, but kids do awful stupid things."

This, it turned out, was about all Edna had to offer. Her memory began failing her.

Krantz stepped back in, warning that lying to a grand jury was a criminal offense. "What happens to someone in a courtroom when they don't tell the truth, what do you think?" he asked.

"What's that?" she asked.

Krantz repeated the question, louder.

"What happens?" Edna asked.

"Uh-huh."

"Well, they lied."

"Uh-huh, and what does the court do to people who have lied?"

"I don't know. I guess put them in jail."

"And you know why you're here."

"Couldn't help but know it."

"So, I'm going to ask you a question. Would you lie for Lloyd?"

"No. No. I haven't lied yet and won't start."

Her memory and hearing faded fast from that point on. She had been threatened and did not take it kindly. No, she didn't remember Teddy Welch, her nephew, and no, she knew nothing of Lloyd's life outside his brief stays in her house. Despite Lloyd's rosy-hued memories of her—he still called her "Mom" and "the only one who ever loved me," and so forth—Edna had no affectionate memories of him at all. She said she hardly knew him. Neither she nor Lee had wanted him around. He returned for only a brief period when he was eighteen. Her occasional letters to him in prison were less maternal affection than Christian charity, which accounted for their didactic scriptural content. So why were they bugging her about him?

But continue bugging her they did, at which point the old woman gave the assembled legal talent a master seminar in nonresponse.

"Did Lloyd ever tell you he had been at Wheaton Plaza?" Krantz asked.

"What period of time?"

"Any time."

"In his letters."

"Okay. And what did Lloyd say in his letters?"

"What did he say?"

"Uh-huh."

"Well, all right. I can't really recall. If you want to know, I don't read."

"No. And I'm not trying to embarrass you."

"Well . . ."

"I understand."

"Generally somebody who writes, reads," he said. "Who reads Lloyd's letters to you?"

"Well. Part of them never was even read," said Edna.

"I'm talking about the one where he talked about Wheaton Plaza."

"Well, he said he didn't do it."

Krantz reminded Edna that the detectives had spoken at length to Lloyd. "So I want you to think real carefully before you answer. What did Lloyd say in his letters about Wheaton Plaza?"

"I can't tell. I don't remember. Now, he might not have said nothing. I don't know. But he said he didn't or something like that."

"What if I told you Lloyd has admitted doing it?"

"I'd say he's a liar."

"Uh-huh, and why is that? Is that because you don't want to believe that he did it?"

"What's that?"

"I mean, do you know whether he did it or not?"

"You want the honest truth?"

"I want you to answer my question. Do you know whether Lloyd did it or not? Yes or no?"

"No, I don't know in my heart. No."

"So you don't know whether he's lying?"

"But I know what I think."

And on it went. Edna said she felt sure Lloyd had done no such thing.

"Who writes the letters that you send to Lloyd?"

"What? Who writes them?"

Krantz repeated the question.

"I do."

"You know what you write, don't you?"

"Yeah. Or I think I do."

"And you can read what you write?"

"Sometimes."

"Uh-huh."

"My spelling ain't too good. I have to look up every word I spell."

"You wrote and told Lloyd that the police had been to your house asking about him?"

"Yeah."

"Didn't you?"

"Well, that's probably what I told him."

"Why? Why did you do that?"

"I guess I did."

"You already said that you did."

"Oh yeah."

"And my question to you is, why did you do that?'

"Well, what do you write to somebody that you don't even hardly know?"

"Well, that's my question. Why would you write to somebody you hardly know?"

"Just to have something to write, I guess."

"And he wrote back to you, didn't he?"

"Yeah."

"And in the letter he wrote you back, he talked about Wheaton Plaza, didn't he?"

"I can't say."

Edna slipped and slid out of her questioners' grasp. Sometimes she didn't hear; at other times she started off on her own tangent.

"Listen, you've got to help me here, because I'm slow," said Krantz, finally.

"Oh yeah?"

"Yeah."

"Don't tell me that. Your face is red," said Edna.

"That's blood pressure."

"Oh yeah. You're getting mine up here, too."

Krantz tried a different tack. He asked Mark Janney, "Did she ever make any statements to you, Detective Janney, about this conversation with Lloyd Welch?"

"Yes."

"What did Mrs. Welch tell you?"

"At first she said he told her that he was going for a reward, and then later she changed and said he did not say that."

"Did you hear him?" he asked Edna.

"No. I didn't hear him."

When Dave tried, her hearing further deteriorated. He asked where she had been when she first learned that the Montgomery County police wanted to talk to Lloyd about the Lyon sisters.

"Wait a minute," said Edna. "You talk awful soft. You almost have to holler."

Dave approached her.

"I can bend down here," he said, leaning toward her. "When you found out about this case."

"What's that?"

"When you found out about this investigation from the Maryland police."

"Yeah."

"How did you find out? Did they come to your house and talk to you?"

"First they called me on the phone."

"What did they tell you over the phone?"

"What did they tell me? That they were investigating, you know? I can't tell you what they told me."

"Because that was me that called you."

"Oh, it was?"

"It was."

"Well, you booger."

"And didn't we talk? You remember what you told me?"

"I don't know."

"You told me I had to talk to your son Roy."

"Oh. You know why? Because I don't hear too good."

"Exactly. So we never had a conversation about this case. I simply told you that we were the police department and I needed to talk to you, and you said, 'You need to talk to my son.' And you went as far as to give me Roy's cell number."

"Oh now, well, maybe I did. I don't know."

"I know, because I had that conversation with you."

"Yeah?"

"Absolutely."

"All right."

"And we never, ever talked about this case."

"Now, somebody did."

Katie took her turn. She challenged Edna's assertion that Lloyd could not have committed the crime. Amid Lloyd's correspondence they had found a recent letter from Edna that began, "Hate to say this but if you did anything like they say you don't need to be out. . . . I need to whip your ass when you was a boy. So make it [prison] your home. You don't need to be out. A man do this to children need to be cut up like a pig and P out of a straw."

She admitted writing it.

"Yeah, but I was mad," she said.

"Okay? Mad about what?"

"Mad about all the accusations and stuff you-uns make, which we didn't know nothing."

"So the accusations we made, made you write a letter to Lloyd saying—"

"Well, maybe not you."

"Oh, it was me. I'm the one that's been at your house a couple of times."

Katie then said, "Okay. So you think he would do bad things so he should stay in prison, but you don't think he's capable of doing *this* bad thing."

"No," said Edna, simply, either rejecting Katie's characterization or embracing the distinction—it wasn't clear which.

"You can see why that would be confusing to us," said Katie.

"Well, you know, sometimes I'm confused about what I even write."

"Have you ever described this investigation as ridiculous?"

"Yes. Insane."

"Okay. What about it is ridiculous?"

"Because we had nothing to do with it."

"Has anybody ever said that you had something to do with it, or are they asking questions about—"

"Well, if you think—you, wait. Wait now. You're getting my goat here."

"All right," Katie said. "Bring it. Let's see it. Bring your goats. Tell me. I want to know, and the grand jury. What about this is ridiculous?"

"You want to know how I feel about the investigation?" Edna asked.

"I do."

"You're wasting your time."

Connie and Henry

In a way, Edna was right. Cold cases were more or less defined by wasted effort. When you weren't walking down well-trodden paths, you were pursuing leads so unpromising that others had long ago abandoned them. Yet evidence could emerge from anywhere, even from missteps. They had found Lloyd only because Chris was looking so hard at Ray Mileski. In their efforts to "tickle the wire," the detectives began to range more widely, visiting just about every Welch relative they could find in Virginia, Maryland, and elsewhere—Kim Pettas was living in South Dakota. The Bedford sheriff's office was plugging away at local clan members who appeared to be well outside the inner circle but who might have useful background knowledge. And it was here, on the least consequential edges of the probe—as these things happen—that the investigation at last found something important.

On September 17, two Bedford detectives knocked on the door of Connie Akers in nearby Salem. Connie was the only daughter of Lizzie Parker. She had grown up on Taylor's Mountain, and the detectives hoped she might give them a better picture of that homestead in 1975, and she did. Connie had seemingly distanced herself from the rest of the clan. After her parents died, she and her only remaining sibling, Henry, had had a falling-out over their inheritance and hadn't spoken in years. An articulate, fifty-five-year-old woman living with her husband in a nice suburban home, Connie was well dressed and well coiffed, with short gray hair that swept across her forehead, and wore fashionable glasses. And yet, as far removed from her hillbilly roots as Connie appeared, it turned out she was still surprisingly plugged in.

When she answered the door, she told the detectives forthrightly, "I know why you're here. Lloyd Welch."

The detectives told her that they were just trying to flesh out her family tree to get a better idea of who had been living on Taylor's Mountain in the 1970s. She said she had lived there then with her parents and her three brothers.

"Lloyd is a drifter," she said. "He would come and go. Mother always told me to stay away from him. So I did."

They chatted some more. Connie sketched the layout of the property, helping to pinpoint the location of the family's frequent bonfires. Then she announced that she had something they might want to know.

"Okay, I can tell y'all my story," she said. "I do remember Lloyd in 1975 coming to the house with his wife, or whatever she was. She was pregnant. It was warm weather. I remember getting clothes off the clothesline. He had a duffel bag with dirty clothes in it." Connie said the dirty clothes were caked with freshly dried blood. "He said they were bloody because he had ground beef in it. The only reason I remember it is he told me to wash his clothes, and I told him he could wash his own clothes."

That Connie remembered warm weather and Helen visibly pregnant pinned the encounter to the spring of the Lyon girls' disappearance. Given her distant relation to Lloyd, this was something she was not likely to have known without actually having encountered the couple, so it lent veracity to her account. But the real breakthrough was "freshly dried blood."

Otherwise, Connie seemed uninterested. She offered this single memory and that was it. She repeated that she had little or nothing to do with Lloyd or any of the other members of his immediate family. But the squad found something different on her Facebook account. Connie was conferring frequently with her Maryland cousins about the case. Soon after she was questioned, she wrote to Teddy's wife, Stacy, about what she had been asked and what she had said. She also phoned Pat and Dick's daughter Patricia Ann. She later wrote on Facebook to another cousin, Patricia Ann's daughter, Amy Johnson, and explained that her story was, in part, meant to absolve her uncle Dick. "I called Pat last night to let her know I talked to police," she wrote. "I know Dick did not bring him [Lloyd] down. He walked down with his pregnant girlfriend. That's for having our back."

What did she mean by that last line?

Connie provided her own explanation in another posting to Amy: "I'm really trying to help. I remember some things. I told them today that Dick didn't even go around Uncle Tommy [Teddy's father]. They didn't like each other. There is no way Dick helped anybody do anything bad."

The police also learned that Connie had reached out to her estranged brother, Henry, who was four years older and lived in nearby Roanoke. It was their first conversation in more than a year. She encouraged him to watch the TV news. There was detailed coverage of the police search on Taylor's Mountain. She told another cousin, but not the police, that Henry had been with her when Lloyd and Helen had arrived with the bloody duffel bag and that they had come not on foot but in a white car. The car was significant. A number of the Welch cousins recalled a vehicle that was variously described as a big white sedan or a green or yellow station wagon. Some said it belonged to Dick. Its automatic windows were memorably newfangled. The description of a station wagon, in particular, jibed with the old report phoned in by the IBM employee who had seen a blond child bound and gagged in one on his way to work.

Lloyd's bloody duffel bag, the car (or station wagon), and a raging fire suggested that the girls had been murdered and cut into pieces, stuffed into a bag or bags, and taken to Virginia to be incinerated. Connie and other neighbors remembered one bonfire that had lasted for days and had enveloped the mountain with a dreadful odor. This dovetailed with an odd statement Lloyd had made in the first interview, when asked to speculate on the girls' ultimate fate. He had said they had probably been *killed and burned*.

After learning that Connie had not been completely forthcoming, the squad sought to compel her full cooperation. She was subpoenaed by the Bedford grand jury in October, when, now under oath, she again told only part of what she knew. Recalled two months later, after having been warned of penalties for withholding information, she at last told the full story.

"He placed the duffel bag between the four of us," she said, referring to herself, Lloyd, Helen, and Henry. "It was packed enough to sit up on its own."

"Was the duffel bag ever opened in your presence while you were outside?"

"Yes, because I seen the bloody clothes on top." She described the blood as "like present blood bleeding, but it wasn't dried brown blood to be dried for weeks. So it was, like, a maroon color." She said it wasn't just a spot of blood, that there was "a lot." She said, "It smelled bad. I can remember it smelled bad."

"Smelled bad like anything in particular?"

"Rotten meat."

"What did you do?"

"I must have asked him, how did that happen? And he said that him and Helen were going to camp on the side of the road and that was from ground beef, ground beef that went bad."

The team encountered yet more reluctance from Henry, a frail, prematurely doddering man of fifty-nine with an advanced breathing disorder. He was tethered at all times to an oxygen tank. His ailment caused him to habitually retch up gobs of phlegm, which he expelled vigorously, either into a soiled handkerchief or, outdoors, freely and without much warning—every time he turned his head, Katie would ease away. Connie's other two brothers had died. In one of her Facebook exchanges with her cousin Amy, Connie confided, "My biggest fear is that my last family member Henry was part of it on the mountain." She had told the grand jury that her brother often hung out with Lloyd when the latter visited. When asked how Henry might have been involved, she said, "Henry wouldn't murder the child. He wasn't in Maryland. I meant help bury it. If he helped bury the bodies on the mountain."

"Why do you think Henry would bury the bodies on the mountain?"

"Because his momma would tell him to do it. We always did what Momma told us to do."

Henry had been questioned by the Bedford police on the same day they first visited Connie. He remembered Lloyd as a troublemaker, a thief, someone often in trouble with the law. Significantly, he said that when Lloyd had visited in 1975, there had been talk even then of his involvement in the Lyon sisters' case. This was almost forty years before Lloyd's name had been publicly linked to it. He said that before Lloyd showed up on Taylor's Mountain with "a heavyset girl" in "a big green car," he had heard "Mom and Dad talking about the [Lyon] kids coming up missing and stuff. And, them talking, saying they wouldn't put it past Lloyd to do something like that, so I don't know."

"Why did they link Lloyd with it?"

"Because of the news and everything and everybody talking about it, you know?'

"Back then?"

"Yeah."

"Was Lloyd's name out there then?"

"Yeah."

It had not been.

Before the October grand jury, Henry downplayed Lloyd's surprise visit. It was of so little note, he insisted, that he had almost no memory of it. He said Lloyd and Helen had left the day after they arrived—everyone else, including Lloyd, remembered a weeklong stay. He also recalled a phone call to his mother from Lloyd's father just after his arrival, specifically inquiring about the Lyon girls.

"He asked my mom did he have two kids with him. She said no. So that's all I heard about it."

This was startling and unexpected. When Mark and Katie paid Henry a visit the next day to question him further, he was annoyed. Coughing and wheezing, he protested, "I told y'all everything I knew. Ain't no more I can tell you. It's like y'all are harassing me now. I'm fed up with it."

But Henry knew a lot more. For his second grand jury testimony that December, he arrived with a black bag containing a portable oxygen pump connected to his nose by a plastic tube. He was stooped and looked beleaguered. Told there were discrepancies in his statements, he was warned that unless he sorted them out he would be in serious jeopardy. In a small interview room at the Bedford courthouse, Dave and Mark worked him over hard prior to his formal testimony. It was the only time in this case when Dave remembered losing his temper. He knew Henry was hiding something—Connie's testimony told them that—and he'd had enough. He accused Henry of being directly involved in the crime.

"Do you know what happened to those kids' bodies?" asked Dave.

"No, I do not know. I wish I knew; I would tell you!"

"Did Lloyd come down here to get rid of those two kids' bodies?" asked Mark.

Henry was shocked and frightened.

"I don't know what he did, honest to God! I don't know. He coulda had 'em in the trunk of his car. I don't know. I mean, he was gone for a while and then he came back." Henry speculated that Lloyd might have killed one of the girls with a tire iron on the drive down to Virginia, but emphasized that this was just conjecture.

"When he first got there, what did he have with him?" asked Dave.

"He had his girlfriend with him; that's all I know."

"What else did he have?"

"I don't know. He had some clothes with him as far as I know."

"This is where we're going with this," said Dave, alluding to the grand jury questioning that would shortly take place. "This is the stuff that we need you to tell."

"That's the only thing I seen is the old girl with him and his clothes."

"What were the clothes in?"

"A suitcase."

"A suitcase?"

"A suitcase or a bag or something. I don't remember."

"What color was the bag?"

"I don't remember that."

"Was it a big bag? A small bag?"

"I don't know. Honest to God. It's been so long ago."

"This is important. This is really important," said Dave. "This is for you. This isn't for us, because we already know what the answers are, but we are looking for you to tell us. Because you need to clean this up for yourself. The commonwealth attorney is not liking what he's hearing from these other folks. I'm just being straight with you. So, if you can help us undo this, you'll be helping yourself."

"I think he had a brown suitcase with clothes in it or a duffel bag, like an army duffel bag?"

"Like an army duffel bag," said Dave. "So now we're getting somewhere."

"It was like a brown or, from what I remember, or green, a light green."

"What was in this bag? This is important."

"Clothes was the only thing he said he had in it. Clothes."

"He needed to wash some clothes? Or he needed to do what with what was in that bag?"

Henry protested that he knew no more. Dave now exploded with impatience.

"It was full of bloody sheets and bodies!" he shouted. "It stunk! Connie fucking looked in it! And you were standing right there! And she said you walked away and helped Lloyd. For God's sake, Henry, we're trying to help you!"

"Hell no. Connie's wrong!" he said. "She's telling a fuckin' lie right there."

"Oh, no," said Dave. "She's going to testify to it."

"Oh my God!"

"Right! She's gonna testify to it."

"Oh my Lord."

"She's probably testifying right now."

"Oh my God."

"The same bag that you burned!"

"Oh God."

Henry now gave them a very detailed story, one that he had not spelled out in his interviews or during his first grand jury appearance. He repeated it later that day in formal testimony.

"It was a green duffel bag tied on the top [of the car]," he said. He described it as a big bag that placed on end reached up to his waist. It was cinched on top with drawstrings.

"Were you asked to do something with that duffel bag?"

"Yeah. We had a big fire outside, burning where we'd cleaned off some brush and stuff out in the garden we was going to have for next summer. We had a bunch of wood and stuff we had put up there to burn. And we was out there burning it. And he [Lloyd] said, 'I got some old clothes and stuff in this old duffel bag here.' He said that the old dog that had belonged to the girl that was with him, he said they had the car jacked up and the dog got underneath the car. Said the car rolled off and killed the dog. He told her that he'd bring it down there and bury the dog on the property there. And he said, 'Well, why don't we just throw it over in the fire and give it, like, an Indian burial?' "

Henry said the bag had red stains.

"He said it was transmission fluid, spilled in the trunk of his car."

"Mr. Parker, I want to caution you," the prosecutor said. "I want you to take your time, make sure you tell the grand jury exactly what you told the investigators, because they've got that on a recording."

"Right."

"Okay. Did you think that what was on the duffel bag was blood?"

"Could have been from the dog. I don't know."

"That's not what I asked you. At the time did you think it was blood?"

"Well, it could have been."

"Okay."

"I'm not saying that it was or it wasn't."

"How heavy was the duffel bag?"

"It was probably about seventy, eighty pounds, because he said the dog was a big dog."

"How many duffel bags did he have?"

"Well, we went out to the fire and throwed one in there. That one he throwed out I never did see that."

"Did your momma tell you to burn the duffel bag?"

"Well, she told me to take it out and burn it in the fire."

"The big, heavy one?"

"Yeah."

"Was anything in that bag when you burned it?"

"He said it was a dog. I never looked into the bag."

"Did he have the bag with him when you first saw him or did he have to go to the car and get the bag out of the car?"

"He had it sitting outside the car."

"Did you throw the duffel bag into the fire?"

"Well, I told him to get it where we could pitch it up in the fire, because it was awful hot, getting close to it."

"Did it take both of you to do that?"

"We swung it like this," moving his arms to demonstrate. "I said, 'Swing it and throw it up in the fire,' so it would be up in there."

Henry said Lloyd threw a second bag into the fire himself.

He was asked about the phone call between his mother and his uncle Lee. Henry told the grand jury that when his mother was on the phone, she exclaimed, "Oh my God!"

"I'm like, 'What is it, Momma?' She said 'You don't need to know. It's on a need-to-know basis.' "

He said later his mother explained to him what was going on.

"What exactly did your mother say?"

"She said it was two kids missing up there in Maryland and they were thinking he had the kids. It was about six months later after she told me, because she wouldn't discuss it with me."

Later in the same testimony, Henry elaborated: "She had said he had two kids, babysitting them that day, and then it was later that she said the two kids had been killed."

"Did your mother ever tell you what was in that bag?"

"No, she never did."

"Exactly what did your momma say?"

"Said it was two kids missing in Maryland and they were thinking that he had the kids."

"Okay."

"And they didn't know where they were at, and they were still looking for them."

"And that was when, how long after he left, that she told you that?"

"It was about six months later after she told me she wouldn't discuss it with me."

"Lloyd was still there though when you and him—obviously—threw the duffel bag into the fire."

"Yeah. Later that night—see, my dad stayed out there to keep the fire from getting away, you know. And Lloyd stayed out there with him the rest of the night tending to the fire."

"How long did the fire burn?"

"It burned for a day and a half."

Henry now said that Lloyd and Helen had stayed with them for about a week, sleeping on the living room floor. On further examination he said the duffel bag had smelled, "like something dead in it. It was a dog. And it was red on the outside of it. I didn't know how long he had had the dog in the car with him." He said the red substance on the bag was "sticky." Lloyd had dragged the bag over near the fire himself, and then Henry had helped him toss it up into the flames.

The detectives had reason to suspect that Henry had been more than just a helper. His sister had told them about his sexual interest in her as a child, including one preplanned assault from which she had escaped. And when they forced him to revisit the episode Henry seemed deeply troubled, to a degree they found surprising. Pressed by Katie about the bags and the fire, and told that Lloyd had implicated him, Henry had broken down.

"Just knowin' those babies wasn't taken care of like they should have been. I couldn't deal with it. If I had heard some babies like that I couldn't deal with it. I couldn't! Myself!" he said pointing to himself. "Oh God, no. I wouldn't be able to do it myself. I'd go kill myself. I'd jump off a damn bridge or somethin' somewhere."

9

Wanna Get High?

Lloyd Welch and Helen Craver

January 28, 2015

A bloody duffel bag, a bonfire, family phone calls from Maryland to Virginia linking Lloyd to the Lyon sisters—the mystery now had a terrible ending. This was not what the squad had been looking for when they zeroed in on the Welch clan, but it was huge. Amid all the man-hours and expertise and effort over the latter half of 2014, the Bedford sheriff's office, off on a tangent, had found powerful new evidence.

Lloyd had admitted being present when the girls were abducted, and now others had placed him squarely at the story's end, the disposal of bodies, or of at least one. The squad had always been coy with Lloyd about what they knew, mostly because they knew so little. Now, encountering him again early in 2015, they at last had something solid he had not told them.

Little had reached Lloyd about the extensive effort that had taken place over the previous half year. Teams of expert consultants had surveyed the wooded landscape of Taylor's Mountain on foot and from the air. Parts of it had been dug up and the soil sifted, work that continued. A persistent search had been made for a car that fit the description of the one used to deliver the duffel bags. If it had carried a bag as bloody as the one described, there might still be traces of the girls' DNA inside. It was not found. The location of the bonfire had been fixed, and the dirt there scooped out and sifted through screens. A fragment of charred human bone was found, along with scraps of singed fabric that might have been worn by the girls or come from the bags described by Connie and Henry. Melted fragments of beads were found that might have matched a necklace Kate had worn, and a piece of wire recovered might have matched the frame of Sheila's glasses. None of these items tested out convincingly. No DNA could be recovered from the bone. As with so many other leads in this case, these bits were suggestive but inconclusive. There was nothing distinctive enough to be considered evidence. In the end, they just confirmed that when you looked hard enough you found things that resembled what you were looking for.

This was true of everything except Connie and Henry. Here were two eyewitnesses to what appeared to be the story's bloody end, whose testimonies jibed, and who had offered them independently. Oddly, their reluctance to tell the full story augmented their credibility. Real evidence.

By January, Lloyd was back in the general prison population. Dressed again in white denim, he looked fitter and better groomed. The gray hair on the sides of his head had been trimmed so short he looked bald, and his white goatee was clipped close to his chin. He was again taken to the upstairs interview room at Dover police headquarters early in the morning. Dave came just before ten, carrying a manila folder and wearing a neatly pressed blue sweatshirt. They had not seen each other in six months.

"What's happening, stranger?" he greeted Lloyd.

"Well, look who it is!"

Dave set a cup of coffee on the table before Lloyd and then walked back out to ask a guard to remove the handcuffs and chains. When they shook hands, Dave grasped Lloyd's arm like an old friend. He promised that this time the coffee was hot, "black and all," just the way Lloyd liked it.

"What have you been up to?" Dave asked. "I see you're not in the orange."

"No, I'm surviving."

"Is it bad in there?"

"Yeah."

"Tell me what's going on."

"I mean, I've got my status back and everything, but I hate all this mouth from these guys. Shit comes on TV. They see it in the papers and shit like that. 'Oh yeah, that's that motherfucker; he's the one who did it,' you know? So I keep my door shut and stay to myself."

He said he'd had a few "little threats" but no attacks. There had been grumblings when stories appeared about the grand jury and the dig on Taylor's Mountain. He knew that his uncle Dick had been named as a person of interest in October and that in December his aunt Pat had been indicted. That had all been reported on TV.

Dave told him that he looked good.

"I'm tryin' to stay positive," said Lloyd.

"I think we're at a good spot," said the detective. "I really do. And that's why we came back. It has been six or seven months. We wanted to talk. We wanted to share with you all of the things—that day we left here, every day since then, I kid you not, including weekends and nights, we've been working on this thing. And I brought a lot of stuff to share with you. I've got a lot of questions for you. There are no charges. I know that's always a concern when we meet."

"Right."

Dave repeated this a few more times. He wanted to make sure Lloyd didn't spook. He called the legal problems encountered by Dick and Pat "unfortunate," and reinforced the idea that all of Lloyd's relatives were out to get him. Pat had been caught lying, although about what Lloyd was unclear.

"Okay. I'm here as a sex offender. I understand that. So, yeah, they're going to say, 'He did it.'"

"There's some things that we need to work out between us," said Dave, "and I think this can be a good outcome, a real positive outcome."

Lloyd suddenly made a point of saying that he had been only seventeen in March 1975. The age of majority in Maryland was eighteen. As a seventeen-year-old, he might be able to avoid being charged as an adult, but math was not one of Lloyd's strengths. "I'm fifty-eight now," he said. "I just turned fifty-eight in December, okay?" That much was true, but if he had turned fifty-eight in 2014, it meant he had turned eighteen in 1974.

Dave didn't argue with him. He was focused on very specific things—Teddy, the duffel bags, and Uncle Dick. Teddy's broken arms and the bloody duffel bags undermined two critical parts of Lloyd's story. Teddy had almost certainly not been involved in the abduction, and Lloyd, who always said he had fled at the first sight of the girls being abused and had never returned, had in fact helped dispose of their remains. Rather than confront him outright, the detective was going to lead him to these contradictions step by step, without showing his hand. He started with Teddy.

"Do you remember when you guys were in the mall or the ride over or the ride back, however you remember it, do you remember if there's anything wrong with him [Teddy], like, physically wrong with him?"

"Besides being gay?"

Lloyd got a good laugh over this.

"No. Well, other than that. Like, was he injured or anything like that, that might have prevented him from doing something? Was there physically something wrong with him that you could actually see?"

Lloyd, ever agile, offered, "I mean, he did have a limp. He kind of hunched over a little bit, but I didn't see no injuries on him."

"He claimed—and it was kind of hard to prove it—that he had two broken arms during that time period. So, we're like, how can you prove it? We were able to go back and get hospital records, and then we were fortunate enough to get a picture of him." Actually, Teddy had done these things himself.

"Humph!" Lloyd snorted emphatically. "Yeah, I heard about him being pushed off a building, but I didn't see no cast on his hands or arms or anything like that, 'cause, I mean, he had a jacket on, so I didn't really."

"Right, but you would think you would have known. And I don't care. It doesn't hurt in any way." Dave said that Teddy believed Lloyd had thrown him into the story for reasons of his own.

"Nah," said Lloyd. "I didn't throw him in. He was there that day. I'll take a Bible and put it right there in front of me—like I said, I'm a Christian now—and he was there that day because he's the one that offered me a ride home. He's the one who said, 'How you getting home?' I said I was going to hitchhike home, and he said, 'Well, we'll give you a ride home.'"

Dave reminded Lloyd that this—along with his most recent account, from the July session—overlooked his earlier and oft-repeated insistence that Helen had been with him at the mall.

Lloyd didn't miss a beat. "She was there for a while that day. But she left because she was going to her mom's house, and I was gonna meet her back at the house, and she asked me to get some ice cream for her because she was pregnant. You know, she wanted to see her mom."

This, once more, elided significant parts of Lloyd's original story that could now be regarded only as completely false—getting on the bus with Helen, his remarking to her about the car he'd seen leaving with the girls, and so on. Lloyd made such edits to his story without hesitation or concern and with no apparent sense of how false it made him appear. Dave moved on. He asked Lloyd to talk about the couple's carnival travels. Struck by how worried Lloyd apparently had been about Helen's memory, Katie had come up with the idea of telling him that his old girlfriend had kept a journal. It wasn't true, but Lloyd wouldn't know that. They would confront Lloyd with some of the things they had gleaned from the wiretaps, presenting them as entries in Helen's journal, which would give them more impact. Lloyd rarely pushed back for long against demonstrable truth. His slippery stories were built around the known facts.

Dave said, "And y'all did some things—and I'm not pointing fingers—it's just that we went and talked to her current husband and she jotted a few things down that you all had done together. She made mention of a green station wagon and about how you broke into a house and stole a gun and a badge. It's just things that we have read through her journal."

Police records showed that Lloyd, during one of his youthful robberies, had stolen a police badge and in another had taken a green station wagon. Since the press conference, the squad had been contacted by other women who, as children, had been approached by a man at Wheaton Plaza in the months before the Lyon sisters disappeared. They said the man had flashed an official-looking badge. And the station wagon appeared in Lloyd's stories, in the IBM man's tip, and in the testimonies of Connie and Henry.

Lloyd looked mystified.

"Stole a gun and a badge? Stole a green station wagon?"

"No, she didn't say you stole it, just that y'all were driving around in a green station wagon."

Lloyd fell silent. Finally, he nodded and smiled broadly.

"That wasn't a green station wagon, that was a SUV," he said. It was green, but it had been a Jeep.

The detective asked again about the vehicle his uncle Dick had been driving when they left the mall. "It was definitely a station wagon? It couldn't have been any other type of car that Dick had?"

"He had a couple of cars, but he was always driving a station wagon every time I saw him."

Dave asked what kind of work his uncle Dick did. The squad had learned that he worked as a security guard but not at Wheaton Plaza. This might also explain the stories about a man with a badge.

"You are probably thinking to yourself, these are kind of weird questions because we have the whole background," Dave explained. "We've got the beginning. I think we've got the end. We're missing the middle." Dave said Lloyd's family, those who were still living, had "taken and built the circle around you, and they basically put you in the middle of it, and they're pointing their fingers at you. You actually said that when we left here—'You're gonna go back and talk to him [Dick], and he's gonna say, I ain't got nothin' to do with this.' And that's what happened. And what they've done is, either through computers or phones, they've tried to develop the story, and we're trying to discredit some of this." In other words, *We're on your side.* "Your entire family has made up this story and it all falls on you. And I said, 'Well, wait a minute'—because there are people out there that have said, 'Well, shit, let's just let it all fall where it may'—and I said, 'No, no, that's not right. That's not the right thing to do.'" Dave was suggesting that others—his colleagues or superiors—wanted to charge Lloyd based on what they had learned. As Lloyd's champion, he was battling his hostile family and impatient prosecutors. "We're not here because we want to lock the world up. We're here for answers, and we're not gonna get the answers if we shut the door."

"Yeah," Lloyd agreed.

"We've got to keep that door open. We've got to keep the communication going between us, because it's obvious to me that your whole family knows. The whole family knows. Now, what they know and what their involvement is, it's gonna be hard, but it's got to come from you."

"Well, see, the one thing is I can't tell you who all's involved and who all's not involved because I really don't know. All I know is, Dickie was driving the car, Teddy was there talkin' to them girls." Lloyd was not about to drop Teddy from his account. He said, "If you look at it, he wasn't a bad-lookin' kid back then."

"Right. And neither were you."

This startled Lloyd.

"I mean, you were a good-looking man. I've heard that from several people."

Lloyd shrugged and laughed.

"We've got pictures of you in your younger years."

Lloyd said that he didn't flirt with other girls. He admitted eyeing little girls in the mall and talking to the Lyon sisters but said he had always been loyal to Helen. This was disturbing and revealing, and Lloyd seemed unaware of what it implied. It had come up several times. Helen was a twenty-two-year-old woman, pregnant with his child. He was eighteen. The girls in the mall he admitted ogling had been prepubescent, and yet, in Lloyd's view—today as well as then—they were already sexual objects in the same way Helen was, potential rivals. He equated chatting with a grade-schooler with flirting or potentially cheating on Helen. But he was just warming up for his newest argument.

"One, how could I have gotten them out of the mall?" he asked. "How could I have gotten 'em away from the mall without those two girls screamin' and kickin'? Now, what that boy [Teddy] said to them girls to get them to go outside, I have no idea."

"You have to have wondered what happened," said Dave. "Like, were they in Dick's house for two days, a week, two weeks? Where did they end up? What did those clowns do with them? Was there more than Dick and Teddy having sex with them? 'Cause that's pretty prevalent in your family. I mean, there's no other way to put it."

"Yeah."

"It didn't matter who you were or what you were, it just happened and it was accepted."

"Right."

Dave had taken the liberty of substituting Dick's house for Leonard Kraisel's. The logic in Lloyd's original version of where the girls had been taken was grounded in Teddy's relationship with the older man. The squad now knew that the relationship had not started until years later. If Dick had been driving the car, however, it was reasonable to assume that the destination basement would have been in *his* house, so Dave just went with it, and Lloyd didn't dispute it.

The detective next began edging the conversation toward Taylor's Mountain. Lloyd entered into another rambling account of his visit back to the mall to bear false witness—he said he still could not remember the actual police interview, recalling only that he had been "fucked up" and "scared." When he'd returned from that, he decided to leave town.

"I said [to Helen], 'We need to go, man.' I told her what I knew and said we need to go. She said, 'Where are we going to go?'"

"Where did y'all go?"

"Just traveling. South Carolina and Florida. I don't remember all the other places we went. I always like warm weather." They discussed various places Lloyd had visited or lived in over the years, and eventually Lloyd came around to mentioning Virginia.

"I went to Thaxton when I was a kid two or three times with Helen. We stayed there for a while because I really liked the area a lot."

"It's beautiful," said Dave.

"It was beautiful. We'd stay for a while, and then me and Helen would leave. Last time I was there it was with Helen."

"Do you remember about when it was?"

"Seventy-six, seventy-seven, somewhere around there. Seventy-eight."

"How long did you stay when you were down there?"

"Couple weeks."

"And who do you typically stay with when you go down?"

"We stayed at Artie's. Right there at that big old house right up there on the mountain."

"Is it possible that you and Helen showed up down in Thaxton right after this incident, just to get away from those family members and this crazy madness that was going on?" asked Dave. "Because you said you left. You had to get the hell out of there. Is it possible?"

"It could be. I mean, it's possible we went there first. I don't know."

"It's important. I want you to think about that. I ain't saying you did anything wrong. I'm saying there may be some . . . the way people are trying to paint this is, 'It was all him; he showed up, he did this; he did that.' And I'm thinking the way this is gonna play out. It's tough for me to gauge, so I need you to kind of interact with me a little bit about this."

Lloyd learned here that his Virginia relatives had talked about his 1975 visit, and, true to form, he did not contradict real evidence.

"It's a very strong possibility that we went there first," he said. "We hitchhiked down there, stayed a week or two. Oh yeah. It's a strong possibility."

"You hitchhiked everywhere?"

"We hitchhiked everywhere."

"How did you carry your shit?"

"Duffel bag."

"Do you remember what the bag looked like?"

"Yeah, it was a green duffel bag. It was my old army duffel bag. That son of a bitch was packed, too. People go to pick that up to help throw it in the car, and they're like, 'Oh my God!'" This comment was telling, confirming Henry's description of the bag as heavy, about seventy pounds.

"Who would normally pick you up?"

"Truck drivers. Christian people. Christian vans. You know, people like that. Just hippies. That's what we were called back then, a hippie."

"Where did y'all eat or lay your head down in between?"

Curiously, Lloyd said they slept "in the car."

"How would you typically eat, use the bathroom, shower?"

"Restaurants. We'd eat at some of the restaurants. Some of the Christians, they would give us money to eat. We'd wash up in the bathrooms, pull into a gas station."

"You didn't have any pets or anything like that?"

"No."

"No cats, no dogs, nothing?"

"No."

So much for the two explanations Lloyd had given Henry and Connie for the blood on his bag—they did not carry or prepare food (the "ground beef" in Connie's story) and did not travel with a dog.

"What some of the folks down there have said is that you and Helen show up with a big green duffel bag, the army bag, and there's something in it."

"Yeah, it was my clothes."

"Was there something wrong with your clothes when you showed up down there?"

"Got rained on a couple of times, so they'd be soaking wet."

"Anything else?"

"No."

"They weren't dirty, like mud-stained? Have any transmission fluid or antifreeze on it or anything of that nature?"

Lloyd said no. He said the clothes would start to smell after a while, need laundering.

"So there would be no reason that the bag would have been tossed in a fire?"

"No."

"None at all?"

"No. I kept that bag for a long time. Shit, me and Helen had that bag, damn, we had it when we went all the way down to Florida and my last daughter was born."

"So Henry never destroyed that bag?"

"Hell no. Ain't nobody ever destroyed it."

"This is the type of stuff that has been put out there," said Dave. "They're pointing fingers. I think you know where I'm going with this."

"I had bodies in there," said Lloyd, grinning and laughing. "Come on!"

"That's where they're going with that."

Lloyd leaned back and laughed heartily. "Oh, that's a good one."

"We can't make this stuff up," said Dave, humoring Lloyd. "I mean, this is the stuff that they're testifying to."

"Wow. So they're saying that I killed those two girls."

"I didn't say you killed them."

"Well, they're saying that."

"That you showed up down there."

"With a duffel bag with Helen that had two bodies in it and threw 'em on the fire?"

Dave nodded.

"Come on. If he threw them in the fire and there was bodies in there, they'd stink like bodies."

Dave said that Lloyd's cousins had in fact described the smell: "Like burning rats."

Lloyd shook his head. "Boy, that's the best one I heard yet."

The God's Honest Truth

Lloyd showed no alarm, but he must have felt cornered here. Dave told him the full story related by Connie and Henry, under oath. Lloyd saw how damaging this was.

"Wow," he said.

This was going to require some major tinkering with his story, and Dave was there to help.

"I try to come in here with the best judgment," the detective said. "I look at it as, okay, seventeen-, eighteen-, nineteen-year-old boy at the time. You're in the mall. You get back to Hyattsville. You see what you see. You're part of the family. They did what they did. Now all of the sudden they put it on you, and who's to say you knew what was in the bag? Who's to say they didn't put the bag in the trunk of the car, and Dick drove you and Helen down there and told you to take it and put it on the fire, with Henry and you not having any knowledge of what was in the bag? You see what I'm saying?"

He was showing Lloyd how to endorse the evidence without admitting he had *willingly* burned a body.

"They could have completely used you, as a nineteen-year-old kid, and it's stuff that we need to clean up. I'm not sure what your involvement and role was, or was it just that you were played as you're being played now, and that's what we're left with."

Lloyd just nodded and grunted affirmatively as he listened. He wasn't buying it.

"Well, when me and Helen went down there, nobody took us down there," he said. "There was no bloody bag or bodies or anything like that. That bag did not weigh no seventy or eighty pounds. That bag probably wasn't any more than twenty-five, thirty pounds. It had her clothes and my clothes in there, and that's all. Oh, it had my razor and, you know, her little makeup [kit]. I'm telling you—and I've never been straight before with you until recently—I'm telling you the God's honest truth. There was no bag with blood, bodies on the fire, and it was not our bag. If there was, that's them, not me."

If the subject matter had not been so grave, it would have been laughable. Lloyd was invoking past lies to sell his current probity: *You can trust me now because I admit I was lying then.*

"Do you remember Dick coming down during that period of time?" he asked. "How can we explain this bag?"

"I do remember me and Helen being woked up at night, hearing a car pull up, but I didn't get out of bed or anything like that. I don't know who it was."

"Do you remember if there was a fire going, like, for a couple of days during that time you were 'woke up'?"

"Could have been. I mean it was dark out. It was like one or two in the morning." Lloyd told him where on the property the fire would have been. He said he thought they were probably just burning brush.

Dave told him about Henry's memory of a phone call to his mother from Lloyd's father, and of Lee's asking whether the two girls were there.

"My dad called?"

"Yeah."

"That's a crock of shit."

"I'm just telling you what they—"

"Yeah." Lloyd shook his head.

"I mean, I can't make this shit up," said Dave.

"Boy, I tell you, they're really trying to bury me, ain't they?"

"Oh yeah. And that's what I mean, why when I came in here I said these are gonna be some hard questions and hard answers. Because this is what people have come up with. And there's gotta be a way we can undo this, because not only have they testified, but about two weeks ago in a certain area on this property, we found the fire and we found what we believe were human remains that were burned."

"You found the fire? Wow." Lloyd began laughing quietly to himself.

"I mean we can't undo the fact that you were at the mall, you saw the girls."

"Yeah, I admitted to that."

"But we haven't made it to the point where they're in Virginia and they're being burned. So, somewhere in between, someone in this family took those girls down to Bedford and burned them."

"What car did I drive?" Lloyd asked.

"That's—"

"I was seventeen years old." Lloyd explained that he didn't own a car at the time and that whenever he had stolen a car he'd been caught immediately. "And my dad called down there and said me and Helen's coming down there?"

Dave said these were things they had been told.

Lloyd again denied it, but the detective defended the story.

"These two [Connie and Henry] came up with this story independent of each other. They hate each other. They haven't talked in years. There's a hatred to the point where they had to be separated in the courtroom. That's how bad they hated. This all has to do with money. Property, wills . . . it's a dispute. Someone had to have showed up down there for them both to say the same thing, and I'm not saying it was you." Connie and Henry, of course, had said it was Lloyd. "So, who else would have had access to a green duffel bag? Help me out here. Who in your opinion would have taken this thing? Because I think it's unrealistic to think, it's almost impossible to think, and I'm just saying this hypothetically, that you killed one or two of those girls, put them in a bag to where they started to decompose with blood leaching out of them—because that's what they described—that you can do this on the side of the road and get into somebody's car with that smell. There's no way."

"There's no way possible," Lloyd agreed. "No."

So long as he adhered to his hitchhiking story, it kept him well removed from a bag stuffed with decomposing body parts. He now suggested that perhaps Teddy had concocted this story and fed it to Connie and Henry. Dave showed him pictures of cars, and Lloyd picked out a station wagon that his uncle Dickie drove. "That was, like, his baby," he said. He was always washing it, keeping it clean. He said the car was more of a yellow color than green.

They took a lunch break, and when Dave returned he got Lloyd to walk through the events of that day at the mall once more. Lloyd repeated his most recent version of the story: leaving the mall with Dick, Teddy, and the girls, the younger girl crying softly in the back seat; getting out at the convenience store to get ice cream for Helen; going back to Dick's house (he had smoothly incorporated Dave's version of where the girls had been taken); seeing his uncle raping one of the girls; going to the mall to give his false statement; and then leaving for

Virginia. Once he and Helen were there, after hitchhiking down, someone arrived in a car, waking him up. He didn't know who it was. He said he heard a man and a woman outside in conversation.

Lloyd said the bonfire had been burning when they got there and was still burning when they went to bed. He also said he had been "scared shitless" when he left for Virginia.

"I mean, I've seen Dick mad before. You know? I've seen him mad. And I didn't want to be nowhere around in case he knew that I actually did see him on top of this girl. You know?"

"Do you think there's any way that Dick or somebody could have brought down one or two? One was burned and maybe the other one was still left alive and somebody else down there did something to them?"

"I can't say. I don't know. I mean, well, possible. I last saw them at his house and that was the last time I saw him. I really didn't know what was going on. I mean, I put two and two together a little bit here, but I didn't think anyone was gonna be hurt, that they were gonna be hurt or anything like that."

"Well, tell me what you put together. It's important to try to figure out how this thing kind of—"

"I just kind of figured, why would my uncle, when he's got a nice-lookin' wife, be with a young girl? I don't know. Maybe he's just trying to live his youth or whatever. You know? I guess I didn't hear right in my mind because at that time, I wasn't thinking about molesting any girls or anything like that. That didn't happen until years later, and I don't know why that happened. I guess whatever snapped. I just thought it was kind of strange that he was with one of them, and she wasn't screaming or anything like that, so I couldn't say if it was mutual at the time or if he was forcing himself and just wore her out or what."

"What if he choked her out?"

"That could have been. I mean, her eyes were closed. She wasn't looking at me or anything like that. Her eyes were closed, so I don't know if he had her drugged up, you know, or what. I didn't see the other girl, so I didn't know where she was at."

"Probably beat her with something," said Dave.

"Could have. I don't know."

"And she was the one in the bag, unfortunately," said Dave, speculating.

"Like I said, I got scared shitless and I left. Didn't want no part of it, and to this day I still don't want no part of it. I mean, if I actually had to get up on the stand and testify what I saw to prove my innocence, I would do it. Right in front of him."

"Yeah, I mean, look what they've done to you."

Lloyd continued to assert his innocence. "Even if you offered me freedom and charges dropped, I still couldn't tell you what happened to those girls and where they're at. Because I had no part in it. I didn't touch them. I didn't walk them out of the mall. I didn't do none of that."

Dave now returned to Helen's journal, Katie's fiction.

"There was some stuff in there, Lloyd, but she's not here to explain it. There was stuff in there about the station wagon with the seats laid back. There was stuff in there about you hurting kids and she felt bad about it. So, you read it for what it is. It could have been out of frustration."

"I believe it was," said Lloyd.

"Or there is truth to it. If someone would just stand up and say, 'Look, this is what the fuck happened!'" Dave banged his hand on the desk. "Then we could go back and figure it out, but that's not what's going on. They're giving these little pieces because they want to remove themselves," which was, of course, exactly what Lloyd was doing. Dave asked him to explain what he thought had happened.

"I think Uncle Dick killed them. I honestly do. Out of frustration, anger, or whatever, you know? Maybe they didn't do what he wanted them to do, and he killed them."

"How long do you think that they were alive?"

"Honestly, I don't know. I can't say if he got rid of them that day that I saw them, the next day. I know my dad used to go over there a lot."

"And, see, that's the stuff that we need to know, because they're testifying that he's the one that called Lizzie."

"He probably did," said Lloyd, accepting what, minutes earlier, he had dismissed as "a crock of shit."

Lloyd was distinctly uncomfortable. He no doubt could feel the probe closing in, and he was still evading, but for once he seemed unsure of his next move.

This Conversation Is Over With

After four hours, Dave left and Katie stepped in. She buttered Lloyd up at length, going on about how much better a person he was than the rest of his family, how much more cooperative he was. Then she pleaded with him to help himself by helping them. They were on his side!

Lloyd listened politely and held fast.

Mark joined them. He sat in a chair alongside Lloyd, facing him, and for a while he just listened to Katie's efforts. Then he started showing Lloyd photos of the materials found at the burn site. The evidence, he said, corroborated the stories his cousins had told.

"We just want the truth," said Katie. "None of us want to keep doing this."

That much was true. The investigation had taken over her life to such an extent that it was causing problems at home. She had left off working on child-abuse cases because they were emotionally exhausting, only to be drawn into the worst case of her career. It was consuming her, stealing part of her soul. She had begun working with a therapist to deal with it. She hadn't told the department about that; she was paying for the therapy herself. Her physical health had suffered. She blamed it on the long hours and the stress. As a mother, she looked at Mary Lyon and could not imagine being in her place. But she took pains not to let any of this show, especially to her colleagues. Before Lloyd, everything she did and said was a performance.

"Look, this is a race," she told him. "We've got all these people that have something to lose at this point. Whoever gets over the finish line first, meaning whoever's gonna come and just break and tell us the truth first, is the one that is in the best position. Everybody is starting to crumble."

Lloyd said he knew nothing more.

Then Mark used a different approach, something they had not tried. He had catalogued Lloyd's lies. The list was nothing short of astonishing.

"I would ask you to think, as I say this, put yourself in a position of a reasonable person. You're a reasonable guy. But if you are a reasonable person listening to this case, what would you think when I get to the end?"

He then reviewed the list, item by item. Lloyd kept trying to interrupt, but Mark wouldn't let him. It was extensive. It started with the original 1975 story, which Lloyd had admitted at the time was mostly a lie. Then there was one he'd made up in his first conversation with Dave. "You say, 'I was never at Wheaton Plaza. I never talked to any police. I don't remember any of that.'"

"No, I said I was there that day."

"No, you initially said that you weren't."

Then there was the failed polygraph administered by Katie. Then it was telling Dave that the kidnappers were Teddy and the older man he lived with. When it was pointed out that Teddy had been just eleven, Mark continued, "you finally come around and say, 'Okay, it was Dick that was with us. Dick was driving the car.'"

Then Mark reminded Lloyd that he had said he thought the girls had been raped, killed, and burned.

"Do you remember saying that?"

"I didn't say raped and burned."

"You did."

"I said raped and killed."

"You said they were probably raped and burned."

"No, I didn't. No."

"Lloyd, I've never lied to you, and I'm not going to."

"Okay. So, when are you all going to charge me?"

"Just hear me out." Mark then explained how their investigation in Virginia confirmed, in fact, that at least one body had been burned.

"Now, again, reasonable person, Lloyd. Two people who haven't talked to each other in two years who get hit up cold by the police and come up with those kind of details on the same story?"

"I'll say it again, when are you charging me?" asked Lloyd, who was growing increasingly agitated. He sat with his arms folded, coiled.

Mark went on, "And now all of the sudden we find human bones in that same location? In addition to those bones, we find material consistent with a green army duffel bag. We find this piece of wire"—he pointed to a photo on a sheaf of paper on the desk—"which is consistent with the wire that was in that girl's wire-framed glasses. We find these beads that are melted together, and we know that one of the girls was wearing a beaded necklace. We find this button from a pair of pants that are the same kind of pants that one of the girls was wearing." In fact, Mark was deliberately stretching the truth here. None of these scraps could be linked to a duffel bag or to what Sheila or Kate had worn, but Lloyd didn't need to know that. "So we've got a problem here, Lloyd."

"Your problem is that I didn't do nothing to those girls."

"Lloyd, you can explain away each little piece, but when you have to explain away everything, what's the reasonable person [going to] think?"

"Well, you all think I did it. I mean, let's be for real."

Mark said he knew that Lloyd left the mall with the girls, and also that he had been on the mountain at the same time they had been tossed into the fire.

"Now, what happened in between is what I'm hoping you can help us figure out, because those two things are fact."

Lloyd now offered, at last, something new. He said his trip to Bedford with Helen was prompted by his fear of his uncle Dick.

"He knew that I knew that he had them," said Lloyd.

"If you are so scared and so upset, why did you go back to the mall and risk being put right in the middle of it?" asked Katie.

"I had a little bit of conscience, a little concern."

"But then you misled them."

Lloyd nodded. She was right; this made no sense. If he were concerned about the girls, why lie to the police?

"Every time we jump a little hurdle with you, your face slams in the mud," she said.

"I felt that if I gave a lie that maybe it would eventually come out," Lloyd explained, unconvincingly.

"But how does that ease your conscience?" asked Mark. "By putting the police on the wrong trail? It makes it worse!"

"I don't know. I was a druggie back then. I was an alcoholic. And I've told you all that I can tell you. I'm gonna say it for the last time, charge me. I'll get a lawyer, go from there. If not, I did not do nothin' to those girls. I don't want to be charged for something I didn't do."

"Then help us sort it out and help us figure out who did what."

Lloyd was fed up.

"Okay. I'm on state property," he said. He stood abruptly, walked to the door, opened it, and spoke to the guard in the hallway. "I'm ready to go, sir. This conversation is over with." Mark leaned back in his chair and grimaced. Then he and Katie stood and started gathering their papers.

"Oh, that's unfortunate, Lloyd," said Katie.

But Lloyd abruptly closed the door and returned to his seat. He was in too deep to walk out. Katie worked to salvage the situation.

"We're sitting here trying to give you the benefit of the doubt," she said. "The last thing we want to do is pin this on somebody who didn't do it."

Katie sometimes tried to simply overwhelm Lloyd. She would start talking, throwing out ideas, her words flowing in great improvisational gusts, easing from one concept to the next, alternately flattering, reasoning, bargaining, confronting, empathizing. Mark called it her superpower; he joked that sometimes suspects would confess just to shut her up. Katie turned it on full bore now. She invoked Lloyd's children, who, she said, wanted this all to be over. She talked about mistakes she had made in her own life. She was somebody who *knew* mistakes. Life, she said, was about learning and moving on . . .

She was still at it when the session passed the six-hour mark. It was a magnificent torrent of cajolery, all of it delivered earnestly and with a straight face.

And finally, Lloyd, as he did at all these sessions, caved in. He sighed heavily, and, interrupting Katie's monologue, which showed no signs of slowing down, he asked the question he always asked before offering something new.

"Okay. Let me ask you this question before—I didn't mean to cut you off. If I sit here and tell you from day one what went down to day two, what's gonna happen to me?"

Don't Worry, You're in Good Hands

Lloyd didn't give the detectives time to respond. Apparently, as he listened to Katie, he had worked out how to modify his story.

"First of all, I didn't kill 'em," he said.

"Okay," said Katie.

"I didn't burn 'em."

"Okay."

"It was not my green bag. It was Lee's bag out of his trunk."

This was new. He had now brought his late father into the mix.

"Okay," Lloyd said, "I did not do that. I can tell you who did."

"Okay."

"What's gonna happen to me?"

"Well, why would anything happen to you?" Katie asked. "If you didn't do the crime?"

"Because I was involved. I was at the mall."

"You asked Dave the same question last time right before you told us about Dick, and I'm gonna give you the same answer that Dave gave you. We can't answer that question for you until we know what your role was and if you were involved in killing them."

"I wasn't involved in killing them, and I wasn't involved in raping them."

"Okay."

Lloyd still insisted that Teddy had lured the girls from the mall. The rest of his story was the same, too, but he revised his account of the car that arrived on Taylor's Mountain early in the morning. He now said that he knew who was in it.

"Dickie came down," he said. "It was about one, one thirty [in the morning]. There was somebody else in the car. I don't know who else was in the car. There was a big ol' fire going, and I seen Dickie and Henry grab a bag and walk over to the fire and throw it in. Me and Helen, after that, said it was time for us to book out, and we left. What was in that bag, to my mind, was the girls."

"Both of them?"

"I don't know if it was both of them or one of them. I honestly don't know. All I know is, yes, me and Ted did pick them up [at Wheaton Plaza]."

"Tell us how that went down," said Mark.

"Just asked them if they wanted to get high, and they said yeah."

"Now, how did that happen?" Mark asked. "Did you approach them inside the mall first? Outside?"

"We saw 'em go in. We tried to catch them and ask 'em if they wanted to get high before they got all the way into the mall, but we didn't get a chance to get to them, so I guess that's why they saw me watching, because I was trying to see who they were hooking up with and where they were going. So I guess that's why everybody said they saw me watching them. We were gonna party, that's all, but I guess you could say in the long run, I got scared and I didn't want any. I told Ted and them, I said I didn't want anything to do with it. Dick did take us all back to his house. I did get out at the store, and I didn't want anything to do with it. I was scared."

"Who set this up from the beginning?" Katie asked.

"Dick, I believe."

"So you guys were at Dick's house when this went down?"

"Yeah, he said he had some pot."

"Okay, let me ask you this before I forget. Was he dressed in a certain way?"

"He had his security uniform on."

"Dick did?"

"Yeah."

This was plausible, both the uniform and the pitch about smoking pot. In 1975, marijuana was a craze. It had moved aggressively from black America and the fringe hippie subculture to white suburbia. Many youngsters, especially teenagers, were eager to try it. This new version of the story was believable in another way. Grabbing two girls had been carefully premeditated. In Lloyd's earlier version, Teddy had just happened on the Lyon sisters. Dick sending Lloyd into the mall (Teddy's involvement, despite what Lloyd said, was highly doubtful) to lure the girls made more sense, especially with what the team had learned about Welch men. Dick's uniform also made sense.

"He said it would be easier," explained Lloyd. "The girls would probably not be as scared."

The uniform also would have made it less likely for a bystander to intervene if the girls had objected or tried to pull away.

"So, did you guys formulate this plan?" Katie asked. "How is this set up?"

"It took two days for them to talk me into going into this plan," said Lloyd. "He [Dick] said, let's go party with some young girls."

"Okay."

"You know?"

"And 'party' to you means he was gonna have sex with them probably."

"Get high and shit like that. To me, back then, partying was gettin' high, drinkin', you know."

"So that's a way to buy you in, because you were part of that scene?"

"He just said, 'Look, I'll drive you up to the mall. I've got some pot. Just find a couple of girls that look like they might want to party or something like that, bring them on out, [we'll] bring them back to my place, we'll get high, we'll have a little sex.'"

There were shopping centers closer to Dick's house, but Lloyd said they chose Wheaton Plaza because it was farther away. It was less likely that they would be seen by anyone who knew them. Lloyd still insisted that Teddy was part of this plan and that he must have been wearing a coat or a jacket that covered his arms.

"He drops you guys off," said Katie. "How long did it take you to find the girls? Convince the girls?"

"About an hour, hour and a half at the most. We went walking around. Like I said, we saw those two go in, and we said, 'Hey, how about them two? They look like they might get high,' or something like that. And then I guess you can say we followed them around, starin' at them or whatever to see who they were hooking up with."

"So the whole story about Helen is not true?" said Katie.

"Yeah. Helen wasn't there."

"Okay."

"Yeah, and the job thing. I was gonna go up there and put in applications, but I didn't that day."

"What do you say to the girls to get them to come out?"

"We asked them if they wanted to get high. If they liked to party. They didn't say no. They didn't say yeah. They didn't say anything. They said, 'I don't know, let's see.' "

"And they just follow you guys?"

"Well, they walked out with us."

"And at some point, you've been very clear from day one that the little one starts crying. What makes her start crying?"

"I guess she got scared when she saw an older person in the car."

"Does he say anything to them?"

"Alls he said was, 'Don't worry, you're in good hands.' "

At that point Lloyd reverted to his old version of the story. He got in the back with Kate. Teddy and Dick sat in the front on either side of Sheila. They drove around, he said, for about two hours, which seemed inordinately long, but Katie let it pass. When he told Dick he wanted out, his uncle turned around and gave him a dirty look, "like, *Don't say anything.*"

"So you know in your gut that shit ain't right," said Mark.

"Right."

"Because this is a planned situation. Of course, they have no idea that they are going to be killed and burned."

Lloyd said that when they were all still in the car, Dick made a comment about the girls, "Going to meet their Maker."

"That's one of the main reasons why I got scared and got out of the car."

Lloyd said that when Dick showed up on Taylor's Mountain more than a week later, he was driving the same station wagon—it was yellow according to Lloyd. After Dick and Henry threw the heavy bag onto the fire, his uncle drove away.

The detectives pushed for more, but Lloyd was finished changing his story for that day.

Katie thanked him. "I pray and I hope that this story that you told us is really true."

"It is the truth."

"It makes a lot of sense to us," Katie said.

Dave came back in for a few minutes before the session ended. It had lasted almost seven hours. Lloyd was worried.

"I just wanna know what's going to happen to me," he said to Dave. "I mean, my involvement was helping to get the girls in the car, and that was it. I didn't touch 'em. I didn't rape 'em. Didn't have sex with 'em. Didn't kill 'em. Didn't carry them down to Virginia. Didn't do none of that. I was a scared-shitless little boy, you know?"

"Well, we'll work through it," Dave said, noncommittally.

Lloyd had now greatly strengthened the kidnapping case against himself. It had been planned. He had lured the girls with pot and led them away. He had driven off with them. Lloyd still had his immunity letter, but that wasn't going to help. That had been contingent on his not having committed a crime.

And Lloyd knew it. In one of his last comments to Dave that day, he remarked that the letter "ain't worth shit now." He was right.

10

The Whole Thing from Beginning to End

The Welch family property on Taylor's Mountain Road

Can't Tell You No More

Cops beset poor Henry Parker. Increasingly frail and bent, rolling his oxygen tank to his front door, he groaned when he recognized the ones on his snowy porch on February 24, 2015. They had driven up in an unmarked pickup.

"I don't know what's goin' on!" he exclaimed, before they'd said a word. "Y'all keep buggin' me, man. I ain't got nothin' to say to you guys no more. I told you everything I can tell you."

Henry's condition had worsened in the cold months since his grand jury testimony. He was miserable and could feel his time slipping away—he would last only one more winter. He couldn't sleep and could not take pills to help him sleep, because he feared, with his lung ailment, that in deep slumber he might stop breathing altogether.

"I'm traumatized with all this shit," he said. "I'm thinkin' about going to see a head doctor like my sister done. I mean, this is fuckin' me up!"

Word had gotten back to Henry that one of the cops working on the Lyon case was a brother of the Lyon girls, which in his mind framed his ordeal—it was a family feud. The men visiting him, Virginia State Police agent Lee Willis, Sergeant Jon Wilks, and investigator Mike Mayhew, from the Bedford County Sheriff's Office, assured him that they were local—their drawls made that much plain—and while it was true that Jay Lyon was a cop up in Montgomery County, Maryland, they assured Henry that he was nearing retirement and was not working on the case. Henry wasn't buying it.

"I want you to leave," he said.

"No, we're not going to ask you any questions," said one. "We're gonna show you something. We want to show you what Lloyd's been saying. Remember we told you that Lloyd was trying to throw you under the bus? Well, we're gonna show you. We're going to show you what he is saying so you can see it's Lloyd, not us, making up a lot of shit. We know you think we're lying our asses off to you, so we're gonna show you we're not bullshitting you."

On a laptop, they played for Henry a piece of Lloyd's January session, wherein he explains to Dave that it was Henry and Dick who threw the heavy bag onto the fire.

"There was a big ol' fire going, and I seen Dickie and Henry grab a bag and walk over to the fire and throw it in," says Lloyd. "Me and Helen, after that, said it was time for us to book out, and we left. What was in that bag, to my mind, was the girls."

"'To my mind'?" repeated Henry, scornfully. "He knows what was in the damn bag."

"We know," said Wilks. "We don't believe a word he is saying. We believe it was him and you threw it on the fire. He's puttin' Dickie—he's getting his picture plumb out of it. We know that."

The detectives hoped that this might anger Henry enough to convince him to tell them more. They believed he knew more but understandably feared further implicating himself. If he heard Lloyd naming him, maybe he'd feel compelled to refute his cousin. But it didn't work. Henry still said he thought the bag held a dead dog.

"I didn't even see Dickie," said Henry. "He [Lloyd] drove down in a car. I found out later that Dickie came down and took him back up to Maryland. Some girl was with him. He drug it [the bag] over from the car."

The detectives explained that Lloyd had confessed to planning the abduction of the girls from the mall.

"So, he's thrown himself into a chargeable offense," said Willis. "Even though he has minimized his other part in it, he is saying he was part of the conspiracy to abduct these girls. He's also saying other people helped him do it. And we have to believe somebody helped him do it. He couldn't do two girls at the same time."

They assured him again that they did not believe Lloyd. They were not looking to charge Henry with a crime.

"We are looking for you to give us some assistance on what's up on that mountain," said Wilks. "You have to know there was some girls in that bag, not a dog. You're smarter than that."

"But I *don't* know."

"But knowing what you know today—"

"I still don't know no more about what was in it," Henry said. "Anybody who sits there and opens their mouth can tell you anything."

"Well, they can, but usually they don't open their mouth and say they are guilty of a class-one felony that's gonna get 'em fifteen to thirty years in the state penitentiary. You know what I mean? He's acknowledged that part of it, which is the crazy thing."

"We've the first part, and we've got this bullshit ending," said Mayhew. "We're trying to get you to help us sort out this bullshit ending."

"I can't tell you no more than I told you," said Henry.

It was the same everywhere they went, in Virginia and Maryland. The Welch family had either lawyered up, shut up, or given—they said—all they could. The wiretaps were off, the grand jury proceedings at a standstill, the digs and lab tests winding down. The enormous effort had moved the case forward, but only by inches. It had provided a few awful glimpses of Sheila and Kate's end.

There remained, again, only one fruitful avenue. The one person who always had more to say.

February 25, 2015

The day after the interview with Henry in Virginia, the Lyon squad visited Lloyd for the eighth time.

Dave burst cheerily into the gray interview room at Dover with coffee and a doughnut. In a departure, he was wearing a crisp blue dress shirt and boldly striped tie.

"I'm dressed up for you," he said. "Look at me."

"Yeah, what the hell's that for?" asked Lloyd. He was still in his baggy prison whites, a black eyeglass case clipped to the front pocket. They bantered like old buddies, Lloyd reviewing once more his doomed hopes for release, and Dave, listening as if for the first time, full of his seemingly guileless bonhomie. Lloyd was in denial. He certainly grasped the seriousness of his predicament, yet carried on as if nothing had happened. Dave gave the routine recitation of rights and then announced that there would be another Virginia grand jury in March. He asked if Lloyd would consider appearing.

"We're trying to develop a case against your uncle, so the strategy was to bring you to grand jury to testify, obviously with your permission." He said it would entail a drive of several hours, "so our department actually went above and beyond, and they were looking at getting an RV and allowing myself and Mark and Katie to sit with you in the RV and drive you down there."

"I'd love it," said Lloyd. "I'd love a nice ride."

Dave said that they would try to coordinate it so that Edna would testify again on the same day.

"Why not give Lloyd a bone?" he said he'd told the others. "His mom's there. Why not let them come into a room like this and talk? You haven't seen her for how long?" It had been decades.

In anticipation of this jaunt, Dave explained that he wanted to spend this session "clearing up" Lloyd's story. He said the other principals, Dick, Pat, Teddy, Henry, Connie, and others, would also be recalled.

"So they're still blaming it all on me, ain't they?"

"Shit, yeah. They're blaming it on you."

"'Lloyd did it. Lloyd's in jail.'"

"That's the easiest thing to do."

Reflecting back on the long, damning chain of falsehoods Mark had recited in their last session, Lloyd allowed that he looked guilty, and if he was hoping for reassurance from Dave, he was disappointed.

"You got it," is what the detective said.

"I agree with you one hundred percent on that," said Lloyd. "Looking at it on paper, the way he said it, it's like, damn, Lloyd did do it, you know, or he was there."

The task today, Dave told Lloyd, was to shift that blame to Dick. This was not, in fact, his primary objective. The squad did believe Dick had been involved, so anything more about him was welcome, but the primary goal was to coax still more about what had happened from Lloyd. He was going to try to get himself off the hook by damning Dick, but no matter what else he said at this point, he would share culpability.

Dave asked for more details about how the kidnapping was conceived.

"The original plan was me and Teddy would go into the mall, find a couple of girls that looked like they might want to party or something like that, ask 'em if they'd like to get high, bring them out, we'd all get in the car, and we'd go up and get high, you know, and party. That was the original plan. Not one thing was mentioned about sex. Just to party. Nobody said anything to me. Nobody said, 'Hey, we're gonna bring 'em up and have sex with them.' You know?"

This was, of course, beyond belief. Dick had been a thirty-year-old man. The idea that he would plot to lure two little girls to his house in order to get them high or drunk and have a few laughs was ridiculous, as was Lloyd's contention that he had been only an innocent ride-along. But Dave played along.

Lloyd said he went to Dick's house that morning. His uncle was wearing his security guard uniform. They rode with Teddy in Dick's yellow station wagon.

"We went to the mall and saw the two girls. There was a bunch of them walking into the mall. I heard Dickie say, 'Well, what about them?'

I didn't know who he was talking about at first." Dick pointed them out, and they watched the girls enter the mall.

Dick stayed in the car, Lloyd said, while he and Teddy went after them. They offered the girls a chance to smoke dope.

Lloyd recalled Sheila answering, "Yeah, I'd like to try."

"That was all, you know?" he said. "'Oh, it sounds like fun,' you know? Kids."

Dick pulled up to the curb as they exited with the girls.

"Okay, you said one got in the front and one got in the back," said Dave.

"Right."

"The young one was in the back."

"Yeah, I think that was . . ." Here Lloyd encountered a new problem. If the girls had left with them cheerfully, looking forward to smoking dope and hanging out, why had the younger one been crying in the back seat? "Like I said, I don't know if she was really cryin' or not. I don't know. It sounded like she was." He whimpered softly to illustrate. "But that could just have been a sniffle, because she had her head turned the whole time. She didn't say nothin'. The girl in the front didn't say nothin'. They didn't ask where we were going to party or anything like that, you know."

In the previous session, Lloyd had told Mark that they'd driven around for two hours. Dave pointed out that this didn't sound right. Hyattsville was only about fifteen minutes away. Lloyd insisted that he'd never said two hours—he didn't seem to realize that all these interviews were recorded. Several times he joked about it, once telling Dave he had checked the desk drawers looking for a recorder when he'd been left alone in the room. "Because how in the hell does he remember everything I said?" Lloyd asked. But he never got serious about the question. Dave would swiftly change the subject.

Lloyd continued recalling the ride away from the mall.

"I know there was some joints already rolled up. I know Dick smoked pot. I was smoking one in the back. The girl [Kate] was sitting over there, she didn't smoke at that time. I should have asked, 'Are you okay?' or something like that, but I wasn't thinkin'. I was gettin' high."

"Ah, see, to me, I don't think that that's odd," said Dave, who in fact found the whole situation horrifyingly odd. "Look at it this way. If you're loading two girls to go party, in your mind you're partying, you're hanging out. In Dick and Ted's mind—you don't know what they talked about but—more than likely they're talking about having sex with these two girls after they get them high and drunk, right? I mean, I'm just sayin'."

"Right. But I guess what scared me the most is when we got up there by the university [University of Maryland], Dick didn't turn all the way around. I guess he was talking to Teddy or somebody, and he said, 'Well, you know, they can always meet their Maker.' You know? I guess that is what scared me the most, because I didn't know what the hell he was talking about."

"Why do you think he said that?'

"I don't know. They [Dick and Teddy] were having a little whispered conversation back and forth to where I couldn't really hear them too much."

"I said, 'Hey, can you drop me off at the store there. I'm gonna get some ice cream.' "

"Let's break that down," said Dave. "Something had to happen where it pissed Dick off. Why else would he have said that? Were they throwing a ruckus? What happened?"

"No! They weren't raising their voice or anything like that."

Dave asked, "How do you go from 'I'm gonna have sex with these girls' to now suddenly thinking about killing them?"

"I believe that the little girl in the back is the one who was getting him upset because of her little sniffle."

Lloyd stuck with his story that he had exited the car, bought ice cream, and walked back to his father's house in Hyattsville. He retold the story of returning to his uncle's house the next day, when he saw one of the girls being raped. Four days later he had gone back to the mall to tell his misleading story, and then he had panicked, he said. He and

Helen left to hitchhike to Virginia the following morning. He repeated his story about seeing Dick show up early in the morning on Taylor's Mountain and watching from a window as his uncle and Henry lugged a heavy bag out to the fire.

He decided now to admit that Lee had called ahead to alert Lizzie (Lee's sister)—the call Henry said he'd overheard. Lloyd continued to deny the rest of what his cousins remembered. When they reached the end of this version, Dave again asked him to speculate about the girls' fate. Lloyd said that he believed it was Kate Lyon's body in the bag that went on the fire.

"When you looked out the window and they put the bag on that fire, you knew exactly what was in that bag," said Dave. "I mean, there was no doubt in your mind."

Lloyd nodded.

"You don't drive five hours to throw trash on a fire in Virginia at one thirty in the morning."

"No, you don't. I agree with you about that."

Sheila Lyon was still alive in the car, Lloyd speculated, and was passed on to Henry, who abused her for a time and then killed her—Henry had told a story about him, so Lloyd now told a story about Henry. But he said he was just guessing.

Each time Lloyd made a change to his narrative, it triggered a cascade of ill-considered implications. Dave had learned to spot these and pounce. Dave now pointed out how improbable it was for both Lloyd and Helen to have arrived at Taylor's Mountain *coincidentally* on the same day his uncle Dick showed up with a body in a bag. If Lloyd now admitted that his father had called in advance, that showed something else.

"That's the preplanning that they put together to bring the girls, live, dead, one dead, one alive, down there," said Dave. "That's what we're talking about. It's been a week, eight days from the day they went missing until they ended up in Virginia. There's no feasible way that Dick kept them in his house without your aunt Pat knowing. Think about it."

"Yeah, I agree with you, but where he kept them I don't know."

"If Dick has these two girls—whether they are alive or dead—in his house, there had to have been a lot of chatter about what are we gonna do as a family? How are we gonna resolve this? Can't just open the door and say, 'Get out.'"

"Right."

"I'm thinking, normal folks, made a mistake, now we're left with this mess. That's all that was talked about. There has to be a moment of panic."

This made too much sense for Lloyd to deny.

"Yep. I was suckered into going up there, but nobody told me what was going to happen. Nobody said anything to me. Like I said, I was the black sheep of the family."

"Let me put it this way," Dave said. "Did you get suckered into going to Virginia to let them know they need to start a fire? Not knowing what you were really doing? And when you got down there they show up with this car and a bag? Did you go down to lay the groundwork?"

"Nope."

"So they just literally followed you down there?"

"I don't know if they followed me down there or not. All I can say is, he showed up knowing I was going to be down there."

"Why wouldn't he have given you a ride?"

"Me and Dickie didn't see eye to eye like that. We weren't that close. I mean, he got me to do that there, you know, to talk the girls into partying and stuff, but as far as me and him sittin' and havin' a conversation? Nah. Never happen."

"But he trusted you enough to go out and do something like this."

"I guess he figured that me being high all the time, me leaving all the time—"

"But look at the ace in your pocket. I mean, let's say in the nineties when you get hit with this [child-molestation charge], you could have looked at them and said, 'Hey, I've got something on my uncle.'"

Lloyd nodded.

"So he trusted you enough that you wouldn't say something. Why?"

"I'm . . . that's a good question," said Lloyd, folding his arms and leaning back. He had clearly never considered this. And Dave was right.

The abduction of the Lyon sisters, the most notorious unsolved crime in the region's modern memory, would have been an ace indeed. It might have given Lloyd real leverage. He had complained bitterly about the unfairness of his prison sentence. Here was something he might have traded to reduce his time. And by Lloyd's own account, there was no love lost between him and his uncle. He had no good answer.

"After so many years I did forget about it," he said, weakly. "I honestly did."

Who forgets kidnapping two little girls? If this was going to be his play before the grand jury, Dave suggested, he might as well give it up and confess to the whole thing. It wouldn't fly. In Henry they had an eyewitness to—a participant in—throwing the bag on the fire. Connie corroborated it. Henry said he'd done it with Lloyd; Lloyd said Henry had done it with Dick.

"Is Lloyd the one telling the truth?" Dave asked. "Is Henry telling the truth? Now, Henry is in a bad situation because emotionally he doesn't know how to deal with it. I think as he's gotten older, he's gotten soft."

Lloyd nodded and grinned.

"That's weird, because Henry used to be a nasty little ass."

"His health's bad. He knows he probably has only a couple more years, if that, to live. What would bother Henry the most? Do you think there's direct involvement?"

"I would," said Lloyd. "I would say that it's tearing him up so much because he got involved with one of the girls. Like I said earlier, something went wrong. It's already went so far, and he killed 'em, and it's tearing him up. See, it's eating me up inside but in a different way. I didn't kill them. I didn't rape them. I just walked 'em out of the mall and got them in the car. I'm guilty of that. That's as far as I'm guilty of. Them doin' what they did is tearing them up more. It's not tearing me up that they're dead. It's tearing me up that I even got involved. There's times I could kick myself in the ass for even getting involved into going and getting them, but as far as them dying and me having a hand in it, I can't say it's tearing me up."

He repeated his belief that Dick gave Henry the older girl.

"He had sex. They told him to get rid of 'em, and this thing about the tire iron?" Henry had earlier speculated that Lloyd might have killed one of the girls with a tire iron on the drive down from Maryland. "He's probably saying the tire iron because that's probably what he used." Lloyd laughed. "I mean, that's the only thing I can think. Why would he say a tire iron?"

"That's what I said. It's an odd thing to say. What do you think Henry would have done with the second girl?"

"He probably put her in the fire."

"Do you think both of them went in that fire?"

"Yep. If Henry killed her."

Lloyd said the fire reeked so badly in the morning that it made Helen nauseated.

When We Got There

Wearing Lloyd down worked. On interview days he was awakened early and kept waiting in Dover police headquarters. He would sit alone and shackled for hours in the interview room before the squad arrived. Then they tag-teamed him. Chris stayed back, watching on a monitor. Dave would engage Lloyd for hours on end, taking him back over the same ground again and again, alternately wooing and threatening him, offering him what looked like avenues of escape. His story wasn't good enough, Dave kept telling him. If they were going to make charges stick against his uncle or his cousin, they needed something more. They needed verifiable details. Through it all Lloyd kept lying, and Dave mostly just absorbed his whoppers and excuses without contradiction. He repeatedly assured Lloyd that somehow all of this was working to his benefit, urging him to fight back against his family. After a lunch break, Mark and Katie would work Lloyd over for hours more. Katie played stubbornly on his conscience, stressing how certain she was that he had one, what a truly decent fellow he was at heart, how in her eyes he was always trying to do the right thing, tenaciously egging him on to display this inherent decency. Mark continued to bang away at all the obvious holes in his story.

And every time, Lloyd broke. For all his vaunted street smarts, he never seemed to catch on to how he was being played.

On this day Lloyd got his lunch break after four hours with Dave. He was given his choice of take-out food, and the detectives always brought back additional orders from the same place for his guards. Lloyd consistently disappointed them by selecting Arby's. When he'd finished eating, it was Mark and Katie's turn.

"We're back," said Mark.

"Are you surprised?" asked Katie.

Katie had prepared an elaborate backstory about Helen's invented journal. It was, she said, "My big thing that I've been working on." Showing a flair for fiction, she explained that the journal had gotten waterlogged, and that Helen's handwriting was so small it was hard to decipher, so it had taken her some time to make sense of it.

"It had some emotional stuff, but I didn't want to come in here and give you bullshit, so what we did was send it to the FBI lab, because they have ways of re-creating, you know, gluing stuff and putting them in air containers and getting stuff back together."

"I never knew she kept a journal," said Lloyd, skeptically.

"She didn't, I don't think, when she was with you. It was very clear that you were kind of the love of her life, you know." Katie was laying it on thick here. "And I'm not saying that to blow smoke up your ass. I mean, her husband was—what's the right word?—alienated by that, which I think you can understand." Katie went on and on about the diary that did not exist.

Katie sat behind the desk, and Mark took a chair alongside Lloyd, who was silently chewing gum. She began by presenting an entry that described a room with a pool table at Uncle Dick's house: a room that had a bed on the floor in a closet. This was a tidbit they had gleaned from the wiretaps and from a new tip offered by Teddy Welch. Still struggling to free himself from suspicion, Teddy had called with a recovered memory. He said that on a visit to Dick and Pat's house, he'd heard the click of pool balls and had followed the sound upstairs, where he opened the door to an attic-like room that had a pool table—this is where the couple said their pool table had been. Teddy said he saw Lloyd at one end of the table, and Helen sitting on a mattress tucked into a small closet, watching. Sitting on the other side of the table were two blond girls. Teddy said he had then been called back downstairs. The detectives wondered why he hadn't mentioned it earlier—this was after multiple police interviews, a polygraph session, and several grand jury appearances. Since they were always accusing him of holding something back, Teddy explained, he had been working hard to recover whatever memories he could.

He was convinced that this brief encounter explained why Lloyd had chosen to name him as the kidnapper. Lloyd would have recalled being seen with the girls, so he had acted to head that off by blaming Teddy. To the detectives, it was hard not to view Teddy's recovered memory as tit for tat.

But to test out the scenario, Katie said Helen had written of the upstairs poolroom in her diary.

"Yeah, that was in the back room where the pool table was, yeah," said Lloyd. "Right off the living room."

"It sounds like she [Helen] is describing something like an attic almost," said Katie. "Like a finished attic."

"Oh, we really never went up there. . . . We stayed at Dick and Pat's maybe two or three different times." Lloyd said the room upstairs was kept locked.

"She talks about this time there was a mattress in the closet, a pool table, and she speaks about two girls being in this area with you guys."

"Yeah. Could have been the kids. I don't know. Not the girls from the mall. It could have been Pat's kids. I don't remember that. That's got me confused."

"I'll bring the copies next time so you can see them," said Katie. "But it sounds like you and her and these two girls, and so I was wondering if somehow you guys ended up staying there because you needed a place in the interim and didn't know that the Lyons girls were there and [they] ended up being in that room with you guys."

Katie was really pushing it here.

"Nah. We didn't stay at Dick's house. We were at my mom's house. When those girls came up missing we were at my mom's house."

"Well, they didn't come up missing. You guys took them from the mall."

"Well—"

"Right? Okay?"

"I'm saying when they were announced missing," said Lloyd.

Katie forged on. "Okay. The only thing that she said was, something I wanted to share with you, was that she hopes someday that you would do the right thing and make peace with this situation."

Lloyd said nothing. He shook his head and then flipped his right hand dismissively, as if to say, *I have no idea.*

"Obviously, I'm telling you that she was able to piece this—I don't know if you guys had a conversation—but she was definitely able to piece some of this stuff—"

"I never told her about them girls. Could she have pieced it together? Knowing Helen? Yeah."

"Oh, she did. I mean, I'm reading that she pieced it together."

Lloyd seemed unaffected by this. The diary ploy didn't appear to have troubled him at all—though it had—so Katie dropped it. She went back over Lloyd's most recent version, and let him know that, as it now stood, he had still failed to produce enough verifiable information to nail Dickie.

"You've told us the beginning part. We're piecing together the end part based on the stuff you've already told us and stuff that other people have told us. The middle part is what we really need to hammer him on, because you're saying, basically, that he had these girls and he's the one who brought them there [to Virginia]. What we're looking for are unique facts that we can hammer him on where he can't refute, you know. Somebody killed them. Somebody kept them alive. He [Dick] has got his damn hands full. He doesn't care if Lloyd and Helen are going to Bedford. You know what I mean? We can't go and present to a grand jury in trying try to put something together against Dick that [says] you are there and then consequently these bodies just end up there. You know what I'm saying? Like, it doesn't make sense?"

"I know it looks like Lloyd's the one who did it."

"Well, sure. And that's what everyone is painting. And if you had a part of it, tell us! Clearly you were a teenager that got pulled into all this bullshit. You know I'm a little bit more sensitive than the average guy. You and I have had some heart-to-heart conversations. It sucks to be the outcast of the family. It sucks to be the one who nobody wants around and feel unloved, so I get that. 'And these people finally want to have something to do with me. I'll go smoke some dope and party with these girls if that makes me fit in.' But there are holes that don't make sense. I'm not saying that you did more, but you knew more about what happened on the back end of this, and you just don't wanna say anything, because you don't want to be involved. But the truth is, you're already involved."

Lloyd didn't budge. He reiterated his story about hitchhiking, about seeing Dick pull up in the middle of the night with the bag. He was sure Dick and Teddy had sex on their minds when they went for the girls, but not him. He was loyal to Helen.

Now Mark leaned into the conversation.

"When we talked the last time, you told Katie and I that it took Dick about two days for him to talk you into it because you were scared."

Lloyd nodded in agreement. He had said that.

"What were you scared about?"

"I didn't want to get involved in going and picking up girls, you know? That was really not my scene."

"Was it that there was going to be some trickery involved to get these girls? That's what it seems like, that he's wearing a security uniform to make them feel safe."

"I don't know if at that time you could say there was trickery or anything like that. Like I was saying, I really didn't want to cheat on Helen."

"Let me ask you this. If Dick hated you so much, why would he involve you in his plan?"

"I think I was being used."

"Well, I get that sense, too."

"Because I was the one who walked around that mall the most."

"And approached them?"

"Yeah."

"You're the sacrificial lamb," offered Katie.

"I was the one with the headband. I was the one with the long hair. I'm the one who looked like a total hippie, you know? Yeah, like you said. I was the lamb. The sucker."

Lloyd then offered a little more detail about luring the girls. He watched them for a while, and when they were alone he approached them. He said he asked, "Have either one of you ever gotten high before? Ever thought about getting high?"

He replayed how the conversation went:

"I've thought about it," said Sheila, "but I've never done it."

"Well, I've got a little pot, and I'm just hanging around here. Would you like to get high?"

Sheila said yes, but Kate balked. "We can't do that," she said.

"Oh, come on," Sheila urged her. "It isn't going to hurt us. Everyone is doing it."

Katie immediately cast doubt on that dialogue.

"These girls didn't smoke. I mean, they were ten and twelve."

Lloyd said that was how it happened.

"Their parents say there's absolutely no way that they would have gotten in the car with strangers," said Katie.

"Well, their parents lied."

"It's not that they're lying. You know, parents want to think the best of their kids."

Mark asked why, if Dick had decided to drive all the way to Wheaton, because he did not want to be seen picking up girls close to his house, did he bring the girls back to his house?

"That's a question I've asked myself so many times, and I can't answer that because I don't know. All I know is he got high down in that basement down there, and that's where he did all of his partying then. I guess he felt safe in that area."

Again Lloyd said that he got out of the car at the convenience store. Here is where he had decided to take his stand. He had innocently participated in taking ten- and twelve-year-old girls to "party" with his pedophiliac uncle. The rest had come as a shock to him—although not enough of a shock to impel him to take a single step to aid the girls. Mark scoffed. He leaned toward Lloyd and fixed him with a steady, troubled gaze. He spoke very calmly, asking again why Dick would have taken the girls back to his own house, where his wife and children lived.

And then Lloyd tripped up. He said that Pat wasn't home "when *we* got there."

Mark did not draw attention to it immediately; he just ran with it.

"So, you guys pull in the driveway, do you all go back around to the basement?"

"I shouldn't say *we* pulled in," Lloyd said, backtracking fast. "I'm saying *they* pulled in. Pat was at work. I can see the house when I'm walking by the tracks."

"See, and that's the kind of thing the jurors are going to get tripped up on, because when you said just a minute ago—"

"I said *they*."

"—when *we* pulled into the driveway."

"When we pulled in, yeah."

"All right? And if you pulled in, if you didn't get out at the store, that's fine."

"No, I got out at the store and got ice cream."

"You established a lot of credibility with us now, and we completely understand that back then you didn't know where this thing was going," Mark lied. "And you were scared and all that stuff. If you went to Dick's house from the mall, that doesn't change things as far as the way we're looking at all this."

"No, I did get out at the store."

"Lloyd, did you get back in the car?" Katie asked. "Because, honestly, it doesn't make sense."

"Yeah. I walked down the railroad tracks You can see their house from the railroad tracks."

"But hear me out," said Katie. "You're saying that they dropped you off, and you went about your business, and you didn't know anything until the next day, and now you're putting yourself looking at them pulling up to the house with the girls. So it doesn't matter if you were in the car, it doesn't change anything other than the fact that we can believe in you. Because it doesn't make sense."

"I understand," said Lloyd. "It doesn't make sense."

"Because it doesn't make you any less guilty or more guilty. If you're in the car when they pulled up to the house—already you said somewhere in your mind you knew there was probably going to be sex, not necessarily that you were gonna participate—what curious nineteen-year-old boy isn't gonna go and see what's gonna happen? They [the girls] weren't that much different in age than you. There were totally different things goin' on back then."

Katie was smoothing the path for Lloyd. She was allowing, for purposes of easing Lloyd's concerns, that having sex with prepubescent girls was somehow a *normal thing*, especially in the anything-goes 1970s.

"I can understand important parts where you want to take yourself out," she said. "This isn't one of them. I know it's in our nature to protect ourselves, and I get it. But it just doesn't make sense. I've got a pretty good Lloyd bullshit meter. Mark has a good Lloyd bullshit meter, as you know."

Lloyd chuckled to himself. This was true.

"You know, because you always end up giving it up to us anyways," Katie said.

Lloyd laughed, leaned back, and threw up both arms in an attitude of surrender.

"Okay, goddamnit! Damn. I did get out at the store there and get some ice cream. We drove to the house. I got out. I left the house. There was nobody at the house. I said I was leaving and I left."

This retreat was telling. Katie was right; it made little difference whether Lloyd got out at the store or a few minutes later at the house. But the shift revealed Lloyd's whole method. He told the truth up to a point, but then extricated himself when things turned bad. He removed himself from the scene. When trapped into admitting he was present, as he was here by his own slipup, he became the innocent victim, a sucker, a patsy. Just easygoing Lloyd, along for the ride, exploited.

Having loosened up a little on this, Lloyd offered some more information about those first few hours of the Lyon girls' nightmare. He said they initially drove all over the area, smoking dope in the car. He said Teddy was blowing marijuana smoke into Sheila's mouth in the front seat, while Kate whined in the back. "She really didn't want to go, but her sister talked her into it," he said. "I guess you could say she was acting up. She did ask her sister at one point, 'Are we gonna go back to the mall anytime soon?' "

It evoked such a sad scene, Kate with her head averted in the back seat, staring out the window, wondering where they were going, who these men were, and what might happen to them. Lloyd said his uncle responded by encouraging the ten-year-old, saying, "Why don't you get high!" This was also about the time that Dick, clearly annoyed, told Teddy, "They can always meet their Maker." Later, Lloyd said, Sheila took her little sister's hand as they got out of the car and led her into the basement room.

The detectives picked away further at Lloyd's story. Why would he have gone back to Dick's house the next day if what his uncle had said—"They can always meet their Maker"—so scared him? All of Lloyd's reasons were feeble. He wanted to say goodbye to a cousin. His uncle had good dope.

"Lloyd, did an anonymous nine-one-one call ever go through your head?" Katie asked.

"No."

"Just because you were saving your ass?"

"Yeah."

"Okay, fair enough."

"I didn't want to go to jail."

"Fair enough."

"It was me who was at the mall."

"Right."

"It was me who everybody saw, you know? I mean, y'all have got a picture of me." He was referring to the old police sketch.

"Right."

"Or close enough."

"That's the kind of honesty I'm talking about. Because that's not an easy thing to say, but it's the truth and it's fair, and we don't judge you any. In fact, we are happy that you say it."

"Yeah. Nine-one-one just—"

"That's a hard pill to swallow," said Katie, finishing the thought for him.

Lloyd nodded.

"Knowing that this little girl was getting raped and possibly drugged, dead, whatever?" she asked. "And you could have prevented it, and you didn't because you were preserving yourself."

"Yeah."

"That's the kind of stuff that we are looking for."

Lloyd finally acknowledged unequivocally that he had gone to the police with his false story because "I didn't want them to come lookin' at me. Because I didn't know if somebody had seen me talking to them." He had been, he said, "covering my ass."

Mark pushed him once more on what happened in Virginia.

"You were involved with this thing in the beginning. It ended. And you're there when it ends. It's like a *coincidence* that you just happen to be there?"

"Coincidences happen."

Mark laughed.

"All through life, coincidences happen," said Lloyd.

Then Katie launched into another of her empathetic stem-winders. She believed in her heart, she said, that Lloyd had been sucked into the crime by his uncle, that these were "shitty people," that he was the only decent and honorable one in the family, that he was "a teenager trying to do better with Helen," and that he had gotten into a bad situation because of drugs. She said he had fled to Virginia because his uncle had probably threatened him, and that he had kept his mouth shut about the whole thing for forty years because he was frightened. His family had set him up, essentially framed him to take the hit for the crime, and now they were all free, "living their lives," trying to make sure that the blame came to rest solely on him. *They were getting away with it!* He needed to come clean so the detectives could help him *protect himself*. Dick was the evil one here. He had probably done this multiple times and gotten away with it! "He's still getting away with it!" she said. Lloyd had a chance to bring him to justice, avoid being made the scapegoat, *and* unburden himself. "We can't unless you do," she said. "I wish you would just let it out. Let it go. If that means you have to cry, if that means you have to punch something . . ." Katie was on a roll.

And almost six hours into the session, true to form, Lloyd once more buckled—or seemed to. He started rubbing his eyes. He announced that he was tired. Then out came the question: "What's gonna happen to me?"

And as they always did, the detectives finessed the answer. He had already confessed to having helped kidnap the girls. They did not tell him so, but this alone was enough to lock him away for the remainder of his life. They wanted more. They wanted to know exactly what happened.

"You've asked that question so many times," said Mark. "What's going to happen to me? You said something earlier today: 'Everything I've said hurts me.' And that is absolutely true, and it's true because what you have said up until this point leaves you looking bad." Mark was returning to Dave's argument, that Lloyd needed to tell them more about what happened, *in order to defend himself*.

"Okay," said Lloyd. "Do you want Dave in here too, so all three of you can hear the whole story?"

The Whole Thing from Beginning to End

Helen's invented journal would pay a dividend after all. It had evidently been gnawing at Lloyd. Told that Helen had written of their being with the Lyon girls some days after the girls' disappearance, he was faced once more with tangible evidence—or what he thought was tangible evidence. Lloyd rarely resisted provable facts. Katie's artful fiction would now force another maneuver.

When Mark left to fetch Dave, Lloyd pleaded with Katie, "I just don't want to do no more time. I want to get out."

Katie was not about to dash his fondest hope, not while he was still talking. She dodged it.

"Look, I've seen you struggle," she said. "This is just you and me talking now. The reason you want to keep giving us more is that you want to do the right thing. It's just time. It's just time. You're tired. We're tired, and nobody is taking care of you."

"But the only problem with this all is I tell you all everything, the whole thing from the beginning to the end, and it's still my word against theirs, and there's more of them than there is of me."

Mark and Dave entered. Dave, who had removed his tie, pulled the chair Mark had been sitting in even closer to Lloyd and leaned toward him. Mark and Katie sat behind the desk.

"Okay," said Lloyd, leaning back in his chair and clasping both hands behind his head. "March twenty-third. Dick approached me and Teddy with this plan to go up to the Wheaton mall, like I said, to pick up a couple of girls, party with them, have sex with them." This was a new admission; Lloyd had always insisted on just the euphemism "partying." "I told him no, I don't want to do that. I'll party with you, I'll party with the girls, but I'm not having no sex with those girls. I'm with Helen. She's with child. I said, 'As a matter of fact, I don't even want to be in this. You can leave me out.' Couple of days later, he talks me in. Says, 'Look, I got pot, man. I got plenty of pot. Got some good drugs. We'll all get high,' and stuff like that. So finally he talked me into going up there. I go up there. I go into the mall. I saw the two girls come walking through. I followed them for a while. I approached them and said, 'Hey, do y'all wanna get high?' You know, I did say it that way. 'You wanna get high?' And the older one said, 'We've never gotten high before. We don't do that.' I said, 'Well, we'll try it. Everybody's doing it. I mean, it's the seventies. Peace, love, and rock 'n' roll.' And the older one finally said,

'Yeah, let's get high.' The younger one said, 'No, I don't want to go.' And her sister said, 'Oh, come on, we're just going to get high,' you know? So, we go out of the mall, and Dick pulls up. I don't know where Teddy came out of, but he came up behind me. The older girl got in the front, like I said. I got in the back. The other girl got in the back, and we drove around for a while, started getting high. Ted was giving shotgun to the girl [blowing marijuana smoke directly into her mouth], and we were just talking up front there."

The detectives noted that Lloyd had inadvertently placed himself in the front seat, and since they had long ago stopped believing in Teddy's role, it made sense. Nobody pointed it out, and Lloyd continued his new tale.

"The other girl, she still wasn't saying nothing, just like I said. I don't know if she was crying or what. I didn't offer her anything, because she just looked like she wanted to be by herself. I finally get the ice cream, because I did tell Helen I would get some ice cream for her. We go back to the house there, and Dick, at the time, I guess, was bickering with Teddy about something. I don't know what it was, and he said, 'Well, they can always meet their Maker.' You know how that goes, and I got out and I said, 'Oh, wait a minute, I'm taking this ice cream home. I don't want to. Y'all do your thing. Have a good time.' And I left. I did not go back to that house until the next day, and it was, like, out of curiosity, to see if the girls were okay or if they were still there or not—" Here he had taken to heart Katie's suggestion that as a teenager, knowing there were going to be sex acts, he would have at least been curious to see. "Helen was with me, but she didn't go downstairs. I did. I saw Dick raping the one girl, and her eyes were rolled [back]. Like I said, I don't know if she was on a high or drugged or what, because Dick could get drugs all the time. I backed out. About that time Teddy come, I don't know if he came around this way [around the outside of the house to the basement entrance], and I said, 'Hey, I'll see you later. I don't want to be around here.'"

Now Lloyd offered his explanation of Helen's supposed diary entry about them spending time with the girls days later.

"Me and Helen left for a while. I guess it was the next day, next morning or whatever, Dick and Teddy had come over to the house and asked me and Helen if we would watch two girls, just babysit for a while, you know, and that's true, and I said, 'What two girls?' and he said, 'You know, the girls that you got a hold of.' I said, 'You still got them little girls? What are you doing with them? I thought you were gonna send them home.' And he said, 'Oh, they want to stay for a while. They like getting high.' So we went there. We stayed for a while."

It was, of course, absurd. You kidnap two little girls, who have now been missing for days and are the objects of a mass, bicounty, hugely publicized manhunt; and you have seen your uncle raping one of them, who appears drugged; and you then, with your girlfriend, agree to "babysit" them, accepting your uncle's explanation that they are *enjoying* themselves? It got weirder.

"At his house or at your house?" Katie asked.

"It was his house."

"Okay."

"We watched them. Helen, she played with them and everything like that. Helen always loved kids. I guess, at the time, she didn't really know what was going on. I guess we watched 'em for about four or five hours. They weren't hurt or anything like that. Nothin' was ever mentioned about them having sex or anything like that or getting them from the mall. Dick finally came back upstairs."

The detectives noted that the girls had now been moved from the basement party room at Dick's house to an upstairs room. Lloyd had added a bizarre new scene to his narrative, and like most of his fictions, it appeared to be at least partly truthful. It corroborated things they had heard in wiretaps and interviews. Family members had several times alluded to something untoward going on in Dick's upstairs poolroom. Then there was Teddy's new story. Lloyd, in an effort to help himself, had just placed another rock on the growing pile of damning evidence.

He continued: "Pat, I don't know where she was at, at the time. I don't know if she was sitting out on the front porch and just wanted some time alone or whatever. Finally, they came back in. Me and Helen left. Dickie gave Helen a little bit of money for watching 'em for a couple of hours. We went back to the house [Lloyd's father's house], and I guess you could say that it kind of bugged me of what was going on. . . . They didn't have no marks on them like they were punched on or tortured or anything like that. They had clothes on, so I couldn't tell what was on their body or anything like that, but none of them said anything about, 'Hey, are you gonna get us back up to the mall?' or anything like that. I don't know what they said to Helen, because Helen was the one who watched them mostly. A couple of days later it just kept eating at me, eating at me, eating at me, finally I decided it was time for me to go to the mall and get my name cleared out of this, because I didn't want no part of it. Dick came over to the house one time, talked to Lee, I don't know what they all talked about. He saw me, and he said, 'Look, don't say a damn word about nothin'. You don't know nothin', just get out of here. You're talkin' about going to Virginia for a while. Go there. See everybody and disappear.' I took that as a hint. You know? I went to the mall. I told my side of the story. When I ended up talking to the police, I got really scared then. Left. Me and Helen hitchhiked. It took us a day and a half to get down there hitchhiking. About that time, our clothes were a little mildewy, because it was a little cold outside that night. We stayed in the woods. We got the clothes washed. We ate dinner about twelve thirty, one thirty, somewhere around there. It was late. We were in bed asleep. A car pulled up, and Dick got out of the car. The reason I know it was Dick was because he was wearing his T-shirt and it was the [his] car. He went to the back. He opened it up. He pulled a bag out, and I knew right then and there that something wasn't right. Something happened to them girls. I was too scared to say anything, just like I've been all of this time. Henry came. I don't know where he was at the time. I don't know if he was down by the fire or where he was at. He helped him [Dick] carry the bag down there. They threw it on the fire. Came back to the house. They talked a little bit. Dick looked up there toward the window like I was, like he could see me lookin' out the window or whatever. He got in the car. There was another man in the car. I didn't know if it was Lee or who it was. He never got out. I didn't see him. About that time I laid my head back down, and I said, 'Oh shit.' Helen said, 'What's wrong?' Said, 'Dick was just down here. I don't know what was going on, but he threw something on the fire. I don't know what it was.' I didn't want to tell her what I was thinking. We got up that morning. We ate breakfast. I told everybody, 'Look, thank you for the hospitality and the food and everything like that. We're gonna head down south now.' We walked outside, and it smelled real bad. That's why I said it smelled like rats." In fact, it had been Dave who said this. "Helen got sick to her stomach. She brought everything up. She said, 'What the hell is that smell?' I said, "I don't know.' We left. Forty years I didn't say nothing."

Katie pointed out that Henry and Connie directly contradicted him.

"I understand that," said Lloyd, confident now that he had fully stated his new version of the story, one that incorporated all that he had absorbed from the detectives. He had once more removed himself as far as possible from culpability. This was his new story, and he was going to stick with it.

"Everything I just told you is the way it went down. Everything."

They worked on him for another hour, but Lloyd was done. They finished by talking up the proposed ride in the RV down to Bedford for his grand jury testimony.

"Is there anything we can do for you at the jail?" asked Dave.

"Get me the hell out," Lloyd said.

They laughed. Dave said the grand jury appearance would happen in a week.

"It's all of them against me. I already know that."

"Well, you get your day, and that's what we want to do."

Lloyd would never appear before a grand jury.

11

A Trick or the Truth?

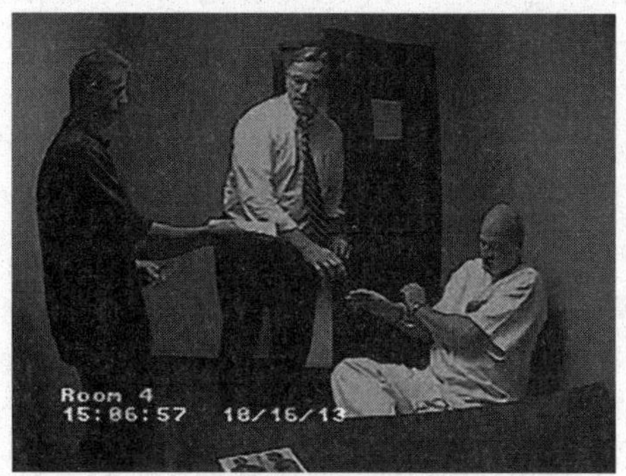

Deputy State's Attorney Pete Feeney and Detective Dave Davis with Lloyd Welch

God as My Witness, No

Wiry, flinty, and truculent as ever, Dick Welch emerged from months of innuendo and intense surveillance a battered man. He was about to turn seventy but seemed older. In addition to his heart trouble he faced a frightening array of accusations. Various family members had accused him of ugly and violent behavior toward them in the past, even of abusing the family dog. Lloyd had named him as the man who had planned the kidnapping of Sheila and Kate Lyon and who then presided over their gang rape, murder, and dismemberment.

Dick denied it all, and if he was lying, he was a lot better at it than his nephew. He said little, and what he did say was simple and consistent. Indeed, he behaved like someone wrongly accused, bewildered and frustrated by wounding falsehoods and at times appropriately indignant. It helped that he seemed so harmless. The man with the menacing look in old snapshots—lean, with combed-back dark hair, long sideburns, a tight T-shirt, and a smirk—was now "Poppy." His voice would rise to a pleading whine when he was upset, and the squad had gone to great lengths to upset him. Apart from publicly shaming him, Mark Janney had told him, in so many words, that no matter what he said, he was "going down." Virginia's death penalty or at least a life sentence loomed behind the threat. But by February 2015, almost a year after the squad had turned to him, nothing connected Dick Welch to the Lyons beyond Lloyd's word, which was, of course, worthless.

A big part of the story about Dick wasn't credible: that the girls had been imprisoned in his house for a week or more before being killed. It had not been a big house, and living in it with him were his wife and four children. It had been across the street from the county courthouse and just a stone's throw from the Hyattsville police headquarters. Someone surely would have noticed the two little blond girls the entire region was looking for. It was, frankly, far more likely that Lloyd had invented Dick's role, just as he had Teddy's, to deflect attention from his own guilt. Dick was not an educated man. He said he could neither read nor write. But he wasn't stupid. He was about the only one in the family who had nothing to say. He had stayed off the phones during those months of surveillance, and when Teddy had paid him that surprise visit wearing a wire, Dick had been entirely consistent. He knew nothing about the case. When he was summoned to appear before the Bedford grand jury on February 6, he came without his lawyer. He had recovered his composure since the browbeating session at his house the previous September. Entering the grand jury chamber, he noticed his now familiar antagonists in the room.

He remarked, "Oh, I see my buddies are here!"

And they went at him for hours, prosecutors and detectives. It was like a nightmare version of the old TV program *This Is Your Life*. All the terrible things said about him were dumped in his lap. Randy Krantz, the Bedford prosecutor, listed all the family members—female and male—who said Dick had sexually abused them as children.

Speaking of Joann Green, Dick's sister-in-law, Krantz asked, "Do you have any explanation why she would tell the police that you sexually assaulted her?"

"I thought we were talking about the Lyon girls," said Dick.

"Well, I'm asking: Did you sexually assault your sister-in-law?"

"No."

"Do you have any explanation why she would say you did?"

"I don't know."

"So it's your testimony under oath that you did not sexually assault her?"

"No."

"Ever."

"Not as I know of."

"Well, what do you mean, 'not as you know of'?"

"I didn't do it. I mean, I don't know where it came from. Okay?"

"Have you ever sexually assaulted any of your family members?"

"Hell no."

"Do you have any reason why other family members would say that you did?"

"Well, they're all a bunch of liars. I know that. You can't believe half of what any of them says. That's why me and my wife stay to ourselves."

Later, Krantz came back at him in the same vein.

"Do you think it is unusual," he asked, "for one person, one person such as yourself, to be accused by multiple people of sexually molesting children?"

"Uh-huh," Dick agreed.

"Your sister-in-law, Joann Green, has accused you of sexually molesting her. Okay? Your nephew—did you ever take your nephew hunting up in Upper Marlboro?"

"Uh-huh."

"What were you hunting?"

"Squirrel."

"Okay, so if he says you took him hunting, that would be the truth."

"Take him hunting? Yeah."

"But if he says you sexually molested him—"

"That would be a lie."

"—that would be a lie. So he's lying, and Joann Green is lying?"

"Yeah."

"Your own daughter says—"

"That's a whole lot—"

"—you sexually molested her."

"You believe that?"

"Yes, sir."

"Not true."

"My point to you, Mr. Welch, is simply this: Would you agree with me that the type of person that would abduct and molest and murder two girls is the same type of person these other people would accuse of sexually molesting them, [someone] that would have sexual interest in children?"

"I'm not that type of guy. I did not. I don't like little girls."

"What do you like?"

"I like . . . I like my wife."

When they came around to asking him whether he had any involvement in the Lyon case, Dick was succinct and firm.

"God as my witness, no."

"Did you transport one or both of these girls—Sheila and Kate Lyon—from Wheaton Plaza to your residence?"

"No, I didn't. I've never been there."

"Did you have sexual contact with either Sheila or Kate Lyon?"

"God as my witness, no."

He gave similar crisp answers to the whole litany of accusations.

"Do you have knowledge of any of these things that I've talked about?"

"No, but I wish I did." He had earlier said that he wished he could help the detectives solve the mystery. "But I didn't."

"Do you have any explanation why people would say that you did?"

"I don't know."

"This is your chance to explain."

"That's what I'm saying. I don't know why I'm getting accused, them saying I did this, I done that. I haven't."

"All right. So your answer is, then, you don't have any explanation?"

"No, because I didn't do anything."

Tud

That is where the case against Uncle Dick stood until May, when the squad found someone who confirmed Lloyd's accusation. Yet another Welch cousin, Wes Justice, a man Lloyd hardly knew, ten years his junior, would tell the grand jury that his uncle Dick had spontaneously confessed to him his role in the crime and had also named Lloyd and Lloyd's father, Lee. Better yet, unlike Lloyd, Wes had no obvious animus toward his uncle. It had taken months to fully pry the story out of him.

Wes's mother, Ruth, was a younger sister to Dick and Lee. Wes was a plumber and looked like one, a disheveled, portly man, unshaven, with a mop of salt-and-pepper hair that was usually crushed under a baseball cap. His family nickname was "Tud." He was a simple man. One of the things he liked to do was fart into Mason jars, which he sealed and kept in the freezer—at one point he showed off this collection to Mark. He would uncork his preserved flatulence around unsuspecting visitors and collapse with giggles at their disgust. Emotional and blunt, Wes had an ambivalent connection to his extended family; he seemed at once loyal and afraid—so afraid that the detectives wondered whether he, too, might have been abused as a child.

On a summer afternoon in 2014, at about the time the full-court press on the Welch family began, Wes stopped by his uncle's house in Hyattsville. He said he was driving past, taking a break from a job in Washington, and saw his uncle mowing the lawn, so he pulled into the driveway. In the conversation that ensued, Wes said, his uncle told him about the Lyon case investigation and "came out and said that he raped those girls."

This was the version Wes told the grand jury in May 2015.

"When Dickie was telling you that the girls were raped, who did he say was involved in their rape?" the prosecutor asked him.

"Lee."

"Lee Welch?"

"Lee Welch and Lloyd."

"Lloyd Welch. And who else?"

"That's the only thing he told [me] was them two and him," said Wes.

He said Dick told him how the girls had been lured by Lloyd from Wheaton Plaza, and then raped repeatedly on a pool table in Dick's house before being killed. They had been taken to Taylor's Mountain—Wes was uncertain whether they were alive or dead at that point—in a green station wagon owned by his cousin Jimmy Welch. The car had then been hidden in a dilapidated barn on the property.

The first time the squad had heard this story, or part of it, was the previous October, after Wes and his cousin Norma Jean Welch were subpoenaed to appear before the Bedford grand jury. Conferring beforehand by phone, Wes told Norma Jean that he was worried he would be asked about "a green station wagon" that he believed had been used to carry the Lyon girls south. Norma Jean, who was trying to be helpful, passed this along to the squad—this is what ultimately prompted the exhaustive and futile air and ground search of Taylor's Mountain. On the same day Norma Jean called, Mark and Katie had driven to Wes's house in Prince Frederick, in southern Maryland.

They knocked on Wes's door on Halloween, a few hours before trick-or-treaters would be out. Wes was startled to see the detectives, and rattled. He couldn't imagine why they had come all that way. And he was not ready to tell the same story he would later tell the grand jury. As his grandchildren played in the next room, he sat with his wife, Robin, a large blond woman who was considerably more poised than her husband, and swore he knew nothing about the case apart from what he had seen online. But he confirmed his remarks to Norma Jean about a green station wagon, which was something that had not been part of any public discussion. Mark and Katie wanted to know where he had heard it. At this, Wes melted down. Sobbing, he stormed from the room and the house. Robin called after him, telling him to calm down and tell the truth. Mark followed him out to the yard.

"I'm trying to think of who I heard it from!" Wes shouted in frustration.

"I know your heart is in the right place," said Mark. "We know you don't want to get involved."

Pointing to Wes's grandchildren, Mark invoked John and Mary Lyon. "Can you imagine those two beautiful kids you've got in there? They know their kids got raped, got murdered."

Wes expressed his revulsion and disbelief that *anyone*, much less someone in his own family, could do such a thing.

"That station wagon might be the key to the whole thing," said Mark.

Wes calmed down. He then told Mark that his uncle Dick had mentioned the car to him in their August conversation. He repeated this when he appeared before the grand jury for the first time, in November.

"He [Dick] just popped up out of the blue about a station wagon up in the mountains in a barn," he told the jurors. "He said it's covered up. And I think he said there's blankets in the back of it."

"Why did that pop up?" a prosecutor asked.

"I don't know."

Wes said the car had belonged to his cousin Jimmy Welch. At the close of his testimony, he had added something intriguing. Summing up, the Virginia prosecutor had stated, "Here's the thing. Obviously, something very terrible happened to those girls. Okay? Age ten. Age twelve. Okay?" And Wes had responded, "I understand. Something—you're right. Something terrible happened, *cut them up, burned them up*, or something."

Here was an echo of Lloyd's own original speculation, which Wes could not have heard. It prompted the squad to invite him in for another chat in Gaithersburg on April 26. When he didn't show up, Mark and Katie went looking for him. They found him at home in Prince Frederick that evening. Wes said his phone was broken, so he hadn't been able to call and cancel, but this, the detectives told him, was not the kind of invitation to be ignored. A number of people were about to be charged with perjury, Mark said, and Wes was on the list.

The plumber was horrified. How could they connect him with such a terrible thing!

"A lot of people have tried to obstruct our investigation," Mark explained. "The prosecutors are pretty fed up."

The detective had brought a transcript of Dick Welch's grand jury testimony and, bluffing, told Wes that his uncle had talked in detail about their August conversation. Mark said Dick's account had contradicted Wes's about a number of things (this was not true).

"It's hard to think that a seventy-year-old man would remember more than you," said Mark.

Wes panicked. He pleaded that he'd told them everything. All he knew was that his cousin Jimmy's car had been involved. For this they were dragging him into it! He had been ten years old when it happened! What could he possibly have known?

"I'm actually here for your benefit," said Mark. "The grand jury doesn't believe you don't know more."

Wes repeated, almost spitting the words, "Dick did not mention about no girls. Nothing like that."

Mark asked again how the subject of the station wagon had come up.

"It's been so long," said Wes. "I have totally blocked it out!"

Katie tried to soothe him. She told him he was the one person they had interviewed who actually showed some feelings about the matter. "The only one who shows any semblance of caring," she said, using the same approach she often employed with Lloyd. "We know you have a conscience," she said, and then added, "but there's no way in hell you can forget this stuff."

Wes complained that they were "jumping down my throat!"

"It's about doing the right thing," said Katie.

They talked about closure, and Wes agreed that the Lyon family deserved some. "I just can't believe it," he said. "It's unreal how anybody could do something like this."

"We know you are a good guy," said Katie. "People put you in a bad spot because they told you something."

"Did you hear that?" Robin said to him. "They think you're not telling them something."

"No one wants to charge you, but not just one but *three people* have told us things they told you," Mark said, exaggerating. "It's hard to believe you don't remember." He pointed out the remarks in Wes's grand jury testimony about the girls having been "chopped and burned."

"How come 'chopped and burned'?" Mark asked. "It actually happened."

"Nobody told me that," said Wes. "Nobody never."

"Of all the ways, the *exact* way."

"Dick never said that to me. I just blurted it out on the stand."

"We don't want to get you hemmed up," said Mark. "We are trying to lead the horse to water."

After much more of this, Wes fairly *shouted out* his uncle's name.

"It came from Dick! He wanted to go up and smash the car. He was all nervous and upset from him and Teddy, and he started blurting stuff out. He wanted to go to the mountain, find the car, smash it, and get rid of it."

Mark reminded Wes that he had been given immunity before his testimony in November, and that the agreement was still in effect.

"You need to try harder," urged Robin.

"This has got to come out today," said Mark. "We're out on a limb here with the prosecutor."

"Dick has no remorse," said Wes. "He don't care."

"Your wife wants you to come clean," pleaded Katie. "We don't understand why you're holding back, unless you had something to do with it on the back end."

"Even if you went down and did something with that car, you aren't in trouble," said Mark.

"He [Dick] said he wanted to find the car—Jimmy Welch's—and destroy it."

"Why would he blurt all this stuff to you?" Katie asked.

"I guess because Tommy Junior [Teddy] scared the shit out of him." (There had been, in fact, nothing whatever threatening in Teddy's recorded conversation with his uncle.)

Mark wondered whether Dick had brought up the car because he wanted Wes's help.

"He didn't say anything, Mark. I didn't say anything. He wanted to smash it all up, flatten it, I guess."

"Don't guess," said Robin. "You're making it worse."

"I'm not making it worse! I just don't want to fucking deal with this!"

"You are involved in it!" said Robin.

Wes blew up and marched outside again, and again Mark followed, talking to him in the yard.

"It's not going to go away," the detective said.

"I know it's not going to go away."

Mark asked him if his reluctance to get involved was more important than resolving the case for the Lyon family.

"I don't know anything else!" Wes insisted.

"You know, and I know you do. I'm here as your friend. I've gone to bat with the prosecutor. He has a list of all who are going to be prosecuted. I'm here to get you off that list. The only way is for the person with the goodness, you, to step up. Not just the bullet points, the details. The details of your conversation with Dick."

"I told you everything I know."

"There's more. You are covered as long as you tell the truth."

Wes broke down. He sobbed. He repeated his disbelief that a member of his family could be involved in such a thing. Mark told him it wasn't just Dick and Lloyd and Lee, it was also his aunt Pat and his cousins who helped them cover it up. He painted a dark picture of Dick, especially, suggesting to Wes that the Lyon girls had not been his only victims. Women in his family had been victimized, other strangers. He suggested that Dick had kidnapped, raped, and killed others.

"You hold the key for all these people," Mark said.

And Wes finally told a fuller story, the one he would repeat in May before the grand jury about his uncles and Lloyd, about the girls being raped repeatedly on a pool table, about his uncle Dick asking for help disposing of the car that had carried the girls to Virginia. When Wes was done, Mark asked, "What *is it* about this family?"

"What's gonna happen to Dick?" Wes asked.

"Should he be allowed to live another day free?" Mark asked.

"Hell no."

"Why didn't you tell us back then?"

"I was scared. I was really scared, Mark. Two young kids being raped by freaking old men. I just can't believe it. I need to take stuff more seriously. Wow. I feel sick now."

Wes was, the squad couldn't help noticing, a lot like his cousin Lloyd. It was just as hard to wring a full story from him, and, after they finally did, they were left wondering how much of it was true.

Feral

It had taken effort, but the squad could now more clearly picture Lloyd at age eighteen. They could look past the sad, pasty, wily, shackled old man who met them in the interview room and see teenage Lloyd, lean, dirty, mean, and high—stoned, speeding, tripping, or drunk. He had been feral. In ordinary times, this might have made him stand out, but in the late 1960s, during and after the Summer of Love, at about the time he was cast off by his family, many teenage boys were growing their hair long, dressing shabbily, infrequently bathing, and freely experimenting with drugs. Lloyd ran smack into the hippie movement in its heyday. For most, this period was a fling, youthful defiance of middle-class suburban norms. But for Lloyd it was no pose. He really was poor, desperate, dirty, and up for anything. And for the first and only time in his life he actually fit in. By 1975 the hippie movement had faded, but Lloyd hadn't changed. He was then part of a class of shaggy vagabonds thumbing their way around the country on back roads, camping in the woods outside suburbia. Like Lloyd and Helen, many were heavy drug users. Flower power had gone to seed. They still proclaimed, as Lloyd would proclaim, the fading mantras of the hippie moment—free love, mind-expanding drugs, and the all-encompassing "If it feels good, do it," but few had considered what such a credo might mean to man like Lloyd Welch.

The hillbilly subculture that produced him has been described in more recent years by author J. D. Vance as "a permanent American underclass." The Welches had never blended into white-collar suburbia. In Hyattsville during the 1960s and '70s, they had lived clustered in the same run-down apartment complexes and eventually in houses on the same run-down blocks, reproducing rapidly. They were marked by their distinctive hill-country manners and dialect, trapped in low-paying jobs with few prospects, cantankerous, prone to violence, colliding frequently with the police, and, sealed in the intimacy of their crowded homes, carrying on vicious old habits.

Lloyd had been an outcast even from this. Abused and abandoned by his father, reclaimed only to be cast out again, at age eighteen he was already an outlaw, stranded on the fringes of a prosperous world beyond his grasp. Although still haunting his family, he was homeless, often camping with Helen in the region's shrinking wooded patches. After he had been publicly linked to the Lyon case, three other women had surfaced with stories of a man who had either assaulted or attempted to lure them as children—all in the mid-1970s, all before the Lyon girls were taken. Each described a man who resembled Lloyd. There was the unsolved case of a fourteen-year-old girl who had been raped by a man who emerged from a patch of woods adjacent to her school. Others said the man had approached them in the mall flashing an official-looking badge, claiming he was an undercover security officer. One girl had refused to leave with him. Two others, in a separate incident, had gone with him, getting into a car before thinking better of it. One had jumped out while it was moving. This caused him to stop, at which point the second girl bolted. If the man in any of these encounters had been Lloyd, the incidents suggested he had been perfecting his approach.

In a twisted way, it made sense for Lloyd to prey on children at the mall, for several reasons. For one thing, he could do so anonymously. Unlike the old small-town Main Streets, where everyone knew everyone else, centers like Wheaton Plaza drew from a wide and densely populated region. Strolling in the mall was more like walking down a city sidewalk; occasionally you would run into someone you knew, but mostly you did not. A sea of strangers was the perfect hunting ground for a predator. And Wheaton Plaza made sense for a deeper reason. Malls were suburbia's gleaming showcases, lined with high-end stores stocked with goods Lloyd could not afford, displaying colorful, oversize ads for a lifestyle beyond his reach. They drew clean and prosperous families with credit cards and shopping lists. Living in the woods with his girlfriend, Lloyd would not have known how to take the first step into that world. And while he was not the sort to reflect on such things, much less articulate them, he must have resented the plenitude, all the comforts of money, family, and community that he lacked. As Lloyd himself had put it, "I was an angry person when I was young." And if he felt scorn, or rage, how better to strike back than to stalk the very thing the mall's privileged customers most prized? The pretty little girls he saw there, to whom he was perversely attracted, represented everything he was denied. Might such a man, driven by lust and rage, steal them . . . drug them . . . ravish them . . . kill them . . . dismember them . . . *burn them*?

It was a theory. In it, perhaps, was the outline of an answer to the old crime's deepest mystery, the one that had bothered me through the years. Who would do such a thing? And why?

None of these ideas were conveyed to Lloyd, of course. The detectives continued to pretend he was, at heart, *a really good guy*, eager to do the right thing, whom they were ever-ready to take at his ever-changing word. They did so because for them to learn what had happened to the Lyon sisters, Lloyd would have to tell them, even though he had every reason in the world not to. He wasn't going to stop talking. In addition to his other motivations—to find out what they knew, to break the monotony of his days—they now realized how much he was enjoying himself. This extended dialogue was a game he believed he could win. And often the detectives wondered whether he was right. At times it felt as if he was leading them in circles.

At each visit, the squad tried to bring him evidence, real or invented, strong enough to make him recast his story. From the first it had worked this way. Confronting him with his 1975 statement—a thing he could not deny—had compelled him to admit he'd been in the mall, which had compelled him, in self-defense, to name someone else as the kidnapper. He'd seized on Mileski because that's who the squad put in front of him. After they removed Mileski as a possibility, he had offered up Teddy, not knowing that his age and broken arms would virtually rule him out.

He had correctly surmised that Teddy and "an older man"—Kraisel—would appeal to them. When that scenario was disproved by the time line, and it was pointed out that he and Teddy would have needed an older accomplice with a car, he'd named Dick, another shrewd choice, as it turned out, given the family's stories about his uncle. When real witnesses placed Lloyd squarely in Virginia with a bloody duffel bag, something he could not safely deny, he'd edged his cousin Henry into the picture—after all, Henry was one of those who had named him.

The one constant in all these shifts was Lloyd's effort to move himself off center. Present but *not involved*. The logical contortions this required were both repellent and laughable, such as "partying" with two scared little girls and then "babysitting" them during days when they were being drugged and raped. But with each new twist, Lloyd revealed more.

Friction

Three months passed. Lloyd's promised day before the grand jury, and his visit with Edna, did not come.

Dave had meant it when he'd made the offer. The Lyon squad had got the RV authorized and intended to wire it up. The detectives had planned to use the trip as a pretext for another long interview. Dave would ride with Lloyd, and the rest of the squad would follow in another car, listening. They could then switch up, do their usual tag-team routine. They would take Lloyd up to Taylor's Mountain first to see whether anything there stirred more memories, and then on to the copper-domed courthouse. Before the grand jury, he would be under oath. Because Lloyd so feared additional charges, it might help pin him down.

But their partners in Virginia had balked. The Marylanders were wearing out their welcome. Bedford had thrown open its doors at first, but when the work produced so little, the relationship grew strained. The sheriff's office had fought to conduct the digs on Taylor's Mountain itself—a point of local pride—spurning the FBI's evidence-recovery experts, recruited by Montgomery County, a move that had delayed the work for months and disappointed the squad members, who had been pleased by the FBI's willingness to help. When the digging yielded little, there remained the suspicion in Maryland that the wrong people had done it. Then there was the matter of indicting Pat Welch for obstruction. The point, as the Marylanders saw it, was to pressure her to testify more candidly, but after being charged, Pat was not reinterviewed. Months later she pleaded guilty and was released on probation. Instead of turning up the heat, the Bedford team had let Pat get off effectively scot-free. There were other instances when the squad felt a lack of eagerness below the border. Bedford was a small community and a close one. Some of those targeted by the probe were, in the eyes of local officers, good ol' boys they knew well, whose protests found a welcome hearing. The Virginians, for their part, were increasingly disinclined to let these obsessed cold case detectives order them around.

These tensions may or may not have contributed to Bedford's refusal to bring Lloyd down. Inviting Lloyd into its jurisdiction for any reason other than to try him for murder was a step too far. Guarding him, figuring out where to confine him overnight, would have been costly and risky. Compared with the thousand-man Montgomery County Police Department, the Bedford County Sheriff's Office was a storefront operation. A security detail to keep watch on Lloyd for several days would have put a strain on its routine patrol duties. The RV ride fell through.

But Virginia was still helping. After the trip was nixed, Chris, Dave, Mark, and Katie contrived to use the refusal to shape their strategy for the next encounter with Lloyd, which was set for Friday, May 1. They were met in Dover by a team of Virginia detectives.

This time they hoped to scare the truth out of him.

May 1, 2015

Dave reentered the familiar interview room carrying the usual two cups of coffee.

"My brother! What's happening?" he said, and then, anticipating Lloyd's usual lament about having been roused early and kept waiting, said, "I know. Don't yell at me."

"Man, I've been up since two o'clock this morning," said Lloyd. He had been dozing in the chair.

"If it means anything, you look good," said Dave. "You do. You look like you've lost a little weight. You look like you're in better shape. You do."

The praise perked Lloyd up. He did look healthier. He said he had been working out.

"This [session] is really for you," said Dave. "And I'm going to explain everything to you. Where we are at. Where it's going. And this may be the last time that we meet."

"Uh-oh."

"No, no, no, no, no. Not in a bad way."

Dave said the promised RV drive had fallen through because of a conflict with Virginia. That much was true, but Dave put his own spin on it: Bedford wanted to charge Lloyd immediately, and the Lyon squad, in his corner, was frantically trying to fend it off. He showed Lloyd the standard forms outlining his rights—"this nonsense," he called it.

"Nothing has changed on the form," he said. "There are no charges."

One of Lloyd's more curious failings was a grandiosely erroneous estimation of how much control he had over his circumstances. He now told Dave that he had been drafting his own blanket immunity agreement—one that would guarantee he would never be charged with anything in the Lyon case. It was a guilty man's dream. No prosecutor would ever agree to such a thing, but Lloyd had visited the prison's law library and drafted one. He had originally planned to insist that it be endorsed before he set foot in the grand jury room, but, he said, he had decided against it. Seeing how eager the squad was for him to testify, and being the magnanimous fellow he was, he had planned to shelve it, telling himself, as he related now to Dave, "I'm not going to put them through that hassle, because I'm trying to get out of here. I'm trying to start what little life I got left, trying to do good." Since they had never come for him, he'd missed the chance to make the grand gesture, but he wanted Dave to know about it. The detective changed the subject.

"You look real good," he repeated.

"Huh?"

"I said you look *real* good."

"Not bad for a fifty-eight-year-old man?" he said, holding up his right arm and flexing his biceps.

"When can you get out?" Dave asked, as if they had not discussed this before, and as if that were still an option. It was a topic that always cheered Lloyd up. "How many years you got left?"

"Well, see, that's the thing. On paper it says twenty twenty-four [the year 2024], but with the good time and stuff like that building up, if I don't get charged for none of this right here, then I could be out of here by twenty-one [2021], at the earliest." He had not been granted the five-year dispensation he'd sought in 2013.

"So you'll be—six years—you'll be, like, say, sixty-five."

"I've done a lot of rotten things in my life. And in the nineteen years I've been incarcerated here, this has taught me a lesson that I never want to learn again. And, like I said, I found the Lord, and I really want to start helping people and stuff like that."

They talked about how much the world had changed, especially the advances in technology. Dave marveled at what he had read of the new Apple Watch, which had been released the previous month. "It does everything your phone and computer does, and it's a watch!"

If he were set free that day, Lloyd said, he'd have exactly eighty-two cents of his own. Delaware would give him fifty dollars and some clean clothes.

"You can't even get a motel for fifty dollars!" said Dave.

"So, what happens to me is, I get violated, and I'm right back in the system."

Dave commiserated: "It's a huge problem that nobody wants to seem to think about."

In time they got around to business. The detective had, he said, new information, "because, like I said, this is more about you today. I've spent a lot of time with you, and we've built up a pretty decent relationship."

"I think we have. And I don't like cops. But I'll be honest with you—this is from the heart—I actually do like you and the rest of the team. You know, I talk to you more than I talk to them, but I've actually come to respect you three. I've actually come to respect you three more than anything else in the world, because—y'all are officers, don't get me wrong on that—it's because you're human beings. I don't think you're gonna throw me under the bus."

"No. And that's why I want to explain everything to you, because we've always tried to be up front with you." This, of course, was not true. He had been duplicitous from the start, and so had Lloyd. It was the game.

"Let me tell you something," said Dave. "It wasn't easy to get here. There was a lot of people that said, 'No, we're done communicating with him.' There was a lot of shenanigans that went on. Part of what got shut down was the grand jury."

"So, they wanted to charge me, put it all on me?"

"It's looking like that. And that's why it's an important day for both of us."

"I've already come to the conclusion they're going to pin it on me."

"Well, let's see what we can get here today. Our county in Maryland, Montgomery, has always been about answers. When we came down here we wanted answers. So, what? We hit you with a charge? You're already in jail. So what difference does it make if we charge you? You're not going anywhere. So, it was all about answers. But then you get other agencies involved, and things start to change. It was like fighting tooth and nail, with some folks saying we've invested two years of our careers in you. We believe in you. Give us one more shot. I said, 'Give me an opportunity.'"

"Yeah. I've implicated myself so much. I realized it when I left [the last session] that I was fucked."

"And that's what I said," Dave explained. Today was a chance to back away from the ledge. Dave said he'd brought his lunch and that they would eat together and "kick back," but first he wanted to run through the whole thing once more. Lloyd retold the story of his uncle Dick's efforts to recruit him, how he and Dick and Teddy drove to the mall. When he got to the part about talking the girls into leaving with them, Dave interrupted.

"All right. Let's stop right there. You've got three or four people that see Lloyd Welch in the mall. No one has ever said anything about Teddy."

"Right."

"No one has ever said anything about Dick, because he was outside in the car. So you've got Lloyd Welch."

But Lloyd refused to take Teddy out of the picture. He walked Dave through the same story he had told last time, but in this version, he now claimed, preposterously, that he did not know when he went back to the mall to give his statement that the girls he had seen at his uncle's house were the Lyon sisters. He now said he thought the girls were just runaways. This ignored much of what he had told them in the previous months, about seeking the reward money, about trying to deflect police interest in himself. It was as if he had never said those things. This appeared to be something he had worked out in his cell during the previous months, a new strategy. It showed a staggering lack of awareness. He seemed to completely buy that Dave was here to help him craft a self-defense narrative, untethered to facts, into which he could plug new, more favorable particulars for old problematic ones—and that no would notice or care!

"So I was going to use them two girls who I thought was actually running away." His choice of the word *use* here was revealing. "You know what I'm saying? Because at the time, I really didn't know their names or really know their faces or anything like that. Like I said, they never said, 'Help' or anything like that when we looked after them. So I thought they were running away."

Otherwise he stuck to the version of the story he had told three weeks earlier, seeing Dick drive up at night, the bag, the fire, the horrible odor. Dave sat through it all, pointing out once or twice how jurors might see through it—Lloyd transparently removing himself from the picture at every stage. But it wasn't good enough. Virginia's prosecutors weren't buying it, Dave explained, because they were more intent on nailing him than on learning the truth. In short, Lloyd was about to be charged with murder.

"Does the DNA from the bones show that it was the girls?" Lloyd asked.

"Got one fragment that shows," said Dave, falsely.

"Now, the question is, how did Lloyd get dead bodies from point A to point B?" Lloyd said, speaking of himself in the third person.

"That's why we're here, because there's lots of stuff in between that we've got answers to. And that's why I'm back. I begged," said Dave. He said he wanted to see whether Lloyd could give him answers that matched up with what they already knew. This was a timeworn interrogation tactic and a stretch. They knew little more than what Lloyd had told them.

"It's hard for me to believe that you don't have some of the answers that you left out," Dave said. "And I get it."

Lloyd altered his story a little. Earlier he had said that he and Helen had gone to Virginia because Dick had told him to get lost. Now he said he had been *asked* by his uncle and his father to go. He said Dick visited him at his father's house and recommended that he and Helen leave earlier than they had planned. "It would be best if you got out of here," he said Dick told him.

"And was that because he knows you were seen at the mall and he knows it's going to hit the media?"

"Uh-huh."

"And now he's worried that you're going to get caught, which is going to implicate him, or you're simply going to turn on him?"

"Yeah. And Lee did make a phone call that we were coming."

"Let's stop right there. Let's not leave anything out. And what I mean by that is, I'm not saying you're holding back. I'm not saying you're lying. I'm thinking from a person outside, taking my feelings out—I mean, I really do care for you—but if you're supposed to be going down there, and Dick has come up with this plan that he eventually is going to come down there with these girls, whether they're alive or dead, why wouldn't he give you a car to drive? Or you and Helen ride with him? Why would you try to hitchhike to Bedford? Explain that, because that logically doesn't make sense."

Lloyd clung to his hitchhiking story. This was crucial. It freed him from having been involved with transporting the Lyon girls to Virginia. He knew that any such involvement would mean more trouble. So he argued again that he and his uncle didn't get along well enough for Dick to offer him a ride. Besides, he said, he and Helen would not have wanted to spend five hours in the car with Dick.

"So, they were dead or alive when you left?"

"They were alive when we left. What happened after that, I don't know."

"Who had sex with them?"

Lloyd said he didn't know.

A Trick or the Truth?

The most important thing, Dave said, was to know who killed Sheila and Kate and where.

"I can give you my suspicion," said Lloyd.

"Give it to me."

"I honestly think it was Dick and Lee. I would think that the girls had had enough; they wanted to go home," Lloyd said, as if Sheila and Kate had initially been keen on their abduction and rape. "Dickie didn't want to send them home. He would be charged with rape and kidnapping and all that. And he decided to get rid of them. And knowing him and Lee were as close as they were . . ."

This was a breakthrough. Lloyd was now coming to the actual murder scene. Dave just let him continue.

Lloyd said the girls wouldn't have been killed in Dick's house. Dick and Lee would have taken them somewhere else. "Where, I don't know." Both men were married and had children living at home. Too many people. He suggested that the girls might have been drugged, knocked unconscious, or even strangled, and then carried up to the railroad tracks that ran near Dick's house or over to the Anacostia River basin, a small tributary that winds down from the northeast toward the Potomac. There they would have been chopped into pieces and put into the duffel bag or bags. Either that, Lloyd said, or Dick and Lee had set off to take the girls to Virginia, and one girl "had gotten out of hand" and was killed on the way.

This was more than Lloyd had ever told them about the girls' ultimate fate. Dave deliberately did not remark on it.

"We've got theories," he told Lloyd. He explained how stories gained credence because of provable details. "I'll give you one because it sticks in my mind. There was a red Ford Pinto station wagon stolen from a Ford dealership right next to the mall the day the girls were abducted. That car was recovered by PG [Prince Georges] County an eighth of a mile away from Dick's house [about a half-hour drive from Wheaton Plaza without traffic]."

Lloyd lifted an eyebrow and smiled.

"And because I stole a couple of cars, the theory is that Lloyd took the car," he said.

"And in your original statement you said that the car was red."

"Oh Lord," Lloyd lamented. "Oh Lord."

"You see?"

"When I first started talking to y'all, back then I was bullshit," said Lloyd. "But everything I've told you in the last year, when I started telling you about Dickie and stuff like that, it started weighing on my conscience. I'm fifty-eight years old. I've held this shit in too long. It's . . . I can't tell you who killed them."

Dave thought he could. He said, "If I told you that I know that Dick killed them, damn near can prove it—I can't prove whether you helped, didn't help. And I can tell you how he killed them, and obviously we know where they ended up. Now, in my mind, the only thing that you're holding out on is some knowledge, just because of the family and the tightness. And because I already know, and you can tell me some of those details, then I could go back and say, 'Look, he told me what we already can prove.' That helps *you*."

"But then that implicates me."

"How does that implicate you?"

"Okay, let's just say I know how they were killed; I know where they were killed; I know who killed them. Then that implicates me being there when they were killed."

"But that's the trust that you and I have to develop. I'm not here tricking you."

Dave said that a family member had come forward who was "very little at the time," but whom Dick trusted—he was talking about Wes Justice. "It was like pulling teeth to get this guy to testify before the grand jury, and finally he broke, and he broke bad. He laid it all out for what Dick told him. And if you were able to back that up—"

"See, that's the problem—"

"If not, then it stands as Lloyd, Lloyd, Lloyd." Then Dave extended his hand. "Out here is Dick and Teddy. And we can't prove any of this shit."

He told Lloyd in effect, *I think there's more you could tell, but you're worried that you're being played.*

Lloyd concurred. "Is it a trick, or is that the truth, or . . . you see what I am going through?" he asked.

"I can't give it to you, because if I do, then they're just going to say, 'Nah, you spoon-fed him that, and he gave it back to you.' You've already hinted around at it before."

"I have?"

"Yes. I want to say that it was in the last interview that you hinted around it. And that's what really drew our attention to what this guy [Wes] is saying."

"Can you refresh my memory of me hinting around?"

"Had to do with the bag. One of the things you corroborated was that your dad, that Lee, had a bag just like yours."

"Yeah."

"That's part of it, but think about what you said when you were being blamed for them being put in the bag, about how they wound up in the bag."

"Oh, chopped up?"

Dave made a gesture with his hands, as if to say, *Voilà!*

Lloyd continued, "Because he said it was bloody, and I said, Well, the only way that I could think about it is if they were chopped up."

"No, what you actually said—you got pissed because you were being accused of killing them. And what you did is, you threw your hands up and said, 'What? Am I supposed to have chopped them up and put them in a bag?' What was told to this person by Dick is that he chopped them up."

"Now, see, I will say that he did," said Lloyd. "I mean, I know for a fact, because he had a little section outside where he chopped wood and stuff like that, because he used to sell wood. Now, he did have an ax, and he did have a hatchet. And he kept them very sharp. And he kept them down in the basement with his other tools. But for me to say that I actually saw him do that, I can't."

"So, you're told by your family to get the hell out of Dodge," said Dave.

"Basically, that's exactly the way it was."

Lloyd had come a long way. He had suggested that his uncle and father had killed the girls and dismembered them. Then he said the station wagon his uncle Dick had driven to Virginia afterward, to deliver the bloody duffel bags, belonged to his aunt Pat or possibly to her father.

"There's two problems that we have to unfuck here," said Dave. These were the stories told by Connie Akers and Henry Parker about Lloyd's bloody duffel bag. Both witnesses gave very specific accounts of Lloyd delivering the bags, and both were believable. Their stories jibed. Lloyd had contradicted both—two against one. Here, again, was plausible evidence that Lloyd would have to explain away.

"Wow," he said, staring the obstacle in the face.

"Yeah. So, we have to undo that and somehow figure out Dick's role in this mess."

"Yeah," said Lloyd, intently collaborating. "So, Henry and Connie are saying, 'Lloyd did it.' Lloyd and Helen didn't show up in no car." He bragged about how powerful his legs were from all the walking he did when he was young. He said he had no memory of encountering Connie with a bag of dirty clothes. He grew angry just talking about the story told by Connie and Henry, and announced that he was done trying to protect anyone in his family. "I tried covering them. I tried to leave it alone, walking away. And I did it for forty years."

"I've got my own opinion," said Dave. "But there's got to be something that you can give me that I can back up, because I have my opinion. And it's good—it's a good opinion of you, and it's a very bad opinion of Dick. And it's easy for Connie to do kind of what you did in the beginning. You'd give us some truth. You just interchanged people."

"Uh-huh," Lloyd agreed, and then came up with a motive for Connie to lie. "I honestly think that Connie had a crush on me. I honestly do. And she was pissed off whenever I'd show up with Helen."

"So explain to me why—"

"Why she would lie on me?"

"Yeah."

"To save Dick's ass, is what I think."

"Right," said Dave. "Because how easy would it be if the true story is that you simply just showed up down there? Dick comes down because that's the plan they came up with when you left. They said, 'We got to do something, the shit's on, Lloyd's been back at the mall, he's been seen, and now he's lied to the police, it's eventually going to come home, we got to do something.' They panic. I don't know where they were killed. More than likely, they used an ax and chopped them up because that's what he [Dick] told this other family member. And I was trying not to lead you."

"Right," said Lloyd. He liked how this was going. Dave had caught the spirit of the thing.

"If there's one person in your corner, it's me," said Dave.

"Right."

"Because I don't want to see you get charged with capital murder in Virginia if you didn't kill them."

I'm Fucked Now. I'm Dead.

After a lunch break, Dave returned beleaguered.

"Holy smokes!" he said.

"What?"

"I was going to come in here and eat with you, man, but they beat me up something awful out there."

"They beat you up?" In Lloyd's world the expression wasn't metaphorical.

Dave explained that the prosecutors and police from Virginia, who were waiting eagerly in the next room, were going press charges against Lloyd unless the squad could extract something new from him, some verifiable fact that corroborated his version of events.

This was, of course, a ploy. The commonwealth attorney's office was being very cooperative, not clamoring at that moment to press charges.

"It's a mess," said Dave. "The first thing I said to them when I walked in there is, 'I believe him one hundred percent. I believe him.' I said, 'There are some things that may differ a little bit than what we've been able to prove, but it's explainable.' But what they said is, 'Look, it's a whole lot different than what he said the last time.' And the way they're looking at it is, *you're going in reverse instead of forward*. And I said, 'Well, what do you want me to do?' So I figured we'd come back in here."

Dave told him how absurd "babysitting" the girls sounded.

"If you were told, simply sit your ass in that poolroom and watch these girls, and the girls were tied up or gagged, and that's what you saw, and that's why you went and watched TV, because you didn't want to be a part of it, I can understand that. It's a little more explainable than you were 'babysitting,' and they didn't say anything. That's bullshit. It was Easter Sunday. It was her [Sheila's] birthday. I'm, like, wait a minute."

"But that's the whole thing," Lloyd protested. "They didn't say anything to me."

"Did they look scared? We're talking about a ten- and twelve-year-old girl."

But Lloyd stuck with it. "I mean, back then, who was scared? It was all free love and partying and shit like that. Those girls were never tied up. I didn't see them tied up, so I can't say if they were tied up. And not one of them said, 'Hey, I want to go home,' 'Hey, this is Easter weekend, you going to let us go? Help us?' Anything. They didn't say nothing.

They didn't talk to me at all, you know. He showed me where those girls were at and just said 'babysit them.'" He said Helen would have done something if she thought the girls were being abused.

This, Dave reiterated, was inconceivable. Kate had been crying when she left the mall, days earlier. She would have been frantic. He talked about the childlike drawings and writings found in the girls' rooms and schoolwork.

"They were kids, man. They were coloring! This wasn't two girls who were going to smoke and drink. And now you're talking about being in a stranger's house for five days? And who knows how many people have run through [raped] them? And it's Easter Sunday and one of their birthdays?"

"Uh-huh."

"How can—"

"I didn't know it was her birthday."

"It doesn't add up."

"I understand that. You asked me earlier if one of the girls looked like they were drugged. And I told you the older one looked like she was drugged. I believe both of them was drugged." He offered a theory. He said he thought Pat was a nurse—she wasn't—and that would have given her access to needles and drugs. Lloyd was flailing now. He floated the idea that the girls may have been running away from home because their father was abusing them. Dave said these explanations were not going to help him.

"You understand completely now that we need to try to make something work," the detective said. "And if we don't, then we're left with a pile of shit. Both of us are."

Lloyd would not alter his story.

"Why would you guys hitchhike and then have them follow you down in a car?" Dave asked.

"Why? I didn't even know they were coming down. I didn't have a car."

"Did you ride with them?"

"We actually hitchhiked. Me and Helen hitchhiked out of there."

"How are we going to explain what Connie says and what Henry says?"

"They're lying. They are totally lying. We did not come down there in a car."

Lloyd looked beaten. He said he was resigned to taking all the blame, unfairly.

"How can we undo it?" asked Dave. "How can we switch it back?"

"I mean, I could sit here and say, 'Hey, I saw Dick chop them up.' I'd be lying. I could say, 'Hey, I knew they were taking them down to Virginia.' I'd be lying. You see what I'm saying?"

"Uh-huh."

"I can only admit to what I know. I can't fabricate that I saw him chop them up. I can't fabricate that I knew they were in a car and that he was just going to take them down. I can't. I didn't drive down in no car. And I'll put a stack of Bibles, anything you want. I did not drive down in any car with any bags in it and throw anything on a fire. That was—no."

The more adamant Lloyd grew protesting his truthfulness, the closer he was to admitting a lie. It was as if he built a wall around a falsehood, and when facts started pressing in, he pushed back harder and harder until he could resist no longer. Then the wall completely collapsed. They were getting close to that point again.

Dave continued pretending that he was Lloyd's ally. He *believed* Lloyd. He pleaded for some detail, one demonstrable fact, that would prove Lloyd's story.

"I have a very strong idea where those girls were killed at, very strong idea," said Lloyd. He described a bridge near Dick's house, a span over the Anacostia River. "You know where the house used to be at?"

"What house?"

"Dickie's house."

"Uh-huh."

"You know where the bridge is? On Buchanan Street, the bridge that goes across? You know the little river than runs down there?"

"Right."

He said Dick had a spot beneath that bridge where he liked to hang out.

"I'm pretty sure that's where they were killed," he said. "That would probably be the logical place for him to take them, because it's under a bridge and it's right there by the water. There should be some family members to tell you that he used to go down and do a bit of fishing there. I mean, he was down there quite a bit. Nine times out of ten that's where I'd say he took them. I'd say he drugged them and took them there, and that's where he did what he had to do."

The bridge, Lloyd said, would have provided him with cover. "Nobody would even know you were there. And if you did it at nighttime, nobody would see you."

"Why would you struggle with telling me that?" Dave asked.

"Because even though I know they're turning against me, I still have some kind of love for parts of my family. I don't like turning against people. I don't like being considered a snitch." This despite the fact that he had months ago introduced his cousin and his uncle as the girls' kidnappers and killers.

"Let me put it to you this way," said Dave. "Do you know that's what happened? Because if you're saying it hypothetically, that's not a snitch. That's just your opinion on it."

"Yeah. I mean—"

"I mean, let's just be fucking real."

"Do I know for real that it happened there?"

"Yeah. I mean, you just said, 'Fuck it.' You were holding that as a trump card. I mean, to me, you know for sure."

Lloyd stammered. "Come on, man. We've been—this is too much."

"It's time," Dave demanded.

"Yeah. I do know that that's where they were killed at," said Lloyd. "Did I drive them down there? No."

Lloyd said that the bridge and river were his uncle's "comfort area," but then he backtracked again. He said he could be only "ninety percent" sure. He was now worried he had said too much.

"I don't think you got the death penalty in Maryland. I don't know."

"No."

"Or in Virginia. I don't know."

"They do in Virginia."

"Oh fuck. Oh fuck. I'm fucked now. I'm dead."

Lloyd now said that he saw Dick leave with the girls in a car heading toward the river and the bridge. He and Helen were clearing out, as Dick had suggested, and that was what he saw. Something bad happened under that bridge. "I don't know what, because we kept walking. I didn't turn around and look."

That Is What It Is

Three and a half hours into the session, Mark and Katie took over, pressing home to Lloyd how hard Dave was working on his behalf.

True to form, Mark zeroed in on the absurdities in Lloyd's story. While there were parts of it they all believed, the rest would fall with one blow. No one would believe—he didn't believe—that the girls were trippy and calm days after being kidnapped.

"I didn't say I kidnapped them."

"You said that."

"Yeah, you did," said Katie.

"No, I did not. I said I walked out of the mall with them. I never kidnapped them. I never forced them. I never said 'kidnapped.' "

"Well, whether you used the word or not, it's po-TAY-to, po-TAH-to, it doesn't make any difference," said Katie.

"I said I walked out of the mall with them. I didn't force them out of the mall. I asked them if they wanted to party and get high."

"But the fact of the matter is, whatever the circumstances of their leaving with you, they never came home."

"Right," said Lloyd.

"So you are responsible for whatever happened to them, in the eyes of the law."

"'In the eyes of the law?' Yeah, I guess so."

"See what I'm saying?" asked Mark.

Lloyd said he understood. Mark walked him through the rest. He had seen one of the girls being raped. He knew that was wrong. He did nothing. And then he turned up at the mountain at the same time as the girls, both dead, or one dead and one alive. "So at no point did you do anything to help them or try to help them, you know what I mean?"

"That's true."

"These are the things that a reasonable body of people are going to be thinking. That is what it is. There's no changing that. But that leaves so much unanswered."

Lloyd allowed that he should have done something.

"At that point in time I didn't really think anything was going to happen to those girls," he said, as if abducting, raping, and feeding drugs to a ten-year-old and a twelve-year-old wasn't, in itself, anything. "Like I told Dave, I think Dick panicked when I ended up going back to the mall, and things went sour. I think in reality he wanted to party and he found a couple of girls that he partied with, you know?"

Katie said that if he didn't drop his pose of complete innocence, his family was going to bury him.

"I can tell you that there's a list of people in your family that I hate, and you're very low on that list. We like you. I can tell you who I hate, that I hope burn in hell I hate them so much."

"Pat," Lloyd interjected, grinning.

"They're evil, awful people. Did you say Pat? She's number one. That's funny that you say that, because she's number one. She's a sickening person." Lloyd leaned forward with mirth, his arms folded across his chest. "But the reason we keep coming back to you is because, number one, you know stuff, but also because we think you have redeeming qualities, and we think you are going to eventually tell us the truth. You're a smart guy. You're one of the smartest people I've met." Lloyd smiled and ducked his head shyly; he was eating this up. "You are! You are always ten steps ahead of us. And it may be because you have a lot of time on your hands to be ten steps ahead."

"I watch a lot of *Criminal Minds*," he said, referring to the popular TV series about a team of FBI criminal profilers, then quickly added, "I'm just joking."

"Maybe if I watched it I could figure out how to crack you," Katie said, "but let's call a spade a spade. You've got more, and we're playing a little game trying to figure out what we need to do to get more from you. It's part of the game that we play with you. You know it. You've admitted it before. For whatever reason you are still holding stuff back. And it's self-preservation. And I would probably do the same thing."

Katie went on to describe how she saw the game. Dave, she said, "who really believes in you," would report what Lloyd had said to the rest of the squad. "And my bullshit meter goes off. We don't have the same relationship with you that Dave has." She told Lloyd that after their last meeting, she suspected that he had gone back to his cell and worried about how much he had revealed. "And now you're trying to draw back," she said, "but the problem is that there's things that have happened that you can't take back. And it makes Dave look like a complete asshole if he's sticking up for you."

"I told Dave earlier—didn't he tell y'all?—that Dickie's the one who killed them. He didn't tell you that?"

"No," Katie lied. "I never even saw Dave."

Lloyd retold his story about Dick taking the girls down toward the bridge as he and Helen left to hitchhike to Virginia. "They [Sheila and Kate] looked like they were still drugged up pretty good, because you could look at them. They were just, like, sitting there, you know?"

"Did they look alive?" Katie asked.

"I mean, the girl's head moved, so I figured he was taking them home at the time."

Sometimes the things Lloyd said were so incredible they took Katie's breath away.

"So this man has abducted them from the mall, had sex, drugged them up, and now he's, like, 'Oh, Happy Easter, I'm going to take them home'?" she said. "That's absurd."

"I thought he was going to drop them off somewhere. I mean, I'm a stupid kid back then."

"You're far from stupid now. There's no way you were that stupid then."

Lloyd was not changing his story.

"I try to tell you when you are not making sense," said Mark. "You've got to help us! That leaves our efforts today to try to better your situation floundering."

"We feel like you know more; you are not helping yourself," said Katie. She told him that his use of the word *babysit* was turning her stomach. The girls had ended up raped, murdered, butchered, burned. "They sure as hell weren't being babysat. They were being held against their will."

"Okay."

Again, Lloyd insisted the girls seemed happy. He thought he was helping them run away from home.

"So you thought that after you saw a drugged girl being raped. You can't possibly convince me that you thought that."

"I did."

During the time he *babysat* the girls, Katie asked, uttering the word with scorn, "What were the instructions you were given?"

Lloyd nodded and waved his hand and shouted, "NOW you ask the question you've been waiting to ask! Right?"

"That actually just popped into my head," said Katie, truthfully.

"It's the question that I've been waiting for," said Lloyd.

This was nonsense. Katie had suggested to him that he was playing games with them, and Lloyd liked that idea. It made him seem smart. So now he pretended, poorly, to be engaging in gamesmanship. The whole thing was just . . . off. It made you wonder how self-aware Lloyd really was. His answer to Katie's question was that he and Helen were told to keep an eye on the girls. This answer told them nothing of consequence.

"So, you're not going to offer anything that we don't ask," said Katie. "If you look up *welch* in the dictionary, it says 'people who will not offer up anything unless you ask.'"

"Really?"

"Yes," said Katie. She was joking, but Lloyd didn't get it. "I actually wrote Mr. Webster a letter and asked him to put it in the dictionary. So, unless we ask you the right question, you are not going to give it to us?"

Lloyd shrugged his shoulders.

"Okay, that's fair. That's cool," said Katie.

"Well, some answers I'll give you, but some I won't, because I'm not really trying to get charged with anything. I'm not trying to stay in jail for the rest of my life for something I didn't do."

The back-and-forth continued for another hour. Then came the day's final act, the one they had been setting up. Three Virginia detectives came in—Mayhew, Wilks, and Willis—all business.

Mayhew introduced himself.

"I'm going to be straight with you, buddy. We just went over this stuff with Dave and Mark and Katie. I know you've been talking to them all day. I know you're tired. But we're here for one thing. We're investigating the deaths of the two Lyon sisters. And that's two sisters, not just one. That's two cases. And to be straight up and forward with you, buddy, everyone we've talked to in your family, and we've talked to everyone, believe me. We know a lot, and we know you still know a lot. Now, where we're going to start this at is, we know we've got you the day they were abducted, in between babysitting them, and at the end where the bodies are at. Do you understand that?"

"Uh-huh."

"Do you also understand that in the state of Virginia, you do not have to touch those girls to be charged with homicide?"

"No, I didn't know that."

"Absolutely," said Mayhew.

Lloyd looked stunned.

Unless he could offer something to prove his version of the story, he would be charged with murder.

"You're the one who abducted these girls, you raped these girls, and you killed them. Do you understand where we're coming from?" said Willis.

Lloyd nodded glumly.

"We're here to give you your chance to tell us what you know," said Mayhew. "You've got a lot of people saying, 'Lloyd, Lloyd, Lloyd, Lloyd.' Do we believe all that bullshit? No. We know other people are involved. We know they are all involved. But right now everybody is saying, 'Lloyd.' You're the one who abducted these girls, you raped these girls, and you killed these girls. Do you understand where we're coming from? You already know what we know. What we're here for today is your side. Tell us what happened."

"Here's the situation," said Wilks. "Listen to me. Here's the situation. We sit here and listen to all this bullshit, all we're going to listen to. We have our case. We got it. If you want to take it all, that's on you, buddy."

"I don't want to take nothing," said Lloyd.

"Then tell us the truth."

"I *told* the truth."

"You conspired to commit an abduction that turned into a homicide. And I can tell you, the commonwealth attorney in Bedford County in Virginia, he's a fair man, but he's going to seek justice where justice is deserved. And those two little girls deserve justice. And he's gonna get it."

"And I agree with you," said Lloyd.

"And he's going to get it. Okay?"

"I can't tell you no more than I've already told them."

"That's where it lies," said Willis. "You can either get in contact with one of the Maryland people if some miraculous memory comes forward tonight, but you are going to be charged in Virginia."

Lloyd seemed cowed. Voices were raised. Lloyd said, "I'll tell you what, let's get a lawyer, and we'll go from there!" All three detectives stood up to leave.

"Absolutely," said one.

"Because I don't need to say no more."

"Absolutely, Lloyd," said another.

"I mean, I'm sorry to waste y'all's time."

"Not a waste of *our* time," said Willis. "Not at all."

"You're getting charged for something you *did do*," said another.

"Thank you," said Lloyd as the men left. He called after them, "Have a good day."

Lloyd stewed for a few minutes alone in the room, his arms crossed, a scowl across his heavy features.

This performance by the Virginia team was all, of course, pure theater. When Dave reentered, having given Lloyd some time to decompress and ponder his plight, he asked, feigning bewilderment, "What in the world is going on?"

"You tell me," said Lloyd.

"Well, my friend, there's a whole lot of arguing going on out there. They're trying to pack their shit up, talking about charging your ass."

"Yep."

"What went sideways in this room when they were in here?"

Like an affronted child, Lloyd told on the Virginia delegation. He replayed the conversation for Dave, what they said, what he said, how unfair they had been. "And I told them," he said, raising both hands plaintively, "I can't tell you no more than what I already know! I had three people coming at me at the same time. I mean, the one guy I was trying to be polite to, the other two wanted to have their little hard nose and threaten me and shit like that. So finally I just said, 'Well, let a lawyer handle it.' "

Despite the elaborate charade, and the fact that Lloyd had clearly fallen for it, he still wasn't going to give Dave anything more.

"You don't have a trump card somewhere you're going to pull out?" the detective asked.

"If I did I'd say it right now, just because they're going back to Virginia to file charges against me."

Dave told him this probably wouldn't happen for a month or so.

"I mean, there's nothing I can tell you, Dave. I'm sorry. There's no trump card. There's nothing. Katie asked, 'What do you want for us to do to get the rest of the information out of you?' There's no more information, you know? I'm screwed. I'm . . . the rest of my life in prison probably, you know? I'll probably finish up my time here and go to Maryland for time y'all give me and then go down to Virginia to do whatever time they give me down there. I'll die in prison for something I didn't do. It doesn't make no sense. Going to put an innocent man in jail who did not touch them girls and did not kill them. My trump card was that I believe that Dickie killed them girls down there at that bridge, you know, or did something down there."

"Right, because that's in his backyard."

"Yeah. I'm pretty sure that's where he did it at."

Lloyd ended by asking for a few more days. It was a Friday. He asked them to wait until Tuesday.

"Give me the weekend to rack my brain. And believe me, every time I do rack my brain, I let you know something new."

The Virginia detectives came back in before the session ended to reassure him that he had a few more days. Lloyd told them how bad he felt for having done nothing to help the girls back in 1975, about how his life had changed. He'd become a Christian; he was determined to turn things around.

"I'm not a bad person," he said.

12

My Only Ace

4714 Baltimore Avenue

The Dungeon

You had to forget the narrative. The way to read Lloyd was to look past the story to its details.

The stories were false. All of them. He had sworn on enough imaginary Bibles to fill a garage. He had been standing on a sidewalk in Takoma Park when he saw someone take the girls; he had been in the mall when he saw a man he recognized—Mileski—walk off with them; his cousin Teddy had walked off with them as he watched; he had been with Teddy and Uncle Dick as they drove off with the girls, but he wasn't involved and had gotten out of the car to get ice cream; he had seen the girls being raped but had not been in the room; he had an idea where they were killed and who killed them, but he had not been present; he had seen a bloody bag being thrown onto the fire but had been watching from a window, from a distance. All these efforts to deflect blame only focused more suspicion on him. He was like the Wizard of Oz imploring Dorothy, "Pay no attention to that man behind the curtain!"

You had to look past the misdirection. Running through many of his versions were certain particulars that recurred—stalking girls in the mall; an offer to get high; a station wagon; a crying girl in the back seat; a basement hangout accessed from the backyard; rape; drugged girls; a poolroom; an ax; the girls "chopped up" and "burned"; a green army duffel bag; a bonfire. As if in an ever-churning blender, these stubborn nubs kept surfacing. The more they surfaced, the more they began to look true.

On the Monday after that May 1 session, Dave went looking for the place where Lloyd said the killing and dismembering occurred. It was at a secluded spot under a bridge, the place he had described as Dickie's outdoor haven. He said it was near his uncle's old home on Emerson Street in Hyattsville. Dick went there to fish and drink and smoke. It was his "comfort area." Lloyd was "ninety percent" sure about it.

Dave didn't know Hyattsville well. It was about a half-hour drive from Gaithersburg, just a few exits south off the Capital Beltway. Dick's old house was no longer there; it had been razed to make room for a new and larger district court building.

But Dave knew where it had been, and he went there first. Right away, Lloyd's story didn't add up. For one thing, the location was the last place you would choose to bring two little girls who were the object of a bicounty manhunt. Even back in the 1970s, before the new courthouse had been built, the address had been a stone's throw from the city's police headquarters. There were cops coming and going all the time, lots of squad cars just a few hundred yards away. Lloyd had said there were railroad tracks behind the house and that the bridge over the Anacostia River, where Dick liked to hang out, drink, and fish, was a short distance from the front door. But the tracks were in front, not behind, and across Rhode Island Avenue. The river, which was more like a creek at the bottom of a wide basin, was not even close. The map showed it was four blocks east, across Rhode Island Avenue, across the tracks, through a thicket of auto dealerships and repair shops, down Baltimore Avenue, and then past a long block of old homes on Buchanan Street. It was not a place Dick could walk to quickly or easily. The layout was nothing like the one Lloyd had described.

Dave next sought out Buchanan Street, which Lloyd had also mentioned. Members of the Welch family had once lived there. It was not far away, running southeast from Baltimore Avenue down to the river basin. Dave drove along that route to where it stopped. The dead end looked down to the water. To the left was a rail bridge that angled across it.

Dave climbed the low fence and walked down. The riverbed was much wider than the waterway itself, which was like a creek, much too shallow for anyone to fish. The red-brown bank sloped gradually to the water and then up again on the other side to dense blocks of homes. You could jump the trickle of water, even though the locals called the area "River Park." This was clearly the place Lloyd had described, but it was no secluded haven; the angle of the bridge exposed it to views from neighborhoods all around. With all the dealerships and parking lots in the vicinity, it would have been well lit at night. Dave strolled down to the water's edge, which was littered with the remnants of late-night beer parties and the leavings of homeless campers. He grabbed a few items from under the bridge that looked as though they had been there a long time. Killing and chopping up a human being, even a small one, would spill a great deal of blood, which could leave long-lasting traces, but it was doubtful anything he saw had been there forty years. As Dave looked around from beneath the bridge he was even more convinced no one would choose this spot for murder. It was like being onstage in a theater-in-the-round. Another Lloyd Welch curveball. He walked back up to his car and tossed the items he'd picked up into his trunk.

Dave had begun to lose hope of ever sorting out what had happened to the girls. This was a feeling that at one point or another had come over each member of the squad. For Chris Homrock, who had been involved longest and still headed the team, the lack of tangible evidence had been a constant frustration. His wife, Amy, also a cop, had cautioned him often to at least allow for the possibility of failure, and he had stared it in the face more than once. But these brushes with despair took turns with them all. And then one or the other would turn up something new or think of a different question to ask or an untried approach, and they would all get back to work. Dave was the one taking his turn at despair that morning. Lloyd's story about the bridge was just another in his endless stream of lies. The only things they could be certain of were those confirmed by other witnesses—Lloyd's presence in the mall, for instance, and his showing up on Taylor's Mountain with Helen and a bloody duffel bag. Everything in between was caught in the tangle of Lloyd's telling, a puzzle with changeable parts, one impossible to solve.

Dave was all too aware of Lloyd's methods, how he would take what he gleaned from their conversations and use it to reweave his story. You could see it in the way he picked up on a word or phrase used by one of his questioners and then began using it himself—as when Dave used the word *babysit* when reaching for a reason that eleven-year-old Teddy might have been spending time with his thirty-year-old uncle, and then Lloyd offered the same word to explain why he and Helen had spent time with the Lyon sisters. Such parroting mirrored a deeper strategy; Lloyd assumed not just their words but also their ideas. When the squad had approached him as a witness, he had embraced that. When Dave had shown him a picture of Mileski, he'd immediately spun a story around him. When Mileski was discounted, he'd smoothly shifted gears again, adopting the suggestion—made first by Karen Carvajal—that "an older man" had steered him into the crime. That was when he'd come up with Teddy and Teddy's "friend" Leonard Kraisel. When Dave had suggested that he and Teddy needed a driver, he'd offered up his uncle Dick. And so it went with every new twist. There was reason to believe that his whole tale had been built this way. Without one piece of physical evidence, a good defense attorney would pick it apart. There were certain things in the narrative that seemed certain—Lloyd's presence at the mall and the bloody bag in Thaxton. But what if the rest was all bullshit? Good detectives do more than just assemble their case, they continually test it against contrary scenarios. If Dave gave his misgivings free rein, it was still possible to wonder whether Lloyd had been involved at all, whether the whole case had been built on lies. It had begun, after all, with the lie Lloyd told back in 1975. Having made that mistake, what if he had spun the rest, step by step, in a bungling effort to extricate himself? Or worse, out of some perverse desire for attention? It was hard to imagine anyone doing such a thing, implicating not just himself but virtually his entire family, but Lloyd was nothing if not strange. How had Edna described him? A child lacking something? One with a deep need for attention? What if that was all this was? Were revulsion and public condemnation and the risk of more years in prison better than being locked away and ignored? It might do as an explanation for why Lloyd kept coming back, digging himself in deeper and deeper. The protracted conversation with Lloyd had created nothing as much as confusion. Dave had never met anyone so mendacious. And what else did they have? The descriptions of those who had seen a man who looked like eighteen-year-old Lloyd at Wheaton Plaza. What if that's all they were? A man who looked like Lloyd? The stories told by Connie Akers and Henry Parker were forty years old. All Connie had seen was a bag with bloody clothes in it. Henry kept changing the details. Wes Justice was hardly a pillar of probity. The detectives were told that he often made things up. None of it was rock solid. Despair made everything about the case seem unreal. Every surface of the narrative was slippery. Dave felt lost.

But as he turned his car around and headed back up Buchanan, staring him right in the face across busy Baltimore Avenue was a house he recognized. He had seen it in snapshots in the file. It was the house where Lee and Edna had lived, 4714 Baltimore Avenue, a two-story, white-clapboard wood-frame duplex with pale blue trim and an uneven front porch. This was the address Lloyd had given when he'd made his original false statement, the house where he and Helen had been staying, the one from which they left for Virginia. Lloyd had described seeing his uncle pull out of a driveway with the Lyon sisters in his car, heading toward the river—this now made more sense. The driveway was directly opposite Buchanan Street, which led straight down to the river and bridge. There was no way the girls had been killed down under that bridge, but this house, right in front of him, was one of those stubborn nubs in Lloyd's stories. The location fit Lloyd's description perfectly, once you saw that it was not his uncle's house but his father's.

It struck Dave with the force of revelation. Just as Lloyd always moved himself off center in his stories, so he had moved this house. The detective pulled over, crossed Baltimore Avenue, and knocked on the front door,

A friendly Hispanic woman who spoke almost no English answered. Dave managed to make himself understood enough to say that he wanted to look at the basement. She showed him that there was no way to enter it through the house. You had to go outside, down the porch, and walk along the driveway to the backyard. Steps led down from the yard to a padlocked door. In every scenario Lloyd had spun there was a basement hangout, a place where the girls had been kept. He had placed it first in Teddy's older friend's home, then in his uncle Dick's, but in both it was a room that could be entered only by walking around the house to a door in the rear. This was the room to which the girls had been taken to be drugged and raped. Once Dave understood how Lloyd's mind worked, he knew, without question, this had to be the place.

Dave walked around to the backyard and then down the back steps. The old padlock on the door was not secure. He jiggled the latch, and it opened easily. He stepped into a dark, low-ceilinged stone dungeon, gloomy, dirty, and stale-smelling, heaped with old furniture. It was so hauntingly familiar it raised the fine hairs on the back of his neck. *This was the place.* He knew it. It was exactly where one would stash two stolen, frightened, drugged little girls—two rooms completely cut off from the house above. Even with big commercial properties on either side and a loud and busy road out front, it might as well have been a remote mountain cave. You could do whatever you wished in this space without being seen or heard. More furniture had been crammed into it over the ensuing years, but there were still traces of the old stuff. There were even a few items he recognized from old Welch family photos the squad had seized. If you imagined it emptier, it looked exactly as Lloyd had described it: a couch, an old TV, stereo components, a mattress, and even a back room with a door.

Dave returned the next day with a forensics team. They cleared away some of the old furniture and started testing for traces of blood, squirting

Bluestar spray, a blood-detection agent that bonds with even the slightest trace of hemoglobin and glows brightly under a blue light. The floors and walls of the outer room revealed nothing much, a few blood spots here and there, what you might find in a room used as a work space. Then they cleared debris from the back room and sprayed some more. It lit up from floor to ceiling. It lit up like a *murder scene*. Someone or something had been slaughtered in this room. It had been bathed in blood.

And then Dave knew. All uncertainty vanished. He was even more certain because he had *not* been led there by Lloyd; he had found it himself. He had extracted it from Lloyd's stories, bit by bit—Buchanan Street, the house with a basement that could be entered only from the rear, and all the rest. Here, at last, was something *real*. Blood. Aglow in blue light, the room announced itself as the place where Sheila and Kate Lyon, lured from Wheaton Plaza, had been drugged, raped, and imprisoned, and where at least one of them had been killed and dismembered. Before he had switched the location to a bridge, Lloyd had talked a lot about a basement hangout. It had been, he claimed, his uncle Dickie's sanctuary, a place with a locked door, where Dick went to smoke and drink. But it wasn't Dickie's basement. It was the basement of Lee's house, the one where *Lloyd* had been living, the space where *Lloyd* hung out, smoked dope, drank, and "partied." It wasn't Mileski's murder scene or Kraisel's or Dick's.

It was *his*.

May 12, 2015

They went back to Lloyd just over a week later, at Dover.

Dave's discovery had recharged them all. It finally nailed Lloyd's vaporous tales to earth. It was real evidence. Not by a long shot was it the finish line. There were still many questions about what had happened and who exactly had been involved, but it confirmed that they were looking in the right place. Eventually blood technicians would determine that, while there wasn't enough to extract DNA, the traces of blood in the basement were human.

More immediately, the find gave them something new to bring Lloyd. This session would lead them, finally, to the dark heart of the matter.

It began with Dave's usual cheery greeting and Lloyd's usual complaint about having been awakened early and kept waiting.

"You don't look happy," said Dave.

"I'm not."

"Did you get anything to eat? Anything to drink?"

"Nah."

"Well, we can make that happen."

Lloyd had left the last session expecting to be indicted in days, but nothing had happened. He was confused and depressed. Dave brought him up to date. There had been no charges, he said, because he was still holding out heroically on Lloyd's behalf.

"We have to be able to come to an agreement," Dave said. "Lay out everything as far as where we are, because I have to be able to explain—a lot of it is theory-driven—the real story, the whole story, good, bad, or indifferent. That's what we gotta come up to."

Lloyd said, "I'm at the point where if I'm gonna be charged, charge me, because I've done implicated myself so much."

Everything now worked in the detective's favor, even Lloyd's despondency. He was going to take the murder rap, so why not simply tell the truth?

"Right," said Dave. "You can't really do any more damage than what's already done."

Lloyd was feeling sorry for himself. He said he was resigned to his fate—death penalty, life in prison, whatever. It would come down to his word against his family's, he said, "And what am I? A convict, a druggie—"

"No—" said Dave, trying to check Lloyd, but he was on a roll.

"An abuser—"

"There's some stuff we've done with what you've given us that—"

"You know?"

"You'd be surprised—"

"Yeah, but it's all looking toward me."

"Well, that's the way people want to line it up, and, like I said, we're going to talk about all that."

Lloyd asked whether the Virginia cops were back.

"There's a mess of people here today. I don't know who is here and who is not here, because, you know what I did? To avoid that I came in and asked, 'Is Lloyd here?' I saw the guard sitting, and I came around the corner. I came right in. I avoided all that because that's something I want to talk to you about."

"Okay, you know, at some point I'm gonna end up saying, 'Lawyer up.'"

"And you know what? There's no disrespect to that."

"Yeah."

"There's none."

"I mean, I did it at the beginning, but I've mellowed out and not said anything about a lawyer or anything like that, but if I feel like I'm being hammered too much by so many people, that's what I'm gonna have to do."

"You know what?" said Dave. "We've sat in this room probably nine or ten times. You know what I've never ever done? Never told you anything about me, where I come from, my family. I mean, you don't know shit about me."

"Yeah, I do," said Lloyd. "I know more than what you think I know. Want me to tell you what I do know? You're a cop but you're a good guy. You have a good heart. You have what I call a generosity that goes above and beyond. That's what I know about you. I don't need to know nothin' else."

"Well, I appreciate that."

Dave described himself as "from the country" and "just your average person." He said, "I'll never own a Fortune 500 company. At the end of the day, when this is over, I'll be happy because I can go back to doing my minimal police work until I put in my five more years, and then I'm the hell out of here." This was true. It had always been Dave's approach to the job. He looked forward to leaving it in a few years and resuming life as a civilian, either taking over his father's air-conditioning company or doing construction work. "But what I don't want to see happen in this case is when they make the movie or they make the book, and it's titled 'The Lyon Sisters,' I just don't want it to star Lloyd Welch," he said. "I want to see it 'written by Lloyd Welch.' You know what I mean?"

Lloyd chuckled approvingly.

"When we left here, what you told me in the end [Lloyd's story about his uncle Dick killing and chopping up the girls under the bridge], it was from the heart. I knew it when it came out because I see it every time you do it. I want to say it wasn't Lloyd Welch that had any involvement. Do I believe you saw it? Do I believe you stood by to make sure nobody walked down there? I don't know."

"Oh, you're talking about River Park?"

"You got it."

"Oh, no. I didn't see that."

Dave ignored him. He said he could readily understand how Lloyd might have been drawn into this thing by his family. He was an abused, rejected teenager. He yearned for acceptance. "If you got sucked into this, I can explain it that way," he said. "Give me an idea of what the hell's going on, Lloyd."

Lloyd said he had nothing more.

Dave continued. He said he was so alone trying to hold off the horde of big shots clamoring for Lloyd's head that, "I may not have a job when I walk out that door."

Then Lloyd offered something new: a motive. He said he'd received a letter from a woman who claimed to have known him back in his carny days. She said she had been approached back then by his uncle Dick, who had asked her to make a porn film. This was curious. Other family members had talked about Dick having porn films. Dave asked if there was any connection between the Lyon girls and those films.

"See, that's what I'm thinking," said Lloyd. "I honestly believe that he [Dick] was going to do porn with them, because he had a camera. He did have a camera. Did he do it with them? I can't say that part because I don't know, but I'm thinking that the reason he had them upstairs for Easter, drugged up, is because he was planning on doing porn with them. I told you, he liked young girls."

"I think we're getting somewhere," said Dave.

Did You Find My Weed?

In the previous session, Dave had planted the idea of a "trump card." In the days since, Lloyd had apparently pondered this. Today, he was prepared to play one—his "ace."

Since Lloyd was in a collaborative mood, Dave decided to tell him what he'd found.

"The basement of your old house in Baltimore Avenue, unfinished—"

"The house is still there?" asked Lloyd, surprised.

"Not only is it still there, it doesn't look like it's changed."

Lloyd described the layout of the basement room.

"In the back part there used to be a couch. That's where me and Roy [his younger brother] used to get high all the time. Used to be a little couch, a chair . . . out of the way, out of mind." He laughed.

"Do you know if the girls were in that basement at any point in time?" Dave asked. He told Lloyd about the blood-test spray, saying, "And I think that we're gonna be able to show that they were in that basement at some point."

"They might have been," said Lloyd. "I never saw them there."

"Do you know if your dad had brought them over, because that would be an easier place to keep them. In a basement that's dark. You only have access one way in and one way out. Eventually they were moved to Dickie's for either Easter Sunday or the porn, when you get hoaxed into watching them. I'm trying to fill in some of these gaps."

"Well, I would say that in Dickie's mind he would probably move them over there because Mom [Edna] didn't go down after dark. And if me and Roy didn't have nothing to get high with, we didn't go down."

"Logically, if they were there, and he pulls up in a car, wouldn't it make more sense if he was pulling up to get the girls? Who would pull up with two kidnapped girls in a car on a busy street in Hyattsville? Doesn't matter what time it is. Think about it."

"Well, you see, you could drive all the way into the back there."

"Yeah, I know you could."

"Well, like I told you, when Dickie drove up the first time, and Lee and them were arguing, those girls were not in the car at all, you know?"

"The girls aren't there," said Dave. "Are they in the basement?"

"That's a possibility. It's a possibility, because—"

"What are they arguing about? I mean, start thinking through that shit."

"They're arguing about me going to the mall."

"So what you're telling me without telling me is that your dad was involved in this."

"Yes."

"I mean, let's just put that out there."

"Yeah. He was involved. I mean, that whole argument right there, that was the one reason why I was leaving to go to Virginia earlier than what I had planned, because me and Lee got into a big argument."

Dave walked him through some facts about his father, Lee. He would have been in his late mid- to late thirties at the time, a few years older than Dick.

"It's explainable where your role may fit into this thing, but I can't explain it unless you tell me. You follow what I'm saying?"

"Right."

"I mean, it's not rocket science here."

"I understand what you're saying. I understand."

"You need to tell me just how it went down. Now your dad's involved, and I know your dad and Dick planned this thing and you got sucked into it."

Lloyd was nodding, agreeing. Dave had him.

"Tell me what the hell happened," the detective said, tapping on the desk for emphasis. "It's time. The only way you're not going to eat this is to tell me actually what happened. We can back this shit up."

Lloyd said it would just be his word against Dick's.

"Well, I want to hear your word," said Dave.

Lloyd nodded and then looked down at the floor. He was thinking about it. Then came the question:

"What kind of guarantee am I going to have?" he asked, finally.

"Well, we'll cross them bridges. We can't get to that point until we know what we have."

Lloyd repeated that his uncle Dick had approached him, asking for help in picking up two girls to "party." Then he said the real reason was "to make movies."

"He was into porn, and he wanted to make movies to make money," Lloyd explained.

Dave told him they had heard about Dick's camera. Dick had shown a porn movie on the porch of his sister Lizzie and her husband Allen Parker's house in Thaxton. It had come out in grand jury testimony, and Dick had acknowledged it. It was important, said Dave, because his uncle's testimony corroborated it.

"So don't leave any details out," he said.

"Right." Lloyd said he went to the mall with Dick and Lee. Notably, after months of insisting that Teddy had been the key player in the abduction, he now simply dropped Teddy from the story. The ease with which Lloyd made these shifts never ceased to amaze the squad. He acted as if he had never told the story differently.

Lloyd said he had lured the girls himself by offering them pot, and the older one, Sheila, had dragged her little sister along. Sheila climbed into the front seat of the car between Dick and Lee; Kate got in the back with Lloyd. Dick was in his security guard uniform and was driving his wife's station wagon. Dick gave Sheila a joint, he said, and when she tried it she began coughing. They drove around for about a half hour with Kate sniffling in the back seat and Dick and Lee arguing in the front about what to do next. They eventually drove to Dick's house, and Lloyd left.

When he returned the next day and saw his uncle raping one of the girls, he now said, his father was there too, filming it with Dick's camera. Lloyd left and stayed at his father's house for several days. During that time, he said, he did not know where the girls were. He and Helen were offered money and pot to watch the girls at Dick's house on Easter Sunday, while the Welch family gathered at Lee's. They found the girls, drugged, in the upstairs poolroom. Lloyd said he also saw Teddy at Dick's house that day.

"Whoa, they're still here?" he said Teddy asked him.

"Yeah, I don't know what's going on," Lloyd said he told him.

"Now, I don't know if Teddy had sex with them. I don't know if he was in it or not, the movies or anything like that, but he knew they were there."

This somewhat jibed with Teddy's story, although Teddy said he'd had no idea who the girls were or even that they were in the house until he saw them in the upstairs room with Lloyd and Helen. Lloyd now said that Helen had stayed with the girls while he watched TV downstairs. She came to him once and asked, "Are they all right? They look like they're sick or something." It was after this, he said, that he decided to go to the mall and invent a story, not to help rescue the girls but "to steer them off me." He was worried—as it turned out, with reason—that someone had seen him at the mall. When he returned, his stepmother was angry with him.

"She knew that the girls were with Dickie and them. I guess about two, maybe three hours later, me and Lee get into an argument. 'You dumb fuck, what'd you go to the mall for? The hell did you do that shit for? Goddamn, you stupid idiot,' you know, cussin' at me, calling me all kinds of names, smacked me around a couple of times. I took off, went upstairs. About that time, I guess, Dickie pulled up. I guess Mom had called him or Lee had called him. He came up. Them two was arguing. Like I said, I looked out the window. There was nobody in the car at that time."

When he went downstairs, Lloyd said, his uncle threatened him.

"Get the fuck away from here before you get yourself hurt," he said Dick told him. Then Lee phoned down to his sister's house in Thaxton to tell her family to expect Lloyd and Helen. Before they left, Lloyd said, he and Helen saw Dick drive off with the girls toward the river and the bridge. Then they hitchhiked to Virginia. The rest of his story was the same: the station wagon pulling into the driveway in Virginia in the middle of the night, the bag, the bonfire.

"That's the whole story," he said for the umpteenth time.

This was not good enough, Dave told him. He asked Lloyd again about the bridge, the place where Lloyd said his uncle liked to fish.

"If them girls were chopped up and burned, then that's where he did it," said Lloyd.

"Well, it's hard for me to believe that anybody would take two people, girls, boys, to an area that's open to the public, whether it's one o'clock in the morning, eight o'clock at night. You would expose yourself to the public. Out in the open. Anybody can walk up on you and see what you are doing. It's harder for me to believe they're going to do it in Pat's house. You've got young kids there. You got people. You're right next to a police station."

"Yeah," Lloyd said.

"So the next best spot would have been Baltimore Avenue. Not targeting you, but you brought your father into this thing. What makes the best sense? Where are you gonna hide two girls and keep them out of sight? Their pictures are everywhere. Everybody is looking for them. You're not going to keep them in an open area. You're not going to keep them in Dick and Pat's house. So you've got to keep them down in this dungeon of a basement, dark, one way in and one way out, and there's even a back room with a damn door on it that you can close. So we said, 'Okay, let's go look at it.' We went and looked at it. That's why I know it so well. I spent damn near ten hours in that basement yesterday."

If this concerned Lloyd, he didn't show it.

"Did you find my weed?" he asked. "I lost weed in there."

The quip was revealing in ways Lloyd did not intend. Dave was describing a dungeon-like room that had been used to imprison and kill children; to Lloyd it was a place of illicit fun, his old doping den. From the beginning, Lloyd had demonstrated this startling and apparently unconscious confusion about fun; he made no distinction between "partying" and the worst sort of cruelty. The equivalence was chilling.

"Lee would go down there too," Lloyd said. This was the other pillar of his defense—"there was no crime" was the first; "someone else did it" was the second.

"You can't get to it from inside the house," said Dave. "It's only on the outside."

"Right, and like I said, he had a key to that door."

Lloyd rambled a bit and then suggested that his uncle Dick might have been "trafficking" children. This could have been his plan from the beginning, to make child porn and then sell the Lyon girls to sex traffickers in Virginia.

"And something went terribly wrong, and they had to kill them," Lloyd said. "I honestly believe that's the way it went down. That's my opinion."

"Now, when you say that something went wrong, we've heard that," said Dave.

"I'm honestly believing one of them girls either tried to get away or something happened to where Dickie lost control," said Lloyd. "And him and Lee killed them. Not on purposely now, not that they were intending to do that, you know. I'm believing it was actually a mishap. Unfortunately."

"And then, obviously, when that happens, they—"

"They got scared and took them to Virginia, and they would do the logical thing," said Lloyd, finishing the detective's thought. "Five hours away. Let's get rid of them this way and nobody would ever find them."

"So, in your opinion, you think they were both killed in Maryland and then transported to Virginia? Or just the one that tried to get away was killed, and then the other one was still alive and went to Virginia? Because, I'm telling you, there's some weird shit in Virginia as well, as far as your cousin Henry."

"I'm honestly thinking that the younger one is the one that tried to get away, because she's the one that didn't want to get high and that I was telling you about. She's the one that caused the chaos or whatever, and they killed her, because that bag—like Henry was saying—yeah, it was heavy."

"You caught yourself there, and I caught it, too," said Dave.

Lloyd had been about to confirm how heavy the bag was and had stopped himself, alertly shifting the recollection to Henry. Dave didn't press him on it; instead he reiterated how young Lloyd had been at the time and how readily he might have been drawn into this by his father and uncle. But Lloyd continued to insist he had not taken the bag to Virginia, that he and Helen had hitchhiked there. He stuck to the rest of his story, too.

"Okay, so if they killed her and something went bad, it probably wasn't at Dick and Pat's house," said Lloyd.

"I'm saying that, in my opinion, it was probably at Lee's house," said Dave.

You could imagine the wheels turning in Lloyd's head. The Bluestar spray was actual evidence, and he usually didn't push back for long against hard evidence. Dave showed Lloyd a picture on his cell phone of the basement space, lit up with traces of blood. He said he thought they could get a DNA match (which turned out not to be true).

"It wasn't *my* basement," said Lloyd.

Dave chided him: "Lloyd was in the mall. Lloyd was staying at that house. They ended up in that house. You just follow the logic. That's what I'm saying. That's why I need for you to fill in these gaps. There's only so much we can do with what we're presented with."

"I just don't want to spend the rest of my life in prison for something I didn't do."

"Understandably."

"You know?"

"And there's only one way we can help you."

Then came the question that always prefaced a revelation.

"I feel like I need some kind of immunity from Virginia and Maryland, a new immunity to where I'm not going to be charged with anything ever."

The facts were closing in on him. Dave just nodded.

"And I'm going to be a witness against them. That's what I was, a witness. That's why I stopped asking for a lawyer. I feel like I'm being fucked, I feel that I'm the one—"

Dave bore in: "Who killed the young one?"

After a year and a half of these long interview sessions—they were an hour and a half into this one—they had finally brought Lloyd to the worst of it.

My Only Ace

"The more I say, the more I fuck myself," he lamented. "How many are against me? The whole family."

"Five, six, seven, ten people who don't have any criminal records," said Dave, agreeing.

Lloyd said his family had money and powerful lawyers. "What do I have? Nothing."

Dave wasn't about to console him. This was precisely how they wanted him to feel. He said, "You're starting to get the train of thought now." Dave stressed that there was other evidence—Wes Justice's testimony—to link Dick to the crime.

"Right. Yes. Dickie's the one that killed the young girl."

"How?"

"He killed her with an ax."

"Can you describe the ax to me?"

"It was a wooden-handle ax."

"Long ax? Hatchet?"

"I mean, it was a long handle. He killed her with the ax and put her in that bag."

"In that basement?"

Lloyd pulled back again.

"Yeah, see, I don't even know. I don't know if she was killed there or not and how she was killed. Because I just now realized by me saying she was chopped up and burned that I have implicated myself big-time." He then said he knew of this only because Teddy had told him during a conversation they'd had years later in a bar.

"Did he say what happened to the older one?"

"No. I left before the conversation got any more involved because it sickened me to my stomach that he killed one of them, so I could just imagine the older one was dead too. And I felt shitty for the simple reason because I'm the one who went to the mall that day, and I'm the one who did not help those girls after we partied. I should have took them back to the mall myself, but as a seventeen-year-old drug addict, I was scared shitless, and to this day I'm scared shitless."

Dave noted the phrase "sick to my stomach." It wasn't likely that being told this story in a bar years later, as awful as it was, would have nauseated him. But if he had been present when it happened? That made sense. Whenever Lloyd started breaking new ground, Dave would take him back again to the beginning, to see what else in the story was going to change. Lloyd's version of going to the mall with Lee and Dick stayed the same.

"When we first got the girls, they went to Dick's house."

"Okay."

"Like I told you."

"Where was Pat?"

"At the time, Pat wasn't there. I think she was at work."

"Well, yeah, because you've got your husband and your brother-in-law bringing a ten- and twelve-year-old girl," said Dave.

"Yeah."

Lloyd suggested that for filming, the girls were then shuttled between Lee's basement and Dick's house, where the decor was better. This lasted for about a week. Dave asked what prompted Dick and Lee to kill Kate: was it that she created problems, or were they simply disposing of the girls after Dick had made his films?

"Teddy just told me that the young girl gave problems, and Dick got frustrated and he broke her neck. Now, did he do it on purpose? Did he mean to do it? I don't know. Teddy didn't tell me that."

Then the conversation took an odd turn. Lloyd, again picking up on something Dave had mentioned, said he'd thought about writing a book.

"But who would publish it?" he asked.

Dave encouraged him. "How many letters have you gotten since they put you on the media, from newspapers, TV? Everybody has an interest. This particular case, forty years later it hits the news and it's viral. People are all over it."

Lloyd said he thought his story would be interesting. He had never touched the girls, he said, but he'd led an interesting life. "I had a lot of ass when I was growing up," he said. "I didn't have to force myself or anything like that. I mean, when I lived in Washington, DC, in that runaway house, I had different girls every night, because we just partied together. Nothing forceful or anything like that. We'd all just get together—"

"It was the seventies."

"—and it was free love. Sex, rock 'n' roll."

"Exactly."

He said he was surprised he'd never contracted a venereal disease. "I never used a rubber. Maybe that's why I got so many children!"

Leaving Lloyd with these happy thoughts, Dave took a lunch break. Lloyd ate his usual fast food. Dave returned after consultation with his team with a clarifying statement. He wanted it on the record that Lloyd had been offered no inducements and had not been threatened.

"Basically, you ain't offered me shit," said Lloyd, laughing. "Nothing." He gestured toward his unfinished meal and added, "A sandwich." Then he complained that it was dry.

"I just want to make sure you feel comfortable," said Dave.

"The only person I feel uncomfortable around is Mark."

"Okay, then, we'll keep Mark out of here."

"I understand that he's trying to do his job and stuff like that, but he gets me feeling, like, when you leave, you're the good cop, and he comes in and he's the bad cop. You know what I'm saying?"

"No. That's not what we're doing." This was, of course, exactly what they were doing.

"We get into a yelling match, and I'm ready for them to charge me. *Get me the fuck out of here, I want a lawyer,* you know?"

"But I want to make sure you understand."

"Nah, you ain't twisting my arm yet."

"I just want to make sure."

"Look, I can stay in here and take the blame for going into the mall and bringing those girls out. I can't take the blame for anything after that, except I should have intervened and gotten them away from there. Okay? That I should have done. But as far as sexually assaulting them or killing them or carrying them down to Virginia, I had nothing to do with that. Not one bit. My hands were not in that at all. You know? As far as I know, that was not no plan whatsoever, you know? I just want to make that clear. And I'm going to keep on making that clear so everybody understands it."

"Right."

Dave asked why Sheila was taken to Virginia after her sister was killed.

"I think he, Dick, was not through making porn with her. I think there was more people involved than just him."

"Who do you think those people were?"

"I think it was Henry, because me and Henry are about the same age."

Lloyd said that Sheila had been more compliant. "I mean, she was game to go get high for the very first time. I mean Mommy and Daddy can say, 'Oh, they were just Christian girls,' and 'They color,' and stuff like that, but let me tell you, I know back in my day there was a lot of twelve-year-olds and thirteen-year-olds and eleven-year-olds who wanted to get high. It was back in the seventies and stuff like that." It was of course an appalling stretch to suggest that a thirteen-year-old willing to experiment with pot would therefore be game to have sex on camera with a series of grown men. Lloyd continued, "I'm not saying they were bad girls, and I'm not saying they were good girls, I'm just saying that people were curious back then. In my opinion, she went down there, and they were going to do more porn with her."

Dave then launched into a long, impassioned plea for Lloyd to simply come clean. He said the adults in his family had drawn him into it and that he had carried the emotional scars all of his life. Dave believed none of this; he was edging Lloyd farther out on the limb. He sensed that Lloyd was about to confess to being present for the murder.

"Now you know that you are screwed, in a way, but you have to figure, 'Okay, I'm screwed but if I just let it go and just tell them what the hell happened, then maybe they can do their goddamn job and get out of here and prove what I told them, because it's the right thing.' Let's be done with the games."

"I'm not playing no games."

"No. I know. I feel like a damn psychologist. Let me pull it out of you. Just what the hell did you see?"

Lloyd sighed. He was listening.

"Either it is what it is because you saw it, or you are totally making stuff up."

"Nope. I'm not making it up. Not making anything up."

"Tell me what you saw."

Lloyd was silent, uncharacteristically so. He was thinking hard about this.

"It's time, man," Dave urged. "It's written all over your face."

"Yeah, but . . . ," and Lloyd fell silent again. His head was turned away and he was looking down; his left arm gripped his right arm as if he were physically trying to restrain himself. Finally, he nodded and said, quietly, "Okay. I did see Dickie and my dad."

"What did you see?"

"Down in the basement I saw Lee break her neck, and I saw Dickie start chopping her up, and he had Lee's green bag there. And as they were doing it, Dickie started stuffing body parts into the bag, and Lee started cleaning up the blood."

"Where did it happen in the basement?"

"As you're coming into that back room, the very far back room, back towards there."

Dave asked a few more questions to establish that this had taken place exactly where the blood test had pointed.

"I was actually going down there to get high. I was actually going down to get my pipe when I walked in on it, and I stepped off to the far side to where you couldn't see me, and they weren't paying attention when the door opened, and I saw what I saw, and after it was all done and said, or all done, I booked it out of there, yeah."

"Was that before or after you went to the mall?"

"That was after I went to the mall. The argument between Lee and them was for real, and I was basically threatened to get the fuck out of there. I don't think they saw me seeing them . . . what they did. Me and Helen left, and I never told anybody about what I saw until just now. Yeah, it's been eating me. I put it all away, and this last couple of months I've been thinking about it."

Lloyd gave even more gruesome details: how Kate was flat on her back on the basement floor when Lee straddled her and leaned down and snapped her neck; how Dick started chopping and could not reach all the way up with the ax because the ceiling was too low; how he started hacking at one knee and ultimately chopped her into "four or five pieces."

"I was pale when I went out of there," he said. "Thought I was going to be sick."

He said they'd used old rugs and blankets to soak up the blood and stuffed them into the bag with the pieces of her body.

Lloyd said he was still scared. He talked about what a changed man he was and how he didn't want to spend the rest of his life in jail. He talked about how "scary" his uncle Dick was. He protested that he didn't realize the girls were being abused because "they didn't ask for help." Dave wanted still more details. He asked if Dick and Lee had been covered with blood.

"Yeah."

Lloyd said that both men had cleaned up when he next saw them in Virginia. He said the car they were driving did not belong to them; he believed it belonged to his aunt Pat's father. He speculated that they got rid of the car because it likely had blood in the trunk from Kate's dismembered body.

It had taken seventeen months of repeated interviews and extensive investigation, but Dave and his partners had finally coaxed from Lloyd nearly the whole crime, at least as far as Kate Lyon was concerned—kidnap, rape, murder. He was still evading personal responsibility, but the pose had become hollow. Telling it had affected him physically. The detectives had often urged him to "unburden" himself, but the result of this admission was the opposite. It was more like taking a burden on, not casting one off. He sat hunched in his chair as if under a crushing weight.

And he spoke softly, like a man defeated. He again said he sympathized with the Lyon family's desire to know the truth, but, "I've also got to think of me." He speculated about the consequences of what he had just admitted. "Am I going to spend time in Virginia for the next ten years after I get out of this part and five years in Maryland or ten years in Maryland?"

"You're right," said Dave, meaning this was a legitimate concern.

"Am I going to get to be ninety-nine years old when I get out of prison?"

"No," said Dave. "And I get it, and if you—"

Lloyd still clung unrealistically—pathetically—to his desire for an early release.

"I mean, right now, I've got at most eight years left in this prison at the most," he said. "My max-out date the last time I checked was twenty twenty-four [the year 2024], but with my good time working and everything like that, I can bring it all the way down to twenty-one, twenty-two [2021, 2022]. But if this keeps hanging over me, and I end up getting time, what am I going to be, eighty, ninety years old? Oh!"

"I have no control over what happens above me," said Dave.

"That's why I keep saying, I need a lawyer here. I want a lawyer. I think I should have some kind of immunity, you know, from Virginia and Maryland, showing that . . . I mean, even though I've got the one [the agreement he'd signed over a year before], it ain't no good no more probably."

"No, it's not."

"Yeah."

"It's passed. Those things are like a one-shot deal," Dave said.

"Yeah, but, see, I would want one that says forever, you know? Nothing will ever happen to me. I've thought about how to word it. I got law library on Monday. I've written it up. I'm typing it up, and I think I can bring court papers and stuff like that. I'm thinking about bringing that and presenting it if I ever see you again, which I'm sure I'll probably end up seeing you again."

Dave said that was true.

"I'm just saying, I got to worry about me. That's why I've been leery about saying things. I try to hold back, I guess you could say, aces. Hopefully it will do something for me."

Dave nodded.

"You know? I don't play blackjack, but I'm sure them aces are good in blackjack. I try to hold things to where—"

"It will benefit," Dave assured him, falsely. If this was Lloyd's goal, he was the worst blackjack player in the world.

"Give me something," Lloyd pleaded.

"Right," said Dave. "It will benefit you in the end," he promised.

"Yeah."

Dave said, "I'm not gonna say, 'Lloyd, tell me something, then I'm going to go to bat for you,' because that's not what I'm about. I'm trying my damnedest to make this thing work. Whether it puts you in the middle of it or it puts you way out here"—reaching one hand out—"it's got to be right."

"Yeah."

"The truth is the truth."

"That was my ace," said Lloyd. "My only ace. Really."

"It's not a bad thing. It's really not," Dave reassured him. It was, for Lloyd, a bad thing.

"It's out. It's off my chest. I feel ninety percent better right now. It's a weight off my shoulders."

This was perhaps the biggest lie of all. And, just as at all the other times he'd told Dave that he'd given up everything, there was still more.

13

The Truth Is the Truth

Montgomery County Police Chief J. Thomas Manger and States Attorney John McCarthy announce the murder indictment of Lloyd Welch.

Charged

Just as he'd surmised, Lloyd's fate was sealed. Despite his most recent claim that the real rapists and killers were his father and his uncle, he, and only he, was indicted, on July 14, 2015, for capital murder by the state of Virginia. If convicted, he might be sentenced to death or, at the very least, a prison term that would ensure he'd never again be a free man.

Whatever illusions Lloyd may have had about winning his game with the squad were dashed. His long effort to deflect blame had steered it all to himself. There was only slightly more reason to believe his last story than his first. Lloyd's father, Lee, with his history of child abuse and rape, made a plausible suspect, but he was dead, and his widow, the exasperating Edna, was hostile and unhelpful. Whether or not Lee had broken Kate Lyon's neck and taken part in any of the other outrages was moot. His destiny, one could hope, had been sorted by his Maker—although the ordeals of Sheila and Kate Lyon mocked the very notion of a just God.

Dick Welch was not charged. The prosecutors could not make a case against him. Indeed, state's attorney Pete Feeney, who had supervised the investigation from the start, was inclined to believe that Dick had, as he consistently said, nothing at all to do with the crime. After all, Lloyd had also blamed Teddy, only to drop the accusation completely when it became too implausible. And he had traduced his uncle at Dave's urging. A close study of the interview transcripts showed how, in effect, the detective had led him into naming Dick as the driver who took him and the girls from Wheaton Plaza. "If you tell me who did it—which I already know," the detective had said, and, "We've already talked to that person. . . . He's an asshole." After Lloyd named Dick as the driver, he had continued to embellish his uncle's role, which conveniently shifted blame away from himself. The strongest evidence against Dick was the story told by his nephew Wes Justice, and it was adjudged unbelievable. How likely was it that Dick, so resolute in his denials despite all the effort to pressure him or catch him off guard, would spontaneously unburden himself in a chat with his nephew? More likely, Wes had been caught in a web of his own making after boasting on the phone with his cousin Norma Jean about inside knowledge of "a green station wagon" used to transport the girls. Under mounting pressure Wes had finally just told detectives a story he believed they wanted to hear. They had threatened to prosecute him if he didn't tell it. There was also the possibility that Wes had some deep, unvoiced grudge against his uncle—a not uncommon thing in the family—and had concocted the story as payback. As with just about everything else to do with the Welches, it was hard to know what was true and what was not.

Lloyd's indictment had not been announced when Dave drove down on July 14th to meet him next in Dover. It had been twenty-one months since their first session, and their long dialogue had led where neither had expected. Lloyd had fashioned a noose for himself, beginning with the trip he had made to Wheaton Plaza in 1975. Dave wanted to deliver the news of the indictment personally for two reasons: the cop in him relished the moment of triumph, and the shock might be useful. Lloyd's reaction—anger, despair, fear—might provoke something new.

He always had more to say. They still had not found the girls' bodies. They had learned of Kate's end but not Sheila's. From the start, a primary goal had been to find out what had happened to the sisters.

As he had learned to do, the detective plotted his approach carefully. He would remain Lloyd's best buddy and advocate. He would pretend to be incensed by the indictment, to see Lloyd as the victim, as appalling as that was, the abused, abandoned, frightened boy, drug-addled, craving the approval of his despicable family, and now, decades later, done in by it. *It was all so unfair!* Dave didn't need a script. He could improvise.

They met again like old friends. At this point Lloyd had spent more time with Dave than with any other person outside prison walls for nearly two decades.

"Hey, what's up, bud?" he asked the detective when they met in the upstairs hallway.

"What's goin' on?" said Dave.

They entered the familiar gray interview room with big cups of coffee. Each had a doughnut.

"Who's here?" Lloyd asked.

"Who's here? Me."

"Just you?"

"Unless you ask for somebody to come in here today." Dave was thinking that Lloyd might finally insist on a lawyer.

Lloyd just nodded.

"I just want this to be me and you," Dave said. "I asked for this day out of respect just for you, and you're probably gonna get mad at me for the next five or ten minutes."

Lloyd looked at him quizzically.

"I said you're probably going to get upset."

"Why? You charging me?"

"I'm not charging you."

"*They're* charging me."

"Virginia has indicted you, but we're gonna talk about that."

"Then I need a lawyer."

"Now, listen to me—"

"And I'm taking the Fifth."

"Now, listen to me. I get it, okay? But you owe it to yourself to hear me out. There's nothing that we say in here that can make anything worse. I know you're gonna get mad, okay?"

"Oh no."

"*I* got mad," said Dave.

"I'm not gonna get mad at you."

"No, I got mad, and then I thought about it and said, 'You know what? I can either get mad or do nothing, or I can get mad and give you the respect to come back down here and explain it to you.'"

Lloyd nodded.

"Try to make something positive out of it, because I was mad and I'm still mad, and there are a lot of things still going on that, I took it upon myself to say, 'Let's do the right thing.' I'm here for the two-year-old boy that was in the car [when Lloyd's mother was killed], and I'm here for the eighteen-year-old kid that went to that mall. You got me? And then I started to think about it, and I started to think about the case, and I started—"

"Hey, Dave," Lloyd interrupted. He seemed neither shocked nor angry. He had finished his doughnut. He said, "That was good."

"I should have gotten two," said Dave. And just like that, Lloyd was talking again. He complained about how cold the room was, and Dave reached up to adjust the air-conditioning unit, which also hid the room's camera and mike.

"Okay, where's the camera at in here?" Lloyd asked, grinning and laughing.

"I don't know," said Dave, and then he pointed to something on the ceiling. "What's that thing up there?"

"That's the fire alarm." Lloyd took a sip of coffee. "I'm just fucking with you," he said.

"It's all good."

"You see it on the TV all the time, doing interviews and shit like that, on the camera, and you don't even know it's in there."

"I totally understand."

"No, I'm just messing with you. I don't care if y'all got me on camera or not. What the hell."

"No. If anything, it protects everybody."

"Yeah."

"Like I say, I definitely want to go over quite a few things with you," said Dave. "I don't think we need to relive the thing like we always do. I don't think that that's important. I think there are important aspects that the people in Bedford [haven't heard]—and when I say 'people in Bedford,' I'm not talking about law enforcement but the grand jury members, just common people, just people sitting there listening to this stuff. They only get to hear somebody else's interpretation. They've never heard Lloyd Welch. They've never talked to you. They only get to see what I tell the attorney down there, and the attorney presents it to them."

Lloyd said he did not want to talk to them without being advised by a lawyer, but he was willing to keep talking to Dave.

"What worse can you get?" asked Dave.

"[They might] give me more time," said Lloyd, matter-of-factly.

"No, no no, no, no."

Lloyd just laughed.

"No. This is just the beginning of a process," said Dave. "And, realistically, it doesn't—yeah, I mean, it's gonna change a few things, but it's gonna change them for the better, because we've come over that hump, and now we just need to figure out a way to turn it into a positive is the way that I look at it. It hit me this morning after I got out of the shower. I said, 'You know what? The two-year-old that was in that car, the nineteen-year-old'—"

"Eighteen."

"Well, eighteen."

"Yeah," said Lloyd, laughing again.

"I always fuck up the math. I'm not the smartest one."

"I was eighteen."

"You're right."

Lloyd then lamented his plight at length. He was being charged for something he had not done. He had come to regret what he'd told Dave in their last session, because, when he reflected on it later, he thought, speaking of himself partly in the third person, "I'm really fucked because now Lloyd knows everything that's going on, and he's gonna be charged with everything, because I can't prove nothin'." Again he said he needed to talk to a lawyer. "I'll vote the Fifth."

"Look," said Dave, misleadingly, "I'm talking to you as a man to a man. Not a cop to an inmate."

"Right."

"Okay? Human being to human being, and I know you gotta do your job and that's protect Lloyd Lee Welch."

"Right," said Lloyd. "You know? I've done that all my life. I'm a little frustrated because I thought I was going to be a witness and end up testifying and not being charged with anything, and now I'm getting fucked. I already know that I am." He said he was an admitted child molester, not a killer. He couldn't even kill an animal.

Dave kept on. He was on Lloyd's side. He was working tirelessly on his behalf. He believed him, but it was still important to clear a few things up. It wouldn't hurt Lloyd at this point to finally tell him all that he knew. "If you break it down logically, it makes sense to me now. You're eighteen, and you're thinking to yourself, 'Well, my father was doing a good thing for everybody and was gonna party, now this thing has gotten sideways, but I'm the only one that anybody saw at the mall.' Now you're sweating it, thinking, 'What the fuck? Now what? I can't go back and say anything to a thirty-, forty-year-old man who might beat my ass.' So at some point you go back to the mall because you're sweating it. Your mom, your dad, they don't know you went back to the mall, they still have these two girls. They're doing these bad things to them. *How am I gonna unfuck this thing?* Now all of the sudden Montgomery County police," he knocked on the table to simulate a knock on the Welches' front door. "Because they kicked you out of the station, and now they're looking to talk to you again, but you're not there, and your mom answers the door, and now your dad knows you've been back to the mall."

A guard, hearing the knocking, opened the door to the interview room and poked his head in.

"No, no, that was me banging on the table," said Dave.

"Okay."

"We're good."

Lloyd laughed, and the guard closed the door again.

"Now your family's mad at you. Now you're even more worried that you went to the mall, and the police are banging on the door wanting to talk to you."

"I didn't even know the police went to the house," said Lloyd.

"I didn't either, because it wasn't documented. That's what your mom testified to twice."

"I didn't know anything about that."

"So, they're aggravated. Now your uncle Dick gets drug in, because that's your dad's brother. He needs help. You know, 'The dumb ass went back to the mall. We got these kids. What are we gonna do?' " And that, Dave suggested, was when the decision was made to kill the girls and when Lloyd found Dick and Lee in the basement in the act. "Matter of fact, they probably made you come over and watch it or help clean it up, and that's how they suckered you into carrying that bag down there."

Getting Lloyd to admit taking the bloody duffel bag to Taylor's Mountain would shore up the case against him. It would substantiate the testimonies of Connie and Henry, two of the only pieces of independent evidence, and would definitely place him at both the beginning and the end of the crime. How could he persuade Lloyd to make such a damaging admission? Dave had come up with an explanation that appeared, if not innocent, at least less damning.

Speaking of Lloyd in the third person, he said, "It's because he was told he was gonna do it and he had no option. What other option did you have? Think about it. You had no fuckin' option."

Lloyd just took this in, arms crossed, nodding occasionally, and laughing softly to himself.

Dave said, "So you owe it to yourself to explain some of this stuff, because how does it get any worse?"

"How's it get worse? Me spending the rest of my life in jail for something I didn't do."

"Well, then, we have to clean it up."

"Did Dickie get indicted?"

"Not yet."

"Is he getting indicted?"

Dave said he was fighting "tooth and nail" to make that happen. "We've got to figure out a way to explain some of this stuff that logically doesn't make sense. See how I'm trying to change everything into a positive with you? Giving you the benefit of the doubt?"

Lloyd sat pondering this, leaning back in his chair, nodding, arms still crossed.

"I'm sniffing all around it, aren't I?" suggested Dave.

Lloyd muttered, nodding, saying something to himself that sounded like, "Shut up." Dave wasn't sure, but Lloyd was definitely thinking about saying more.

Dave reminded him that his family had all turned on him.

"Oh, I already know how they are," Lloyd said. "So if I give my side, I'm fucked anyway."

"Who is standing up for you?"

"No one. Well, you are."

Dave told him about "missing evidence" up on the mountain—he was referring to the car, but didn't say what it was—and his cousin Wes Justice, who "flat out lied" to the grand jury and was now facing the possibility of perjury charges.

"The car," said Lloyd.

"The car. He doesn't know what the right thing to do is. To come forward, or is it right to keep lying and see where it ends up? And where we are with him right now is we think he should come forward, because we're damn close to finding it."

"Well, see, the thing is, I didn't drive up to no mall. I'm telling you. Dickie did take me to the mall."

He went back over the kidnapping and the taking of the girls to Dick's house and his decision to leave. "And what I saw in the basement is true."

Then he stopped. He scratched his head. The truth of his predicament was sinking in.

"See, I know once I start, I'm . . . I'm just fucked. I am just really fucked. I'm going to jail for the rest of my life for something I didn't do, man. Just 'cause I know it."

Dave said a lot of people had theories. For instance, he said, a number of people had at first disbelieved his own about the killing in the basement at 4714 Baltimore Avenue because it didn't jibe with their own.

"They found her blood down there, didn't they?"

"Yes." This was not precisely true.

Lloyd sighed heavily.

"Okay. All right. I'm fucked anyway. You know that whole story about the mall thing and shit like that and about the babysitting and shit like that? Yep, I was in the basement. I seen what happened, and I was threatened. Multiple threats. That I could be cut up, too, if I didn't help do what they wanted me to do. The white car is the one I took to Virginia. You know, I did help Henry throw a bag on the fire, and I knew it was a body in there. I didn't know if it was both of them or not. Lee knew. Lee and Dick did the cutting, and I helped clean up a little bit. Not a lot because it made me sick to my stomach. They took the bag and put it in the car and told me to take it down to Virginia, and Henry would be down there with a fire and to throw the bag on the fire, and to come back. I came back. I don't know what Dickie did with the car after that. I know as soon as I came back, they cleaned it up, and Dickie drove off with the car."

Here was the story whole—well, almost whole. It was worth remembering that this was the same man who, a year and a half earlier, had said—"in all honestly"—that he had never been to Wheaton Plaza. Now he had helped with the kidnapping, dismemberment, and disposal. The distance his story had traveled was dizzying. But, still, none of this had been *his* idea; *he* had never touched the girls; he had been *forced* to clean up the blood after the murder and deliver the remains to Virginia. But here it was; they had teased out the whole abomination.

"When they put the bag in the car, they told me to go straight down to Virginia," he said. "Dickie gave me some money to make sure that the car had gas in it and enough gas to get down there and enough gas to get back."

He said the bag they used was Lee's, not his. The younger girl, Kate, "was givin' a little trouble. She was crying a lot and stuff. I think they got scared. I can't say for sure if Dickie had smacked them around or she hit her head or anything like that, because I didn't see all that. All I know is when I went down to the basement what I saw, them chopping her up. I saw Lee put a small piece of leg into the bag, and that's when I got pulled in, sick to my stomach, and I really don't like blood."

He said Dick had used a hatchet, not the ax.

"I don't know how they killed her, but she was already dead. Lee had a bunch of rags around. They had a piece of plywood on the floor. Eventually they got a part of the leg off, and Lee takes a rag and grabs it and puts it in the bag, and I kind of threw up a little bit, 'cause I was sick, and they told me, 'Don't go nowhere.' Dick grabbed ahold of me and said, 'You're gonna do what we say or you'll be next,' and I was scared. They cut both legs off. I think they eventually got part of her arms off, and then they both picked her up and put her in the bag. I think they had everything else in there. They had a bunch of rags to pick her up and put her in. The bag had one of these clip things. You could hear the bag being clipped. Dick wiped his hands as best he could, and he handed me the keys."

He repeated that he had driven a big white car, the 1966 Chrysler New Yorker belonging to his aunt Pat's father. Dick gave him forty dollars.

"I drove all night. Drove down there and drove back, you know. I wasn't down there long. That's what I was told to do, go down there and come straight back. Don't bullshit around. Don't stop nowhere unless you're getting gas. Drunk a lot of coffee because I was tired. That was a tiring trip. Five down, five back. I had no driver's license. I had just learned how to drive that big-ass car. I was taking it very slow, not speeding or anything like that."

He worried when he stopped to get gas that blood might be leaking out of the trunk.

"By the time I got down there, the bag was pretty wet. I got sick a little more, but I didn't throw up. I just got nauseated, and, like I said,

Henry was there. He said, 'Let's go,' and I popped the trunk." They hefted the bag onto the bonfire, and Henry threw more branches on top. Lloyd had blood on his hands and tried to wipe them clean. On the way home, he said, he felt sick, so he pulled the car off the road, rolled the window down, and just collected himself. He slept for a time and then resumed driving.

He arrived back at 4714 Baltimore Avenue at daybreak, he said. He showered and slept. A few days later he and Helen hitchhiked back down to Virginia. Lloyd said he didn't know what happened to Sheila. He believed she'd been killed but didn't know whether it was in Maryland or Virginia. He said he was "eighty-eight percent" certain that Sheila was brought down to Taylor's Mountain and that Henry had done something with her.

"So, who else in the family knows this story?" Dave asked.

"Lee, but he's dead. I guess Henry knows it. I mean, I don't know if Connie knew. I know my mom [Edna], she can say she doesn't know some of the things, but I'm sure she knows that me and Dickie went to the mall, because she told me right there with Helen, 'You don't know nothin'. You're not involved. Don't get yourself caught up. Don't go to that mall.' You know? And I'm ninety-nine point nine [percent] sure Patty knows, Dick's wife."

Dave asked why Lloyd, a year earlier, had brought his cousin Teddy into the story. His cousin had endured months of suspicion and distress and had been forced to lay bare the most intimate details of his life to clear himself.

Lloyd said, simply, "Scapegoat."

Suckered Big-Time

One big question had always been: what would make the Lyon girls leave the mall with a stranger? If they had resisted, there were enough people in Wheaton Plaza that day to have noticed. Lloyd's explanation might make sense. The lure of pot might just have been enough to make Sheila abandon caution, walk out of the mall, and perhaps even get into a car with strangers, much as her parents disbelieved it. Judging by the stories the detectives had gathered from prior similar instances, other girls had gone that far. Sheila was about to turn thirteen, an age when children are prone to do daring, foolhardy things, and in 1975, smoking dope was among the most common forms of youthful rebellion, akin to drinking beer or sneaking a slug from a bottle in a parent's liquor cabinet. It was *cool.* It was easy to imagine a girl just days away from her thirteenth birthday, even a sheltered, innocent girl—perhaps *especially* a sheltered, innocent girl—saying yes, even to a stranger. Ten-year-old Kate would have been stuck. Told to stay with her big sister, she was now being led someplace she should not go. The detail of her crying softly in the back seat of the car, asking when they were going to go back, was heartrending.

Another big question was: how could one abductor handle *two* girls? Even if there had been some willingness to go with Lloyd at first, at some point that afternoon Sheila's mistake would have been clear. This boy was not their friend. At that point it was unlikely, though not impossible, that Lloyd could have handled both girls by himself, but he had Helen, who was so self-destructively entangled with him. She had participated in other crimes with him. Lloyd might also have had the help of his father or his uncle, as he'd said. There was plenty to suggest, if not prove, that both had a sexual interest in children.

Pornography was another possible motive. Before the digital age, films and photographs of children being used for sex were rare. They were difficult to make and hard to come by. The film itself was evidence of a crime, so it had to be developed and printed privately. Purchasing or even borrowing such material was expensive. Making and distributing child porn was dangerous but potentially lucrative.

"They had money," Lloyd said, of Dick and Pat. "I don't know if they made a bunch of movies with her [Sheila] and sold her off or what. I've always been curious to know where the fuck they get all their money at."

Dick and Pat Welch were not well-to-do, as Lloyd suggested, although their pleasant, middle-class suburban home and their cars might have made them appear so to him. There was no proof that Dick made child porn. In his grand jury testimony he had admitted once buying a porn film and showing it on the porch of his sister Lizzie's house, but that was all. The home movies the squad had seized from his house were all conventional family fare.

No matter what Lloyd said, the most likely place for the girls to have been held captive and raped would have been in the dungeon-like basement of Lee's house. Dave was haunted by the possibility that detectives had knocked on the front door, as Edna had testified, while Sheila was still drugged and hidden below.

The rest of this story fit with what they'd learned in Virginia. The detectives didn't believe for a minute Lloyd's claims of innocence—or that, as he'd put it, "I was suckered big-time." Not likely.

If other family members had been involved, then Lloyd's decision to return to the mall and give a statement might well have triggered the girls' killing. And if the detectives had knocked on Lee's door while one or both girls were still alive, it would have made the need to get rid of them all the more urgent. There was the flood of human blood in the basement to prove that. Kate's unhappiness from the beginning, and her age, made it more likely that she had given more trouble. She would have been too young to fully appreciate the danger. Two years older, Sheila might have chosen not to provoke.

This was as far as evidence and reasonable speculation would go. Lloyd was not offering more.

"What happens now?" he asked Dave.

"Like I was telling you, it's gonna be a process. It could be two weeks. It could be three weeks. They're gonna have a hearing of some sort in Delaware to get you moved to Virginia, and then the process starts down there. I'm sure at some point you're going to get legal [retain a lawyer], and we'll have to go through the attorney to talk to you."

"Well, I can tell you right now, if I end up getting charged, I'm going to take the Fifth. Because I originally thought I'd be testifying against them and not being charged for anything. That was my whole thinking."

He was worried he would be attacked in the prison when his indictment was reported.

"I'm just going to have to live with it tomorrow and see what happens. Next time you see me, if I'm in a body cast, you'll know what happened."

"Anything you want to take away or add?" Dave asked.

"Nope. There's nothing more. I'm going to get a lawyer."

The Ride

There would be one more long talk with Lloyd in September. He'd had more than two months to contemplate the hole he'd dug himself. The fallout in the prison had not been not as bad as he'd feared. He'd stayed in the general population and weathered it fine.

He was picked up at the prison by a van that had been wired for sound and driven to Bedford for his arraignment. Dave rode along with two of the Virginia detectives, Mayhew and Wilks, grasping one more opportunity to get Lloyd talking.

Lloyd had been indicted in July, but the law in Virginia required a waiting period before he could be questioned again. So the drive south had been delayed. Prosecutors anticipated that Lloyd's defense would entail suppressing the interview sessions. His lawyers would be likely to claim that he had been duped into believing he had immunity and that he had not been provided counsel after numerous requests. These were not surefire arguments, but just in case, the detectives wanted to capture Lloyd in the van making a completely voluntary confession. So they were instructed not to question him directly about the case unless he brought it up himself.

The squad believed that Dave, Mark, and Katie should be the ones to take this ride with Lloyd. It was their last chance, and by now the three had learned to play him like a violin. But the van was being furnished by Virginia authorities, and Bedford insisted that its own detectives should have the honors. They agreed to bring Dave along—he was unquestionably the one Lloyd saw as his friend. Katie was offended. After all the work she and Mark had put into the case! She was so upset about being exluded that when she complained to her lieutenant she broke down.

Acutely conscious of being female in a world that was predominantly male, she had never dared shed a tear on the job. Afterward, embarrassed by her emotions, she made a mental note that it was time to begin distancing herself from this case.

The drive from the prison took them through fog to the Eastern Shore and the Bay Bridge, then past Annapolis and toward Washington. They passed the Hyattsville exit off the congested Capital Beltway and headed south on Interstate 95 toward Richmond. Lloyd bantered away with the detectives. He was alternately cheerful, happy to be spending the day outside the prison walls, and distressed. Little time passed before Lloyd cleared the first hurdle for the detectives; he started talking about his case unprompted.

It began as complaint. Why had *he* been charged? He was the innocent one, the wronged one. He'd been misled into thinking he was just going to be a witness, and now his very willingness to help was being used to screw him. None of that capability for remorse and sympathy noted years earlier by his prison psychologist was evident. He still showed no sign of apprehending the horror inflicted on the Lyon girls. His concern was all for himself.

He had seen a story in the *Wilmington News Journal* about his cousin Wes Justice's testimony that his uncle Dick had confessed the whole thing.

"He admitted it a year ago to him [Wes]," Lloyd said. "I've got the article. I'm trying to understand how they're charging me with murder when I didn't kill nobody."

The detectives humored him, chatting about a variety of things, noting scenes by the side of the road, discussing traffic patterns, pointing out a rainbow, but Lloyd kept coming back to the crime. He could not have been more helpful if he had tried. He eventually reviewed the kidnapping scene at the mall, placing himself with his father and uncle in the car as they drove off with the girls. He talked about driving the bloody duffel bag with Kate's remains down to Virginia, although at first he said—even with Dave sitting beside him—that he hadn't known what was in it. He admitted hauling the bag to the fire with his cousin

Henry and tossing it in. Then he described the scene in the basement where Kate had been chopped into pieces—contradicting his claim, just minutes earlier, that he had not known what was in the bag. Lloyd could not help himself. Just as the detectives had hoped, he seemed not to realize that the conversation *counted*, that by telling his story to the police he was, once more, officially confessing his crimes.

"I can't believe that you're doing this to me," he said. "How can you prove it was done in Virginia and not Maryland, or how can you prove it was in Maryland and not Virginia? You see what I'm saying?"

"It will all work out in the end," Dave assured him, "as your aunt [Artie] said more than once. The truth is the truth."

"They all know he [Dick] did it," said Lloyd.

Lloyd now threw another relative into the mix, Luke Welch, his late, mentally disabled uncle.

"Lukie and Dick and Dad, I'm sure that's the three. I was just somebody that, whattaya call it, popped up, and they suckered me into something, and I guess with all the abuse and shit like that, and I wanted the attention and shit, as fucked up as I was."

He had gone back to the mall to give a statement because, "I had a guilty conscience, even though I got scared and lied and shit like that."

Well over an hour into the ride, with the van now pushing through rain and heavy traffic, it occurred to him that he was being worked.

"I don't mind talking to y'all, just so long as it ain't being thrown up that I did this and I did that. I don't know if y'all have a recorder in here or not. I used to ask you all the time, where's the recorder at?"

The detectives laughed.

"I'll ask you," said Lloyd. "Do you have a recorder?"

"Yep," said Mayhew.

"You recording me?"

"Yep."

"Okay."

"We ain't hiding it."

"Okay."

"That's to protect us, too."

"Right. I know how to ask for a lawyer."

After that, Lloyd finally shut up about the case. He had at long last told everything he was going to tell. For the remainder of the drive that day, he conversed but said nothing substantive. The detectives kept trying.

"Is there anything you thought of since the last time you talked to Dave that you think you need to tell us?" asked Mayhew. "Anything at all that pops in your head?"

"Nah."

"You think you maybe haven't talked to us about?"

"That's it," said Lloyd.

Hours into the drive, Wilks asked Lloyd, "What's the favorite state you've been to? What ones do you like most?"

"South Carolina."

"Why is that?"

"Myrtle Beach."

"Trying to get back to it?" asked Dave.

"Yeah, I would like to. It's just something about it. I like the ocean. Good people," Lloyd said wistfully. "Oh, lots of things."

The Plea

On September 12, 2017, in a Bedford courtroom, Lloyd Welch pleaded guilty to two counts of felony murder.

He said he had participated in the kidnapping of Sheila and Kate Lyon more than forty years earlier, and while he continued to deny he had raped or killed them, his admission—which stood in sharp contrast to his bizarre notion of "partying"—fell well within the confines of a Virginia legal doctrine defining as murder a killing "in the commission of abduction with intent to defile."

The plea spared him the death penalty, but it meant, as he feared, that he would never leave prison. His sentence was forty-eight years. He would serve his full sentence for child molestation in Delaware and then travel to a Virginia penitentiary for the remainder of his days. He was sixty years old, and he had, from first to last, talked himself into this outcome.

The case against Lloyd was so tangled that the Virginia charge, and his plea, resulted from a desire by Montgomery County, Maryland, to simplify it. The girls had been kidnapped from a mall in Wheaton, which meant that this specific crime fell under the jurisdiction of the Montgomery County state's attorney, John McCarthy. His staff had been supervising the probe for years—indeed, the county office had overseen it since the day the girls disappeared. It was one of the most significant crimes in county history, and one that had touched McCarthy personally. He remembered the day of the abduction well. A law student at night, he had been teaching a high school class at a local Catholic school, not far from Wheaton Plaza, on that day. Like most people in the region he had followed the story closely and felt the general sadness and frustration when no answers came. After becoming an attorney and then a prosecutor, he had become friends with John Lyon, who upon retiring from broadcasting volunteered as a witness/victim advocate at the courthouse. McCarthy had often benefited from John's help during criminal trials. John also worked Friday nights as a bartender at the local Knights of Columbus hall, where McCarthy sometimes retreated at the end of his workweek. So the decision to hand Lloyd Welch off to Bedford, Virginia, was a painful one for him, not least because, as McCarthy reminded me, he is an elected official (since 2006), and winning a conviction in such a landmark case would surely have meant votes.

The decision made sense nonetheless. What real evidence there was strongly suggested that Kate Lyon, at least, had been murdered in Hyattsville, in neighboring Prince Georges County. No one was sure what had happened to Sheila, or where it had happened, but the statements of Lloyd and others suggested that she had been taken to Virginia and killed there. Technically, the case belonged to all three jurisdictions, and Lloyd, through his own statements, had incriminated himself in all three, but his ever-changing story made it hard to mount a coherent prosecutorial narrative. Basing the whole case on the prison interviews was fraught with legal peril. The various inducements, immunity agreements (written and oral), threats, and vague promises during those hours and hours of interviews by Dave, Mark, Katie, and Chris might give a good defense lawyer plenty of weaknesses to exploit, and laws governing police interrogation were especially restrictive in Maryland. The case against Lloyd was stronger in Virginia, primarily because Lloyd's final story of driving human remains to Taylor's Mountain was corroborated by his cousins. Virginia also made sense because Lloyd had several times voiced his fear of being executed, and since Maryland was not a death-penalty state, he was considered more likely to accept a guilty plea in Virginia to avoid death row—a calculation that proved correct. The plea also avoided the hazards of trial, as did the decision not to seek kidnapping and rape charges in Maryland. Bringing him to trial would invite challenges and appeals that could delay, if not upend, his conviction. The principal factor guiding all this tactical legal reasoning, McCarthy told me, was the desire of John and Mary Lyon to bring the case to a close. It was painful for them.

Little of this rationale was explained to the Maryland detectives, who were more than disappointed. They were angry and felt betrayed. They had poured years of effort into the case, endured sleepless nights, extensive travel, tedious legwork, and immeasurable emotional stress. It had consumed them. And after all their efforts to build a case against Dick and other family members who might have been involved, only Lloyd had faced justice. They still had not found the girls' bodies. Their painstakingly built case against Lloyd would never be fully aired in court. It was a bitter pill.

They were justly proud of their work. In the end, the exhaustive effort against the Welch clan in Maryland and Virginia amounted to little on its own, but it had contributed mightily to what was, without question, a sustained masterpiece of criminal interrogation. How do you get a compulsive liar, one with every reason to lie, to tell the truth? Dave Davis brought recognized skills to the interview room, but neither he nor the others were experienced homicide detectives. They made mistakes, some potentially ruinous—Pete recalled his astonishment after Lloyd had signed the carefully crafted limited immunity agreement, and Dave had proceeded, orally, to liberally broaden its terms. Unsure of what they had in Lloyd at the beginning, they had overpromised, saying that he would not be charged. Dave kicked himself for revealing that Helen Craver was dead, and he and Mark erred by holding an unrecorded, off-the-record chat with Lloyd early on—and apparently threatening him. Katie then made the mistake of admitting this! None of the long interview sessions had gone exactly as the squad would have liked. They had felt their way forward, trying one ploy after another, wheedling, lying, flattering, badgering, and coercing.

"We knew we were dealing with a monster, but we had to entertain him in a fashion," said Katie. "That was the best approach with him. We had to keep him talking, had to keep him on our 'team.' We had to endure the 'friendship' and go through the crap to get as many of the answers as we could."

None of them had ever worked on a case like it, and none believed they ever would again. The effort exhausted them.

The path to the truth, or as close as they were likely to get to it, was down a long trail of lies. It was the only way. Lloyd Welch may never have been linked to the Lyon case, or even noticed, much less caught, if he had not gone to the police himself. Nor would he have been convicted if he'd kept his mouth shut when the squad approached him in 2013. Many times in their interview sessions the detectives had suggested that guilt was gnawing at him, haunting him, burdening him, and that down deep he was longing to confess. He wasn't. It is doubtful that Lloyd's conscience has troubled him for a minute of his life. If anything was eating at him, it was fear. Fear of getting caught had sent him back to the mall in 1975, and years later that's what kept him talking. If he had stopped at any point up until admitting that he'd lured the girls from the mall, the case would have been over. For Dave's part, every time he had entered the interview room with Lloyd, he expected it to be the last. Lloyd's clumsy mendacity kept the thing alive.

None of the thousands of man-hours, millions of dollars, hundreds of interviews, grand jury proceedings, search warrants, wiretaps, excavations, lab tests, or perjury indictments had produced a single conclusive piece of evidence. In the fall of 2017, investigators still digging on Taylor's Mountain found a tooth, which was judged on the site to be human and to have belonged to a child roughly twelve years old. The tooth was bagged and sent to the Bedford sheriff's office. When the squad went to retrieve it the next day, to ship it to a lab for more detailed analysis, it was gone. The sheriff's office had no explanation.

"It could have been anything," said Mark Janney, "from incompetence to corruption. We just don't know, and it was never investigated." It crystallized a larger sense of failure.

No physical trace of Sheila and Kate has been found—indeed, Sheila's precise fate is still unknown. The fragment of human bone found in the bonfire site on Taylor's Mountain had insufficient DNA to sequence. The other fragments of fabric and beads and metal discovered—of which Mark Janney had made much with Lloyd—were merely suggestive. The traces of hemoglobin in the basement of 4714 Baltimore Avenue, found by Dave's remarkable creative deduction, were too degraded to provide even a blood type, much less a DNA match. They'd tried hard. Prosecutor Pete Feeney, who had inspected the basement rooms on the day Dave found them, wanted to take out the entire back wall for analysis. When that proved impractical he had portions of the cement block pulverized and sent to the lab. Nothing. What other evidence they had, such as the testimonies of Connie Akers and Henry Parker, made sense only in the context of Lloyd's own words. The sheer expenditure of futile effort in this case was breathtaking, and even after Lloyd's indictment it continued. In December 2016, Dave had met with a historic preservation specialist to review old satellite imagery of Taylor's Mountain, hoping for some sign of where the '66 Chrysler New Yorker was stashed or buried. He found none.

Reconstructing the past from memory is always hard; when the only witnesses are hostile, it's nearly impossible. Soon after I started working on this book, when Dave told me how liars lie about the big things but flesh out their fiction with the truth, I wasn't sure exactly what he meant. This story illustrates his point. To discern the truth, an investigator (or a writer) must *interpret* testimony. You begin by asking basic questions: Who? What? Where? When? How? Why? The answers are then assembled into a narrative, an orderly progression of time, cause, and effect. And yet, anyone who investigates crimes, or who writes true stories, knows how untidy the process is and how readily such stories can break down. Often there are too many causes and too many effects to completely sort out. Human motivation is too hard to pin down, pieces refuse to fit, and memories notoriously differ. Add the passage of decades and the problem gets harder. Evidence gets lost or degrades. Recollections fade. Eyewitnesses die. And even with strong answers to the first five questions, the last—Why?—is always elusive. The best of modern crime stories—*In Cold Blood* and *The Executioner's Song*, to name two—are not *who*dunits but *why*dunits. In both cases we already know who is guilty. Truman Capote and Norman Mailer, the respective authors, were primarily interested in why, and at best they provided only artful speculation, answers that reflected as much about themselves as about their subjects. This is what you get with a "true story," artful, informed, honest speculation. At bottom, this is what we call history.

Lloyd could not care less. For him, truth is entirely fungible. Facts exist only as tools to craft his next argument, to be employed or discarded as the situation demands. And from his perspective, this makes sense. Anyone who could steal two little girls, abuse them horribly, kill them, and then toss their bodies onto a burning pile, is someone for whom *nothing* matters beyond himself. Beyond the sheer barbarity, such acts are completely, horribly selfish. Caught in a lie, Lloyd was never embarrassed or even mildly annoyed. Knocking down one story just required conjuring another, a game he clearly enjoyed. He's still at it, as I found when I visited him myself.

But for me, the deep questions about the Lyon case—Who would commit such a crime? And why?—were largely answered. Lloyd Welch was the answer to the first, even though it's not clear whether he acted alone. The answer to the second, while inherently less certain, was lust and rage. It's too easy to simply write Lloyd off as a sociopath. Cast out of a family that abused him from early childhood, he was a victim before he became a monster. He emerged from a peculiar American subculture that in many ways was locked out of the American dream, even as its members walked the country's streets and sought work in its malls. Much has changed in forty years; many people from Appalachian families have prospered, and clans like the Welches are hardly the most persecuted minority in American history, but traces of that exclusion remain and still generate anger and resentment. Eighteen-year-old Lloyd Welch was a particularly vicious specimen, someone who distilled the absolute worst elements of his upbringing and who lashed out with unspeakable cruelty. The blame is rightly his own, but the crime reflects the world that made him.

Much of the Lyon mystery remains. It most likely always will remain.

"We started this investigation with the idea of finding the bodies, even if we couldn't come up with a criminal prosecution, and sort of the opposite happened," said Pete. "We had a criminal prosecution and never found the bodies."

Despite strong suspicions about Dick Welch and the possibility that other members of the family were involved, as either direct participants or coconspirators, all must be considered innocent. The detectives are pleased and proud of their effort, but they are also disappointed. They have moved on. Unless there is some surprising new find, they are disinclined to look back.

"I don't know what happened in this case," said Pete, finally and simply.

None of them fully believe Lloyd's story. Why would they?

THEORIES

The four detectives have each formed a different theory of what really happened, in ways that reflect, in part, who they are. All agree that Lloyd was the one who led the girls from the mall, that rape and possibly child porn were the motives, and that both girls were subsequently murdered. They believe that Kate was killed in the basement of 4714 Baltimore Avenue and her body thrown onto the fire in Virginia, and they believe or strongly suspect that Sheila was taken to Taylor's Mountain alive, further abused sexually, and then killed and buried there. But each has a distinct narrative to explain what happened in between, why it happened that way, and who was responsible.

Sunny Dave Davis leans toward Lloyd as lone wolf. The detective is likable because he genuinely likes people, so he leans toward the belief that anyone who could commit a crime like this is fundamentally abnormal or, as he put it at one point, "an animal." There was no shortage of reasons Lloyd Welch turned out that way. Dave believes Lloyd had spent time living in the woods near Wheaton Plaza, where it appeared that he in effect shopped for little girls. This accounted for the stories told by other women—girls at the time—who remembered being approached by a man in the mall who fit Lloyd's description; who presented himself as a security guard, showing a badge; and who tried with varying degrees of success to take them away. He'd perfected his pitch by the time he met Sheila and Kate.

Once he'd lured the sisters out to the woods, they were likely drugged and raped right there. He would have had Helen to help—this explained why her name was the first that occurred to Lloyd when he was informed the police were looking for him. Both were druggies and heavy drinkers, even as Helen experienced one pregnancy after another. She may have clung to Lloyd out of some misguided youthful ardor, but there were other reasons. He was a source for the drugs she craved, and she feared him—her family said she would intermittently resurface black-and-blue, sometimes with broken bones. Lloyd colored their relationship in gauzy hues, but their years together had been squalid, violent, and troubled. As some of Helen's relatives told it, she had been more his slave than his lover or his wife. Teddy said that he always pictured Helen attached to Lloyd by a leash. In viewing her this way, it is not hard to imagine her helping him constrain two little girls. This also explained why, years later, Lloyd immediately perceived her as a threat.

Lloyd was not the sort to plan ahead. After abduction and rape, what then? He couldn't just turn the girls loose. Killing them and disposing of them out in the open would have been problematic. At that point he'd decided to take the problem home, to his father's dungeon-like basement, his hangout for pot-smoking. How much help he got from his family at that point depended on just how depraved you believed the clan was. Lee, Lloyd's father, a drunk and a pedophile, might well have welcomed him showing up with two drugged little girls. It would not be out of character. But getting them to Hyattsville required a vehicle.

This is where the red station wagon fits in. Detectives abhor coincidences, and one that had nagged the Lyon case investigators all the way back to 1975 was the theft of that red Pinto station wagon from a dealership adjacent to Wheaton Plaza *on the same day the girls disappeared*. The car was found days later, parked in, of all places, Hyattsville. Lloyd had a history in those days of stealing—or, rather, borrowing—cars. Sports cars were jumped for joyrides, but who boosts a Pinto station wagon? Perhaps someone transporting two little girls and his girlfriend. And, as noted, a red car was one of those stubborn particulars that kept surfacing in Lloyd's stories—Dave had learned to pay attention to those. If Lloyd took the girls to his father's house, he'd have needed a story to explain why he and Helen had them—they were "runaways," or he and Helen were "babysitting" them. Again, these were concepts that recurred.

If the crime had become a family effort, it's doubtful that Lloyd or the other Welches would have envisioned the firestorm of publicity that erupted. Media reports about the missing girls, the plea for clues, the ongoing searches, meant that nearly every eye in the Washington area was alert for two little blond girls. Pressure to get rid of Sheila and Kate would have been strong. Dave imagined members of the Welch family thinking, "They are in our house, it's all over TV. What do we do with them?" Lloyd made his trip back to the mall to mislead investigators. It was at this precarious point, Dave thought, that Kate's increasing anguish and defiance might have provoked Lloyd to kill her. She was chopped up in the basement, possibly with his father's help. Lee then phoned relatives in Bedford, alerting them that Lloyd was coming down with the girls, one of whom was now in pieces in his old army duffel bag. This is where, in Dave's theory, Lloyd's aunt Pat came in. Lee didn't have a car, but he was working part-time for Pat's father. Dave guessed that she arranged for the loan of his big white 1966 Chrysler, which was used, by Lloyd and Helen, perhaps with Lee, to drive the girls to Virginia. The bloody bag was thrown onto the Parkers' bonfire. Sheila, he believes, arrived in the same car, alive, and was given to Lloyd's cousin Henry Parker, perhaps in return for his help with disposing of the bloody bag. Dave speculated that Henry then further abused Sheila, killed her, and buried her somewhere on the mountain. Given the stories about his own sexual predation, Henry had to be considered a suspect, but after his death in 2017, there was little hope of ever proving Dave's conjecture. There had been so much testimony about the terrible odor that spread over the mountain from the bonfire consuming Kate's body—neighbors and relatives recalled it four decades later—that Henry was unlikely to have burned another. By then, Lloyd and Helen had gone back to Maryland and hit the road. They did not return for years. In Dave's theory, only Helen, Lloyd's father, Lloyd's aunt Pat, and Henry were accomplices. Like Pete, Dave suspected that Dick Welch, the prime villain in Lloyd's stories, had not been involved at all.

Katie Leggett's theory is completely different. She has a more jaundiced view of human nature than Dave and sees the kidnapping as part of something bigger. She believed almost from the start that Lloyd was a patsy, duped into his role. Her background in sexual crimes led her to see Sheila and Kate as victims of a murderous child-porn ring, one that stole children to abuse them before cameras and then peddled the film—and possibly the children—to others in their illicit circles. The intense publicity and search for the girls had made them too hot to handle, so they were killed. The squad believed that several members of the Welch family were involved in rings of this kind. "We did uncover a lot of weird stuff that lends credibility to this," she said. "We found two sisters in the same area who were involved in the same kind of thing, and they believed that their father sold them into that situation. We uncovered a lot of stuff that led us to potentially high-powered people being involved." A former CIA contractor, whom Katie described as "shady and guilty of something," had been part of that ring.

To Katie, Lloyd was an ignorant eighteen-year-old druggie, easily manipulated, and incapable of pulling off a crime like this on his own.

Nor had he shown, at that age, any of the sexual urge for children that got him into such trouble later. He had grown, she thought, into a sociopath and child molester, but as a teenager he was not there yet. From what she knew about child molesters, abducting children and sexually abusing them were often separate things. Few abusers were abductors; abusers tended to groom victims in their family or social circle, and seldom murdered them. This was Lloyd's later pattern. Those who abduct children, on the other hand, are much rarer. They take strangers and usually kill them. Lloyd had definitely been at the mall and had helped lure Sheila and Kate away. She did not believe that Sheila would have been tempted by an offer to smoke dope. Among the girls' effects, Katie had read school notes passed between Sheila and a friend who was trying to tempt her into smoking cigarettes. Sheila had refused and cut off the friendship. So Katie tended to believe that Dick Welch, in his security guard uniform, had probably been the prime actor. "'Come with me, your parents are looking for you,' or something like that," she said. The girls were then taken to the Baltimore Avenue basement, where they were held and abused and filmed over the next week by Dick, Lee, Lloyd, and possibly others. At some point they were taken to Dick and Pat's house, perhaps because it made a better backdrop for filming. Some of the couple's children vaguely recalled girls being kept upstairs in a closet off the poolroom, and Teddy Welch had eventually told a similar story. Back in the dungeon basement, with the media storm raging, Katie said, "The *oh-shit* factor kicked in." Kate was killed there, and her body was taken to Taylor's Mountain and thrown onto the fire. Henry Parker then took Sheila, raped her, and killed her, possibly accidentally. She was buried somewhere on that property. In Katie's theory, Lloyd's conviction meant that they had caught only a bit player in a much larger drama.

Mark Janney is less inclined to theorize than either Dave or Katie. He spent years doing drug work undercover, trusting his gut about people, and tends to size them up quickly and sternly. He is also well acquainted with criminal networks and sees one behind this. Mark believes someone was waiting in a vehicle outside Wheaton Plaza when Lloyd lured the girls out, but he, like Katie, doesn't believe Lloyd was capable of planning and carrying out the crime by himself. "He was not sophisticated enough," Mark said. More likely, Lloyd had been put up to the kidnapping by his father and uncle, who knew an eighteen-year-old would have a better chance of fast-talking two little girls than they would. He agrees with Katie that the motive was both to satisfy their own sexual urges and to make a porn film. They then might have sold the girls into sexual slavery. This was their intent. He notes that Pat Welch, interviewed after her arrest on perjury charges, had conjectured that the girls "probably were sold; a lot of that was going on back then." As far as Mark is concerned, this seemed too creepy and specific to be mere speculation. He believes Sheila and Kate were driven initially to the Baltimore Avenue basement, where they were drugged and raped by Lloyd, Lee, Dick, and perhaps others in their family, who filmed themselves in the act. They were taken to Dick and Patty's house at some point, most likely on Easter Sunday, when the Welch family gathered for a meal at Lee's house. Keeping the girls in Lee's basement for that event would have been too risky. Later they were returned. Kate became more difficult to handle, so she was killed there. Mark believes, like the others, that Sheila was killed later in Virginia and buried there.

Chris Homrock also believes that Lloyd could not have done this by himself. After his long investigation of Ray Mileski, it is still hard for him to let go of that connection completely. He believes, like Mark and Katie, that Lee Welch and his brothers were involved in a pedophile ring and that both sex and movies were the motive in stealing Sheila and Kate. He still suspects that Mileski's group was involved, if only on the periphery. The link, in his opinion, was most likely Dick Welch. Chris returns again and again to Dick showing a porn movie on his sister Lizzie's front porch on Taylor's Mountain. The basement room on Baltimore Avenue, where the girls clearly had been kept, seemed less an opportunity Lloyd had seized than something planned. It had a mattress and a sofa and had, in Lloyd's words, "been set up to party." Like the others, Chris suspects that Sheila arrived in Virginia alive and that, as her younger sister's body was consumed by the fire, which burned for days, she was raped and then killed by Henry Parker. There is no proof of this, or of Lloyd's father's and uncle's direct involvement, much less Mileski's, but after all those years of work, that's where Chris's suspicions land.

He had worked on the case longer than the others, and for him the end felt particularly disappointing and anticlimactic. There were still too many unanswered questions. Finding the girls' bodies had always been his primary goal, and in that he had failed. There was no more time to try. Fifteen minutes after Lloyd's plea, Chris and the others were rolled up into another murder case and were up for two days doing interviews and executing search warrants. With Lloyd convicted, the chances were small that they would ever dive back into the Lyon mystery again. One thing consoled Chris. He was convinced that if Lloyd had ever gotten out of jail, he would have taken more victims.

The Perfect Crime

I wanted to meet Lloyd. Mostly I wanted to size him up for myself, but I also wanted to close the book on the mystery that had been with me through my entire professional life. For years after the Lyon story dropped off the front page of my old Baltimore newspaper, its editors would summon me whenever there was a new twist or potential break. I wrote a story when the IBM man reported what he had seen and another when John Lyon was lured to the Annapolis courthouse by the extortionist.

Four years after the Lyon girls disappeared, my city editor, the late Lou Linley, took a call from a psychic who told him their remains were in a field off Route 50, near Baltimore-Washington International Airport. One of Lou's many eccentricities—one that I did not share—was a fascination with the paranormal. He took the tip seriously enough to dispatch me, along with my colleague Bob Douglas (who in later years would become a lawyer and serve as a chief of staff to the governor of Maryland), to check it out. I wonder now, looking back on it, why Bob and I hadn't found a cool bar in nearby Glen Burnie and spent that humid summer afternoon drinking beer. But we were earnest young men, and afraid of Lou—and of missing a story—so we obligingly stomped and sweated through every inch of those prickly fields. We found nothing.

Through the years I continued to wonder about those girls and what had happened to them. In general, the answers were as easy to surmise as they were hard to contemplate. The words one conjured to describe the crime all fell short: callous, brutal, savage, unfeeling, cruel . . . One could, perhaps, see how someone like Lloyd might be *tempted* to do what he did, but indulging that temptation, ultimately, was a choice. It is hard to imagine making a worse one. The only right word for it is *evil.*

To tell this story I had to meet Lloyd, and did so on January 8, 2018, at the Smyrna prison. I had written to him a month earlier, telling him about this book and requesting an interview. I told him the book would center on the interrogation sessions.

"I am eager to hear your own view of [them]," I wrote, "the tactics involved, and your account of how and why your account so dramatically changed. You are, of course, front and center throughout those conversations, so you will be very much present in the story. I would like to make sure I understand it through your eyes."

I knew he had consistently turned down requests from journalists, so I was surprised when he wrote back promptly. He had conditions.

> It will not be a interview intell we talk and come to an understanding. I know you will make a lot of money off this and most likely you have something in the works with a documentary and a book. Just so you know you are not the first person to write me and ask to do a book. I will tell you the something I told them. I can have up to $5,000 in my inmate account.

He then explained how to wire him money.

> If yu don't want to do this and we cannot come to an understanding then I don't want my name on anything or talk about me through someone else's name, for then I would have to talk to my lawyers. I have not heard from the other two yet. All of

> you have intell 1-8-18 to decide. I hope to hear from you soon on this.

I would not be making any deals with Lloyd, and I knew that I did not need his permission to write about him, but decided to meet his deadline anyway. I wrote him to say I would come to the prison on January 8 to discuss his terms. Hearing him out would give me what I wanted most, a chance to form my own impression of him and to ask a few questions of my own.

The visiting room was large and sunny; a barrier about waist high formed a big U that ran parallel to the room's outer walls. There were benches inside and outside the barrier. I took a seat on one of the outer benches. Inmates were led into the center and then found their way to benches opposite their visitors. Sitting directly across from Lloyd felt familiar; I had watched him on video sitting across the table in the interview room for more than seventy hours. Screens don't convey a proper sense of size or mass, and I found Lloyd to be a somewhat smaller person than I had imagined. He looked thinner than he had appeared in the videos, with a pale pink complexion, and his slate-blue, watery eyes were magnified behind his glasses. His white beard and mustache were neatly trimmed. With me he was cordial but all business. If I was expecting to look evil in the eye, or to find someone exceptional, I was disappointed. What I found was an unimpressive, scheming man, capable of charm but only to the extent that it served his own interest, someone natively bright but deeply ignorant and cocky beyond all reason.

He displayed his usual poor sense of situation, believing he had a lot more leverage over me than he did. The terms he repeated, the same ones he had outlined in his letter, were ridiculous, but I heard him out. Then I asked the questions I most wanted him to answer. The prison would not allow me to bring a notepad or recorder to the meeting, but I wrote out what I remembered immediately after our hour was up.

"Why did you keep talking to the detectives?"

Lloyd said had no choice. He was taken from the prison the first time believing he was going to an interview regarding his parole petition, and instead met Dave and eventually Dave's colleagues. He said his repeated requests for a lawyer were ignored. Prison authorities told him, he said, that he had no choice but to continue meeting with the detectives. None of this was borne out by the videos I had watched. While he had, periodically, asked for a lawyer, and once or twice made a move to leave, he had always quickly dropped the request or, in the one case when he actually did stand up to leave, promptly returned to his chair. He had been transparently bluffing. Even apart from the formal consent forms he had signed, his participation throughout appeared completely voluntary.

The detectives, as part of his plea agreement, were no longer allowed to talk to him, so Dave had asked me to convey a message. Since Lloyd wanted money, I was to assure him that his prison account would never be empty if he revealed where the girls' bodies were buried. It wasn't an official offer, but the Montgomery County police had spent millions on the investigation and still didn't have that answer. The relatively small amounts Lloyd sought, Dave had assured me, would find their way to his ledger.

Lloyd said he didn't know where the bodies were.

"I have told them all I know," he said. "Just because a person pleads guilty to something doesn't mean they are guilty of it. I did not murder or kidnap them girls."

Who did?

His uncle Dick was responsible.

"How do you think I would take two little girls out of the mall, kicking and screaming?" he asked. "Who would be able to do something like that? A man with a uniform." He didn't understand why Dick had not been charged. He said he was afraid of his uncle. He had been in 1975. "When he told me and Helen to leave, we left Maryland and didn't come back for seven years," Lloyd told me. He said he was still afraid Dick would target his children.

While insisting on his innocence, Lloyd nevertheless seemed a little proud of whatever role he had played in the crime. I told him of my early coverage of the story, and of all the years I had wondered about it. He noted that it had taken the Montgomery County police almost forty years to link him to the case, and boasted, "I'll bet it seemed like the perfect crime, didn't it?"

He complained about being treated in the prison as a rapist and murderer of children. Someone, he said, might still "put a shank" in his back. Over eighteen years he had earned a measure of respect from the inmates and staff. After he was linked to the Lyon story, he was treated scornfully. All of his things had been taken from him when he was moved to a prison in Virginia for his court hearing, and when he got back, nothing was returned. He said he had nothing. No TV. No clothes. No job.

He said he had enjoyed the interview sessions. They got him out of the prison, and he got to eat something better than the fare in the prison mess.

"That's one of the reasons I kept talking to them," he said, contradicting what he'd said minutes earlier, that he had been forced to do it. He insisted that he had told the detectives the truth throughout, only sparingly. "I was also trying to protect myself."

By the end of our appointed hour I saw no strong reason to talk with him further. I had asked him my biggest questions. I had seen him invent and reinvent his version of the story so often in the videos that I saw no point in inviting him to do the same with me. It would be starting down the same path trod by the Lyon squad in 2013 and would lead me no closer to the truth. But when I wrote back to him a few days later to reject his deal, I added that if he changed his mind about the payment and wanted to talk with me more, I'd come back and listen.

I got another letter from him promptly.

> I received your letter and I am very disappointed in this. So let me say this to you so you can understand what I am saying to you. First the documentary you are doing, you may not use any pictures of me or Helen and you may not use my name in anyway at all. "You don't have my permission to use me at all." Now, as for your book, I do not give you any permission to use my or any pictures of me or Helen in any way. You do not have my approval or authorization to use anything about the Welch's name. You

> may not use any of the interview sessions that you have of me you do not have my permission. I will not tolerate or permit someone to use my name or make any money off of me. Sorry we did not come to some kind of a understanding. Now you have my input. If you want to come see me then you will have to put $300 on my commissary's books before you can talk to me again. My time is money now.

I noticed that, despite his tone, the price had dropped considerably.

Home

Lloyd's plea had been arranged by his court-appointed lawyers, Aaron Houchens and Anthony Anderson, who chose not to talk to me. No doubt they had been horrified to learn that their client had spent more than seventy hours over almost two years gradually confessing his role in the crime to the police.

Any hope of saving Lloyd from himself vanished when the judge refused to throw those interviews out, as his lawyers had requested. The judge found their arguments largely unpersuasive. The "immunity offer" from the first meeting clearly didn't protect him, because it relied, in part, on his being entirely truthful and had stipulated that it would not hold if he admitted a crime. Lloyd had not met either requirement.

Lloyd had from time to time asked for a lawyer. Dave spent more than an hour on the stand explaining how the squad had handled each of these requests, working through a mountain of paper transcripts. Lloyd was repeatedly told he could stop talking and have a lawyer if he wished—and he kept talking. He had never been held in the interview room against his will. In the end, the judge disallowed only the last interview: immediately after Dave informed him that he was going to be indicted, Lloyd had asked for a lawyer. Dave had smoothly changed the subject, offering to talk to Lloyd not as cop to suspect, but as "human being to human being." Lloyd had gone on to talk to Dave at length, even after repeating his desire to consult with a lawyer, making very damaging admissions. The judge ruled that in this instance the interview was compromised. The commonwealth prosecutor did not challenge the ruling, because Lloyd had repeated all the salient parts of that conversation in the van on the ride to Virginia, voluntarily. He had furnished more than enough rope for his own hanging. He was, in short, the worst client a defense lawyer could have.

His case was over at that point, and Lloyd knew it. His shoulders slumped. It had been his last chance.

The day before his plea was formally entered on September 12, 2017, Lloyd met once more with Dave Davis and the Virginia detectives in the Bedford County courthouse. The idea was to allow him one more chance to explain exactly what had happened. Lloyd was the last stone, and, to some extent, he remained unturned. After he signed the papers for his guilty pleas, which he did at the outset of the meeting, both Maryland and Virginia agreed to forgo any additional charges. Lloyd could do himself no further harm. Dave attended because he thought—he hoped—that at long last, with no reason to lie, Lloyd might tell the truth.

No. With his defense lawyers alongside, Lloyd made an effort to appear contrite—to the detective it looked as if he was trying, without success, to summon tears—only to revert to cheerful laughter in the next moment. He offered nothing new. Instead he offered something old, a story about going to Wheaton Plaza to pick up girls that was essentially the same one he'd told three years earlier, as if he had said nothing different in the interim. Large parts of this "new" version had been discredited—he insisted once more, for instance, that his cousin Teddy had been there. Much of it he himself had long since disavowed, yet . . . here it was again. To Dave, it didn't make sense.

And then, as the meeting broke up, after his lawyers had left the room, Lloyd abruptly asked for them to come back. Dave thought, *Uh-oh, now he's going to try to take back the plea!* The detective wondered, since Lloyd had just signed the papers, whether he could. What sort of confusion would this now cause? But Lloyd wasn't having second thoughts. When his attorneys returned, he asked if the immunity proffered him in this meeting would remain in effect if, at some point in the future, he decided to contact the detectives and tell them something new. He was assured it would, but, Dave wondered, to what end? He left even more confused about Lloyd than when he'd started. *Why would he ask that if he had nothing more to say? If he did have more to say, why not do it here and now? Did he think he could use information to gain advantages in prison? Was he just reluctant for the game to end?*

John and Mary Lyon attended his sentencing, their hair now white, both grown thicker and stooped with age. While the crime was a distant, disturbing memory for those of us who had been around forty-one years earlier, the Lyons had lived with it every day and would live with it for the rest of their lives. Sheila and Kate had become distant memories, smiling faces in faded Kodachrome.

John still had his stentorian voice. He spoke briefly and with calm authority. He had only kind things to say. He thanked Chris and Dave and Katie and Mark.

"The last two or three years or so, they have treated Sheila and Kate as if they were their own sisters or daughters," he said.

He ignored Lloyd, who was seated before him. He ended with weary words that the killer would never comprehend, because they spoke to a shared humanity. What John knew and Lloyd could not know was that such deliberate savagery was a thing beyond setting right, beyond the reach of justice, vengeance, forgiveness, or healing. The only right response was despair. One could only embrace the sadness and turn away.

"It's been a long time," said John. "We're tired, and we just want to go home."

Sheila and Kate Lyon

The author and the publisher are donating part of the proceeds from this book to the National Center for Missing and Exploited Children. You can learn more about that organization at http://www.missingkids.com/home.

Acknowledgments

Thanks to the four detectives, Dave Davis, Chris Homrock, Mark Janney, and Katie Leggett, for their patient and generous cooperation in telling this story; and to Darren Franke, who invited me to meet them at Montgomery County, Maryland police headquarters in 2015. Pete Feeney and John McCarthy helped me understand the decisions they made in bringing Lloyd Welch to justice, and I am grateful to Catherine M. Recker of Welsh & Recker PC for her careful early reading and clear legal reasoning. Thanks once more to Matt Ericson for his lucid maps. As always, warm thanks to Morgan Entrekin and the rest of my friends at Grove Atlantic, for twenty years my professional home, who once more smoothly guided my manuscript into a finished book.